Decolonizing Classroom Management

Decolonizing Classroom Management

A Critical Examination of the Cultural Assumptions and Norms in Traditional Practices

Edited by Flynn Ross and Larissa Malone

ROWMAN & LITTLEFIELD
Lanham • Boulder • New York • London

Published by Rowman & Littlefield
An imprint of The Rowman & Littlefield Publishing Group, Inc.
4501 Forbes Boulevard, Suite 200, Lanham, Maryland 20706
www.rowman.com

86-90 Paul Street, London EC2A 4NE, United Kingdom

Copyright © 2024 by Flynn Ross and Larissa Malone

All rights reserved. No part of this book may be reproduced in any form or by any electronic or mechanical means, including information storage and retrieval systems, without written permission from the publisher, except by a reviewer who may quote passages in a review.

British Library Cataloguing in Publication Information Available

Library of Congress Cataloging-in-Publication Data

ISBN 978-1-4758-7359-7 (cloth)
ISBN 978-1-4758-7360-3 (pbk.)
ISBN 978-1-4758-7362-7 (electronic)

Contents

Foreword: The Struggle for Decolonization: Indigenous Peoples
   and Rights   ix
Dr. Marie Battiste

Introduction   xix
Flynn Ross and Larissa Malone

1: Theoretical Framework for Decolonizing Classroom Management   1
Flynn Ross

2: Colonialism, Assimilation, and Dominant Discourse: A Brief
   History of Classroom Management   11
Adam Schmitt

3: Common and Preferred Practices, But Not Necessarily Best:
   Problematizing Classification of Best Practices in Educational
   Research   21
Ronald Cunningham

4: Under the Hood of a Well-Oiled Machine: Revealing Racism
   and Ableism Within Classroom Management Practices Through
   Disability Critical Race Theory (DisCrit)   29
April Coloma Boyce and Maggie R. Beneke

5: Building Belonging in Classroom Learning Communities   39
Erika McDowell

6: Decolonizing Classroom Relationships   49
Dina Strasser

7: Centering Humanity, Love, and Connection in Classroom
   Management   57
   Erica Holyoke

8: From Interest Convergence in PBIS to Co-Generative Praxis   67
   Matthew Green and Jade Calais

9: Reimagining Classroom Management: A Humanizing Social and
   Emotional Framework   79
   *Brandie Oliver, Brooke Harris Garad, Brian Dinkins, Danielle
   Madrazo, and Katie Brooks*

10: Decolonizing Mindfulness: Centering Liberation and Connection   91
    Patricia Benitez Hemans

11: Challenging the Narrative: How Unexamined Behaviorist
    Beliefs Can Sabotage Trauma-Informed Practices   101
    *Jennifer Randhare Ashton, Jessica Sniatecki, and Maria
    Timberlake*

12: Shaking Restorative Justice Clear from Retributive Justice
    Frameworks   111
    Flynn Ross

13: Fostering Social and Emotional Bonds through Indigenous
    Storytelling   119
    José Ortiz

14: Dreaming Communities of Care: Radical World Building with
    Abolitionist Organizers Toward Students' Heartwholeness   129
    Riley Drake

15: Creating Harmonious Classroom Communities by Embracing
    Community Cultural Wealth and Connection-Building   137
    Violet Jiménez Sims and Dana Turnquest

16: A Collaborative Approach of Ubuntu: Dismantling Colonial
    Classroom Management Practices in South African Schools
    through the Spirit of Ubuntu   147
    Amy Sarah Padayachee and Samantha Kriger

Epilogue: Decolonial Theory to Practice: Toward Shared
    Anticolonial Futures   157
    Rebecca Sockbeson, Fiona Hopper, Bridgid Neptune, Starr Kelly

Contributors 167
About the Editors 169

Foreword

The Struggle for Decolonization: Indigenous Peoples and Rights

Dr. Marie Battiste

> Decolonization and anti-colonial work focus on a particular power relationship that is steeped in the settler imperative. It is about creating space and not necessarily filling space for Indigenous Knowledges. (Margaret Kovach, Jeannine Carriere, H. Montgomery, M. J. Barrett, & Carmen Gillies, 2015, p. 43)

My daughter Annie started teaching at the university and noted that many of the instructors were using decolonization frequently in their discourses about their courses or classroom activities. Talking circles, group work, including play in their scholarly activity, collaborative student teacher devising of required outputs for courses were all said to be decolonizing. Upon reflection, she asked me, "Is decolonizing pedagogies just good teaching?" This question, among others involving where and how to start decolonizing the classrooms, have been central questions asked of me at conferences or talks given on decolonization. I am pleased then to begin this book on decolonization with some foundational concepts to situate decolonization broadly and specifically, in the classroom whether as teacher, manager, or assessor.

It is clear to me that education has never been a neutral enterprise. It has been imbued with meanings constructed from the economic, political, social, and cultural ideologies related to race, class, and gender. Socially constructed for an imagined Eurocentric Canadian society, curricula and the larger context of education have not served all peoples equally, nor have certain sectors of Canadian society gained or benefited from Canada's de facto culturally exclusive educational systems. It is well acknowledged that the various colonial educational systems have systematically excluded the rich diversity of the many peoples and cultures of Canada, in particular, of women, minorities, as well as First Nations, Métis, and Inuit Peoples' perspectives, experiences, beliefs, and diverse knowledge systems (Battiste, 2013; Minnich, 1990; Peters, 2016). Further, although equity, diversity, and inclusion (EDI) have been policies initiated to address some of these disparities, omissions, and colonial injustices, they were not developed with Indigenous Peoples in mind and have not addressed Indigenous Peoples' rights and interests.

This is why Indigenous People often do not acknowledge EDI as their agenda, although they are most deserving of its remedies. Indigenous People see EDI as having a broader aim to make one more inclusive (Eurocentric) society largely for diverse communities of newcomers, refugees, immigrants, and the marginalized groups among them, including LGBT2S. Indigenous Peoples have long held that their rights to be different and separate and equal have been part of the treaty-making process and are now guaranteed in the constitution of Canada. Part of the challenge of decolonization is not just additive Indigenous content, diverse teachers from marginalized groups, or EDI remedies, including classroom management, but unpacking the colonial machinery of conventional education and its normalized packaged Western knowledge system so that diverse knowledge systems and the peoples who live with them can survive, revive, thrive, and be sustained for the present and future, and for Indigenous Peoples, their seventh generation. This is not an easy task or a light one of additive work but a deep dive into deconstruction of assumptions of education, learning, teaching, curricula, pedagogies, and systems; the reconstruction of knowledge systems, languages, histories, teaching, and instructional groundwork in cultural appropriate ways; and the reinstitution of love, relationships, respect, flattening of hierarchy, engagement with culture, spirituality, and more than human life-forms. The larger context of decolonization is important in understanding the term and what it infers for classrooms, for teachers, for schools.

Decolonization in education has had a shorter span of operationalization in schools compared to decolonization as a movement, which has had a much longer history. It is a larger international movement with processes and outcomes created first by United Nations law. Since its inception in 1960, several decades of international decolonization have been initiated, attempting to correct global relations built on the colonial empire building and colonial violence that led to unjust removals and displacements of peoples worldwide.[1] After World War II, the United Nations advanced the political decolonization of European empires and provided the necessary decolonizing foundations for the affected peoples.[2] Both inherent human rights and self-determination have been articulated in UN law to become the remedies for existing colonization and a foundation for justice (Henderson, 2007).

Indigenous Peoples had to secure their human rights over more than 25 years of advocacy, negotiation, and diplomacy process laden with politics, frustration, power struggles, and disappointment in the process of drafting and getting the UN Declaration of the Rights of Indigenous Peoples (UNDRIP) (2007) passed and then finally implemented by the states (Henderson, 2008).

The United Nations has provided in the UN Declaration of the Rights of Indigenous Peoples (2007) the necessary foundational standards for decolonization of Indigenous Peoples. In 46 substantive articles of the declaration and 24 preambular paragraph statements, Indigenous Peoples have had their inherent rights clarified, among them to their collective identities, self-determination, and their knowledge systems. UNDRIP further "emphasizes the rights of Indigenous Peoples to maintain and strengthen their own institutions, cultures and traditions, and to pursue their development in keeping with their own needs and aspirations." It prohibits discrimination against Indigenous Peoples and forced assimilation. Article 31 of the Declaration provides for the Indigenous Peoples to protect their knowledge systems and to preserve their heritage from over-controlling nation-states.

The Truth and Reconciliation Commission Canada affirmed the declaration as principles of reconciliation in its calls to action; and since 2016, Canada has been a full supporter, committed without qualification to the declaration. On June 21, 2021, the Canadian government legislated the UN Declaration of the Rights of Indigenous Peoples Act (Canada 2021). The implementation of the rights is not intended to grant Indigenous Peoples new rights but to affirm their inherent rights explained in the seventh preambular paragraph of the UN declaration that the rights and standards are "inherent" or preexisting before treaties, before British and French settlers. It reflects the existing global consensus that Indigenous Peoples are the bearers of inherent and inalienable human rights. These inherent rights corroborate and elaborate the existing constitutional rights of Indigenous Peoples in Canada.

The purpose of this UNDRIP act then is to make Canadian laws, policies, and practices consistent with the rights of Indigenous Peoples. The act agrees to pursue these human rights, through negotiation and agreement, in good faith as partners with Indigenous Peoples. Equally important is using the UN declaration as a remedy for historical and present systemic injustices, discrimination, and racism. Ministries of education then have the obligation as legislated bodies to institute education in Canada to pursue the same purposes, beyond equity, diversity, and inclusion, but in and through decolonization and reconciliation.

Enacting decolonization in education is then both an opportunity and a requirement, not just to reconcile or accommodate Indigenous Peoples, their cultures, language, and knowledge systems in the plans, strategic directions, instruction, pedagogies, and structures of education, but also to apply the concepts of justice and human dignity to all peoples.

Curriculum, importantly, is from where in the educational academy's assumptions, values, and foundations of learning all professions emerge. The Eurocentric disciplinary knowledges, schools, and universities have long held systemic discrimination to Indigenous knowledges and rights and have contributed both to the ignorance of its educated elite and to the systemic discrimination in the systems we have come to accept as normative education. It is now time under the banner of decolonization to end the supreme systemic resistance to Indigenous Peoples' knowledges, languages, and rights. This presents challenges and opportunities to education systems and educators schooled only in Eurocentric traditions, colonial languages, and academic knowledges.

Decolonization had already begun in Canada with the Canada Act, 1982, making Canada an independent nation from the British empire. Along with its Charter of Rights and Freedoms, the Canadian Constitution specifically addresses its responsibilities and relationships developed by treaties and compacts with Indigenous Peoples on whose lands Canada developed its nationhood. Section 35 of the Constitution thus provides the affirmation of aboriginal and treaty rights and establishes the decolonization framework in Canada. With the Constitution of 1982, Canada ended its lingering colonial relations with Great Britain and created its own unique decolonizing agenda. The formal independence of Canada from the United Kingdom could not have been achieved without the requirement that the new patriated Canada assume responsibility for the continuing legal obligations and relations with the original peoples with whom the British sovereign entered into legal obligations of the treaties and compacts in exchange for British settlers to create their own self-government on Indigenous lands.

This constitutional affirmation of aboriginal and treaty rights is then, importantly, the supreme law of Canada under section 52(1), requiring all federal, provincial, and territorial laws to be consistent with aboriginal and treaty rights. These constitutional powers and rights have been consistently upheld by the Supreme Court of Canada and affirmed in federal law. Importantly, decolonization is not just a responsibility of federal government but also of all provincial and territorial governments and its institutions. It requires that its institutions, including education, also reconcile with the constitutional powers and rights of the Aboriginal Peoples.

These rights include, but are not limited to, Indigenous knowledges, languages, governances, and lands as inherent, communal rights that were never given up to settler laws and are protected in treaties, in constitutional law, and now in the United Nations Declaration of the Rights of Indigenous Peoples

Act of 2021. They also involve broad rights to their histories, cultures, socialization, literacies, oral traditions, and education and rights to pass these on to their children. This unique and exceptional protection provides the effective enjoyment of the constitutional rights of Aboriginal Peoples, both collectively and individually. The holistic Indigenous knowledge systems and Indigenous languages are affirmed then as constitutional rights of Aboriginal Peoples.

Most educators do not realize that the Constitution enshrined aboriginal and treaty rights now that UNDRIP is part of Canada or what that means for the schools and education. Most of Canada's educational ministries have relied primarily on principles of equity, diversity, inclusion, and a notion of Indigenization, arising in part from earlier government policy changes to First Nations education coming first from the appeal in 1972 from the Indian Brotherhood of Canada (now the Assembly of First Nations) for Indian Control of Indian education, and federal government policy issued in 1973 for Indian Control of Indian Education. This policy laid out various efforts to engage cultures in the social life and schools, to correct the negative attitudes toward "differences," and established a foundation for establishing and gradually adding to equity, diversity, and inclusion. Scan ahead many decades. Although many gains have been ushered in with these targeted policies in First Nations schools, and following the important Report of Royal Commission on Aboriginal Peoples (1996), provincial legislation and policies have not corrected the cognitive imperialism and exclusions of Indigenous knowledges and languages in education nor fully addressed the racialization and oppressions continuing to remain in Canadian public schools as a result of the disparities in learning from a singular knowledge system.

Decolonization of laws to align aboriginal and treaty rights requires reconciliation. Decolonization of the educational academies then is best explained as follows:

> Decolonization is a necessary and ongoing process of unlearning, uncovering, and transforming legacies of colonialism, as well as utilizing the educational and knowledge systems available to relearn and rebuild the social, cultural, and linguistic foundations that were lost, or eroded through colonialism. Decolonization also requires making space, balancing, generating and enabling diverse knowledge systems to thrive in the academy as well as in and through educational and knowledge transmitting places for Indigenous Peoples, the formerly colonized or continuing colonized nations, peoples, and cultural knowledge systems. (Smith, Golfman, Battiste, et al., 2021, p. 7, https://www.federationhss.ca/sites/default/files/2021-07/report-faq-en.pdf)

The free online report *Igniting Change: Final Report and Recommendations of the Advisory Committee on Equity, Diversity, Inclusion, and Decolonization*

(EDID) (Smith et al., 2021), though directed to making a more inclusive safe and equitable conference among the Federation of Humanities and Social Sciences, is also significant to the work of all educators throughout Canada. It offers a foundation to engage more meaningfully human rights, human dignity, equity, diversity, inclusion, and decolonization in the work of all educational institutions, educators, and academics alike. The EDID report offers recommendations to individuals, organizers, professional associations, and host institutions on an abundance of ambitious, bold, practical, and transformative processes and approaches for igniting change through EDID. Significantly, the report noted that although much work has been put on equity, diversity, and inclusion over the past 50 years, without a concerted effort to decolonization, educational institutions continue to etch away at Eurocentric colonialism and its inequities and values without much success. Decolonization is then the structural change needed to mobilize human dignity and human rights and Indigenous rights in Canada and beyond. The report notes the importance of decolonization:

> The principles, processes, and practices of decolonization are fundamental to a more equitable, diverse, enlightened, and inclusive social sciences and humanities community in Canada. We believe the sustainable future of higher education requires confronting and unsettling the impact of colonial histories, ideologies, experiences, and legacies on disciplines, archives, canons, curricula, methodologies, and pedagogies, as well as on structures of governance, institutional design, cultures, symbols, and ceremonies. (Smith et al., 2021, p. 7)

Decolonization can then be viewed as the two-pronged approach of deconstruction and reconstruction. The deconstruction begins as a cognitive and affective exercise of understanding how oppression has worked to create the inequities, the ideologies that rationalized them, the benefits to those who represent them, and ongoing challenges that racialization, poverty, homophobia, gender diversity, and gender expression have had on diverse groups, and the losses to Indigenous Peoples from being erased, marginalized, and displaced from their lands and their resources appropriated and exploited. It is heavy head work, but it is also heart work, bringing awareness of injustices to understand the harm that was done to many and the complicities across various social constructions of self and other. The hard work appears first to be at the head and heart of each of us, unpacking and dismantling colonialism in the attitudes, biases, prejudices, internalized dominance, and oppression, understanding the ways colonialism has privileged or oppressed each of us and the ways some have benefited from a position of dominance, others from a position of the oppressed believing that they are indeed unworthy and not capable to move forward or that they have been ungraciously affected negatively by colonial actions.

More important to the task of decolonization is the analogy of head, heart, and hands. The hands suggest that many people may be implicated as oppressor or oppressed and further need to unpack our own complicities with injustice to rebuild and restore human dignity in all its forms in human relationality. It then means that the actions and work of reconciliation (TRC 2015) are the responsibilities of everyone. For each of us, then, part of our education roles is to uplift the consolidated vision of decolonialization to emphasize both the advancement of human rights and self-determination of all subjugated peoples against the systemic injustices of oppression.

All learners have the right to the highest standard of a holistic education that encompasses their spiritual, physical, social, emotional, and cognitive development. Further, the consensus is that the foundations of learning arise from within the learners themselves, their languages, from elders and community teachings, respect for traditional parenting (unconditional love, noninterference, support of the learning spirit; building self-discovery and personal knowledge to connect with the spirit/inner voice/visioning), connecting self "in relation" to others and to the natural order; developing appreciation of the depth of sensory, memory, land-based skills in firsthand and secondhand experience; holistic awareness; understanding, insight, heart/mind connection, and remembering from a strength-based self-determining approach.

I conclude with articulating some liberating approaches that are based on a comprehensive understanding of how Indigenous Peoples in Canada assign priorities to their lives in holistic terms, in ways that represent their local ecological contexts and are represented in their Indigenous languages. Land, the knowledge and skills learned in and from living in a place, Indigenous relationships as reinforced in language and culture, ceremony and tradition with elders and knowledge holders, identity reinforcing teachings linking us to the generations of the past with the generations of the future, to the seventh generation and beyond, are not just aspirations. These are the fundamental constitutional rights affirmed in "aboriginal and treaty rights" and are the fundamental aspects of the rights that Indigenous Peoples have worked toward for four decades. What Canada has yet to resolve in their reconciliation with constitutional rights and now with the UNDRIP act are all integral parts of the learning and educational requirements of states, provinces, and schools among Indigenous Peoples, as well as active involvement of parents, elders, and community to build a successful learning continuum and healthy, resilient communities. Indigenous People must actively participate in all aspects of education and importantly, the normative structures that manage the school and the classroom, including in what languages it is to be delivered.

NOTES

1. International Decade for the Eradication of Colonialism (1990–2000), A/RES/43/47 of November 22, 1988, http://undocs.org/en/A/RES/43/47; Second International Decade for the Eradication of Colonialism (2001–2010) A/RES/55/146 of December 8, 2000, http://undocs.org/en/A/RES/55/146; Third International Decade for the Eradication of Colonialism (2011–2020), A/RES/65/119 of December 10, 2010, http://undocs.org/en/A/RES/65/119; Fourth International Decade for the Eradication of Colonialism (2021–2030), A/RES/75/123 of December 10, 2020.

2. United Nations. (1948). Universal Declaration of Human Rights.

REFERENCES

Battiste, M. (2013). *Decolonizing education: Nourishing the learning spirit.* Vancouver: University of British Columbia Press.

Canada. *An act respecting the United Nations Declaration on the Rights of Indigenous Peoples*, SC 2021, c. 14.

Henderson, J. Y. (2007). *Indigenous diplomacy and the rights of Indigenous Peoples. Achieving UN recognition.* Halifax, NS: Fernwood Press.

Kovach, K., Carriere, J., Montgomery, M., Barrett, M. J., and Gillies, C. (2015). *Indigenous presence: Experiencing and envisioning Indigenous Knowledges within selected post-secondary sites of education and social work.* https://education.usask.ca/documents/profiles/kovach/Indigenous-Presence-2014-Kovach-M-et-al.pdf

Minnich, E. (1990). *Transforming knowledge.* Philadelphia, PA: Temple University Press.

Royal Commission on Aboriginal Peoples (RCAP). (1996). *Report of the Royal Commission on Aboriginal Peoples.* 5 vols. Hull, P.Q.: Canada Communications. https://www.bac-lac.gc.ca/eng/discover/aboriginal-heritage/royal-commission-aboriginal-peoples/Pages/introduction.aspx

Smith, M., Golfman, N., Battiste, M., Crichlow, W., Dolmage, J., Glanfield, F., Malacrida, C., & Villeneuve, A. (2021). *Igniting change: Final report and recommendations of the advisory committee on equity, diversity, inclusion and decolonization.* Federation for the Humanities and Social Sciences. https://www.federationhss.ca/sites/default/files/2021-10/Igniting-Change-Final-Report-and-Recommendations-en.pdf

Truth and Reconciliation Commission of Canada/Commission de vérité et réconciliation du Canada. (2015). *Truth and Reconciliation Commission of Canada: Calls to Action/Commission de vérité et réconciliation du Canada: Appels à l'action.* Winnipeg, Manitoba. Retrieved from http://nctr.ca/assets/reports/Calls_to_Action_English2.pdf

United Nations. International Decade for the Eradication of Colonialism (1990–2000), A/RES/43/47 of November 22, 1988, http://undocs.org/en/A/RES/43/47

United Nations. Second International Decade for the Eradication of Colonialism (2001–2010) A/RES/55/146 of December 8, 2000, http://undocs.org/en/A/RES/55/146

United Nations. Third International Decade for the Eradication of Colonialism (2011–2020), A/RES/65/119 of December 10, 2010, http://undocs.org/en/A/RES/65/119

United Nations. Fourth International Decade for the Eradication of Colonialism (2021–2030), A/RES/75/123 of December 10, 2020, http://undocs.org/en/A/RES/75/123

United Nations Declaration on the Rights of Indigenous Peoples, A/RES/61/295 of September 13, 2007, http://undocs.org/en/A/RES/61/295

Introduction

Flynn Ross and Larissa Malone

Welcome to our book. We like to begin as we would with a class: with introductions. This is because who we are as authors matters to our intellectual engagement, just as who you are as readers will influence how you engage with this text.

I am Dr. Flynn Ross, professor and chair of teacher education at the University of Southern Maine. I am a white, cisgender, monolingual, Christian woman in her fifties. Raised in the Finger Lakes of New York, on the lands of the Seneca, I currently reside in Maine on the unceded lands of the Abenaki, part of the Wabbanaki tribes. I am still considered "from away" for multigenerational white Mainers, although I have lived in Maine for 28 years.

I, Dr. Larissa Malone, am an associate professor of social and cultural foundations of education at the University of North Carolina Wilmington. I am an Afro-Latino woman who identifies as Black. Originally from northeast Ohio, I currently reside on the land of the Waccamaw Siouan. I am a former Montessori teacher and a wife and mother to three girls. I often use my personal experience in my writing, and my research typically incorporates elements of my past within a critical lens.

We are both lifelong educators as classroom teachers in PK–12 and as teacher educators. We come to this work humbly, as neither of us is of Indigenous ethnic heritage. We strive to avoid appropriating language, concepts, and the spirit of native peoples and actively confront colonization within ourselves every day. In addition, we both attended and taught in colonized schools and are now part of teacher education programs that, despite best intentions, produce future teachers that often have colonized mind-sets. Although it is not surprising to us that traditional instructional models in teacher education programs have colonization tendencies embedded within them, we were drawn to this project because we noticed that fairly new practices in teacher education curricula categorized as "decolonized" also preserved settler colonialism ways of knowing. We asked ourselves, "In teaching for social justice, how can we decolonize cultural assumptions and norms in these 'decolonized' practices to acknowledge and strengthen the cultures our students bring to the classroom?"

We decided to create a space of connection for scholars who had begun to interrogate this query. We are very excited to have collaborated with the culturally, racially, linguistically, geographically diverse authors in this text. All the authors are educators representing PK–12 and higher education, and each has challenged a particular classroom practice or concept that claims to be socially just but still leans into various cultural assumptions and norms in its own way.

In this book we acknowledge how we stand on the shoulders of those who have come before us to make this discussion possible. In the field of multicultural education with the evolution from culturally relevant (Ladson-Billings, 1995), to culturally responsive (Gay, 2010), to culturally sustaining (Paris & Alim, 2017). We acknowledge that decolonization is a departure from multicultural education and social justice scholarship that aim to reform schooling as it currently exists. Decolonizing calls for totally dismantling schooling as it currently exists, given its history of acculturation and goals of sustaining and promoting Western cultural traditions (Tuck & Yang, 2012). By challenging the settler colonialism that perpetuates violence on the land and peoples through epistemologies, ontologies, and cosmologies, we work within schools as they currently exist. As Marie Battiste calls for in her book, *Decolonizing Education* (2013), incorporating both Indigenous and Eurocentric thinking is necessary to meet today's environmental, social, and economic challenges.

In the following chapters, the authors unpack the cultural assumptions that lay at the epistemological foundation of many classroom management practices used in schools to identify how they perpetuate the control of students and examine the potentials of incorporating epistemologies from other cultures about the development of children and the nature of learning.

As educators and the editors of this book, we situate our practices with the shift from teacher centered to learning centered. Our pedagogical and interpersonal practices aspire to be inclusive, empowering student voice and self-directed learning, and engaged in the community from early childhood through adult learning. In our diverse democracy we acknowledge that we will not always agree, and it is through active listening, engagement, and reflection that collectively we can build new practices, policies, and traditions. We acknowledge the power dynamics of the culturally dominant structures in society that normalize and make invisible the white, Eurocentric, English speaking, cisgendered, Christian culture. We collectively envision a future in learning in which educators "strengthen relationships to support the ecological vision of humanity as a part of the natural world" (Battiste, 2013).

This book is organized in three sections following the introduction—assumptive language, classroom management models, and future directions. In chapter 1, Dr. Flynn Ross provides a theoretical framework for decolonizing classroom management, followed by a history of classroom management in the United States, provided by Dr. Adam Schmitt. The first section challenges the use of assumptive language in an effort to decolonize our thinking. This is initially approached by Ronald Cunningham when he problematizes the terminology of "best practices," followed by April Coloma Boyce and Maggie R. Beneke's parallelism of classroom management to an "old factory model" through disability critical race theory (DisCrit). This section concludes with Dr. Erika McDowell questioning what "belonging" means, Dina Strasser exploring "relationships" with students and their families, and Dr. Erica Holyoke illustrating what "love" looks like in a classroom.

The second section challenges models of classroom management commonly used in school districts, returning to the cultural roots of practices to share possibilities. Dr. Matthew Green and Jade Calais explore how positive behavior interventions and supports (PBIS) have the potential for co-generative praxis. Dr. Brandie Oliver and her colleagues provide examples of how social emotional learning can be a humanizing participatory framework to promote empowerment and agency. Dr. Patricia Benitez Hemans offers the expanded potential of mindfulness in the classroom if we return to its cultural roots. Dr. Jennifer Ashton and colleagues examine how behaviorist beliefs can sabotage trauma informed practices. Finally, Dr. Flynn Ross articulates how restorative justice practices have been adopted into retributive justice mind-sets in practice in schools and the potential for practices to bring healing to schools when practitioners work to understand the epistemological roots of restorative justice.

The last section of this book shares four frameworks for future directions. Dr. José Ortiz illustrates indigenous storytelling practices to foster social and emotional connections for learning. Dr. Riley Drake describes building communities of care through abolitionist communities to support the whole child. Dr. Violet Jiménez Sims and Dana Turnquest capitalize on community cultural wealth to create enriching classroom communities. Finally, the book concludes with a global perspective with authors from South Africa, Dr. Amy Sarah Padayachee and Dr. Samantha Kriger, using principles of ubuntu in schools.

The vision of creating inclusive, culturally responsive learning communities in our widely diverse society requires that teachers be contextually responsive to the communities and students they serve. In this book, similar to Indigenous research methods that acknowledge the interconnectedness of all elements in a system (Battiste, 2013), classroom management frameworks should be about seeing and learning to recognize the rich diversities of thoughts, emotions, and practices in context and having the mind-set and reflection to respond. This collection of works hopes to move the field of education in that direction.

REFERENCES

Battiste, M. (2013). *Decolonizing education: Nourishing the learning spirit.* University of British Columbia, Purich Publishing.

Bell, D. A., Jr. (1980). *Brown v. board of education* and the interest-convergence dilemma. *Harvard Law Review, 93*(3), 518–533. https://doi.org/10.2307/1340546

Crenshaw, K. W. (2019). Unmasking colorblindness in the law: Lessons from the formation of critical race theory. In K. W. Crenshaw, L. C. Harris, D. M. HoSang, & G. Lipsitz (Eds.), *Seeing race again: Countering colorblindness across the disciplines*, (pp. 52–84). University of California Press. https://doi.org/10.1525/9780520972148-004

Gay, G. (2010). *Culturally responsive teaching: Theory, research, and practice* (2nd ed.). Teachers College Press.

Ladson-Billings, G. (1995). Toward a theory of culturally relevant pedagogy. *American Research Journal, 32*(3), 465–491. https://doi.org/10.2307/1163320

Ladson-Billings, G., & Tate, W. F., IV. (1995). Toward a critical race theory of education. *Teachers College Record, 97*(1), 47–68. https://doi.org/10.1177/016146819509700104

Paris, D., & Alim, H. S. (2017). *Culturally sustaining pedagogies: Teaching and learning for justice in a changing world.* Teachers College Press.

1

Theoretical Framework for Decolonizing Classroom Management

Flynn Ross

Critical education and anti-oppressive education begin with the unpacking of Eurocentric assumptions of education, the normalized discourses and discursive practices that bestow ignorance on students, while it bestows layers of meaningless knowledge on to youth that hide the social and economic structures of Eurocentrism, white dominance, and racism. (Battiste, 2013, p. 106)

Marie Battiste, in her book *Decolonizing Education: Nourishing the Learning Spirit* (2013), calls us in higher education to "interrogate the existing cultural interpretative monopoly of Eurocentric knowledges, assumptions, and methodologies" (p. 103). Applied to teacher preparation and our PK–12 schools, this call helps us question our assumptions and opens space for the many different cultures and traditions from which our students come. Battiste (2013) provides us with a vision of "developing 'trans-systemic' analyses and methods (that reach) beyond the . . . distinct systems of knowledge to create fair and just educational systems and experiences so that all students can benefit from their education in multiple ways" (p. 103). She theorizes that creating an "ethical space" for adult dialogues brings together Indigenous and Western thought.

Our hope is that this book may provide one of those spaces. In these spaces we "reconsider how what one chooses (for boundaries and limits) may infringe on another's space or standards, codes of conduct, or the community ethos in each community" (Battiste, p. 105). If educators are truly committed to building inclusive, multicultural classrooms, we must examine the privilege and dominance of Eurocentric codes of conduct and community ethos that we call classroom management.

The progressive vision of schools has shifted from intentional assimilation for the "good of the child" (Sarche & Whitesell, 2012) to creating an ethos of aspiration as a means for liberation. But can schools be places of liberation or is Audrey Lorde correct in saying that *The Master's Tools Will Never Dismantle the Master's House* (1984)? Critical pedagogues (Apple, 1979; Friere, 1970; Giroux, 1988; hooks, 1994) question whether bureaucracies such as schools and higher education can be places of liberation because schooling has functioned as a place of oppression to re-create the status quo. In fact, Lisa Delpit (1995) calls on educators to make explicit the goal of learning the "culture of power" in schools to have access to economic success in the United States, situating schools as places of liberation by learning the tools of the economic system. Recent critical pedagogues use decolonization as a framework for examining our practices, such as Michael Dominguez (2021), who summons teacher educators to provide "concrete models of decolonial repertoires of practice . . . [to ensure that new teachers learn] how to teach while resisting the coloniality that permeates schools" (p. 551). This sentiment is the impetus for developing a framework to decolonize classroom management.

Fundamental tenets, distinct from multicultural and culturally responsive practice, guide and shape decolonization. Based in settler colonialism, decolonization calls for dismantling world views and power structures with a return to Indigenous ways of knowing and being with the natural world. This chapter outlines a theoretical framework of decolonization beginning with understanding that classroom management is inherently cultural and that practices reenforce the belief systems of those in power. How to decolonize our assumptions is illustrated with the example of examining theories of child development. Empowering student agency in a framework of responsive pedagogy provides a means for redressing the power dynamics of the school-to-prison pipeline. Finally, the framework concludes with visions for the future melding together several emerging schools of thought including ecological humanism, abolitionist teaching, culturally sustaining pedagogy, and promoting agency in student learning.

CLASSROOM MANAGEMENT IS INHERENTLY CULTURAL

Behavioral expectations and what is "appropriate" are determined by one's cultural lens. Yet, teacher education programs have taught, and continue to teach, classroom management as if it is culturally neutral, rather than acknowledging that in the United States it is based on Western psychological principles rooted in Judeo-Christian traditions. Therefore, teachers are indoctrinated to believe from the onset of their career that the concept of punishment and rewards, the need to foster compliance and deter misbehavior, and the cultivation of "civilized" behavior is just good teaching rather than a colonized mind-set.

DECOLONIZING OUR ASSUMPTIONS

Critical educators (Friere, 1970; Giroux, 1988; Greene, 2000) argue that practitioners should question everything, investigate the ideological underpinnings of assumptions and practices, and co-construct new knowledge with our students. Decolonizing the curriculum (Ziai et al., 2020) requires educators to interrogate academic knowledge. It is through interrogation of theory and practice that new teachers can be empowered to build culturally responsive, even culturally sustaining (Paris & Alim, 2017) learning environments with their students.

TribalCrit, a subfield of critical race theory (CRT) (Bell, 1980; Crenshaw et al., 1996; Delgado & Stefancic, 2001) is a structural critique of global colonial systems using the frameworks of settler colonialism (Watson & Jepson, 2021) to examine the colonization of people, beliefs, ideas as well as lands. In the United States, decolonization has focused on displacement from land for ownership and extraction of resources (Veracini, 2010), including the use of human resources and thought. Decolonizing classroom management examines the colonization of ideas and beliefs about what behaviors are "good," "normal," and what schools "should" teach. The impact of the teacher enforcing norms, beliefs, and behaviors in the classroom are powerful and often life transforming for the identity and sense of self of individual students. Understanding CRT and settler colonialism can help educators decolonize our assumptions about our practices.

Education in Eurocentric traditions aspires to identify the "truth" and "best practices" through scientific research. In teaching there is no one best model, set of practices, or research-based best practices for every classroom. This can be very unsettling for new teachers who want to learn how to "do it right." Approaching this learning with intellectual curiosity as it relates to classroom behaviors can help take some of the judgment of right or wrong out of the inquiry into what is best for this group of students at this time. Indigenous ways of learning are holistic (Cull et al., 2018), understanding the whole individual in the social and institutional contexts. The means of knowledge production include experience, storytelling, and discussion in relationship with others rather than relying exclusively on the rational empiricism of Eurocentric knowledge.

How We Come to Know What We Know: Example of Child Development Theories

Decolonizing practices begins with identifying these underpinnings of our thinking. For example, child development as a field of study has evolved in the Western psychological tradition that is traditionally taught in teacher education programs in the United States. Jean Piaget, a French psychologist who comes from rational individualist traditions, is credited with being the father of child development. Piaget's work is related to but differs from Erik Erikson's theory of psychosocial development developed in Germany. Studying at the same time in a slightly different collectivist intellectual tradition in Russia, Lev Vygotsky considered language development in community as the foundation for thinking. All these men were white and of Western traditions of rational individuality, linear worldviews, in the Judeo-Christian traditions of religion and morality. Child development as taught in universities has been dominated by and limited to a very narrow definition of human experience, in part because of who was allowed to attend universities, publish papers, and be recognized in their field.

In contrast, many indigenous beliefs about child development are described as the Relational Worldview Model (Cross, 1997), where there are four quadrants: context, mental, physical, and spiritual. The role of the adult in the community is to nurture the child to allow the spiritual identity to emerge and be realized as the child assumes his place in the good life (Cross, 1997; Sarche, 2012). The child is honored as a unique individual, and the role of the adult is to create an environment to allow that individual spirit to emerge and realize its full potential. These differences in understanding about the nature of children and the role of the adults and teachers result in very different actions and implications for teachers and classroom management.

Empowering Student Agency as a Means for Redressing the School-to-Prison Pipeline

A key concept in understanding decolonized classroom management is where the control of behavior lies. Historically, the teacher controls the students' behaviors. Behaviors ultimately can only be controlled by the individual doing the behavior. Others can influence the individual, but it must be recognized that the agency for behaviors only exists within the student. There is a tremendous difference between a behavior plan that is done *to* a child and a plan that is created and implemented *with* a child. Attempts to control a child's behavior can lead to resistance as that resistance is the source of power and agency for the child, especially adolescents. Behavior management that works *with* children or adolescents to empower them to reach their goals and tap into their motivations are much more likely to be successful because they work with the child's motivations.

The framework for decolonizing classroom management aims to redress the school-to-prison pipeline by creating inclusive, empowering, learning environments *with* the students. The legacy of beliefs that children are "born of original sin" and that punishment will deter misbehaviors in rational individuals has led to zero-tolerance school policies that have resulted in the school-to-prison pipeline that is well documented in research and U.S. congressional hearings in 2012 (S. Hrg. 112–848).

Visions for the Future

What might these new ways of thinking and building knowledge about classrooms and communities look like? Teachers can study various models of classroom management with a critical lens and strive to understand the possible unintended consequences of using different strategies, including reinforcing cultural power dynamics. I will now highlight three models that provide glimpses into a vision of decolonized, inclusive learning environments. These include ecological vision of humanity, abolitionist management for joy, and culturally sustaining practices that honor traditions students bring to the classroom. Every classroom must respond to its local social ecology and build the niche for the individual children to thrive.

Ecological Vision of Humanity

Battiste (2013, p. 114) names for us the tradition of an ecological vision of humanity as a part of the natural world:

> a conception of humanity . . . that rests its foundation on place and ecological teachings and practices of what constitutes being human within a certain ecology. Ecology is the animating force that teaches by trial and error, and elders' guidance, how to live and how to be human . . . Ecology privileges no particular people or way of life . . . They honor and nourish a respect for diversity rather than hierarchy and normative preferences.

Ecology as a metaphor extends well to the classroom where teachers help students grow. But again, what is our vision of the garden? Is our ideal garden shaped by our cultural beliefs? Is it the highly cultivated English rose garden? Or the cottage garden that flourishes with little human interference?

Or is it the wild meadow with thin soil that blooms just briefly? Robin Wall Kimmerer in her book (2013) helps us understand how the deep watching of plants brings a wisdom that the controlled observation of scientific learning may miss at first as the empirical control of variables are subject to the assumptions of the scientist.

I am a gardener who has recently removed the colonizing plants of the invasive species in my side yard. I have found joy and great diversity in watching the native plants return to this space. Each plant in its own niche flourishes in its unique way. As a teacher I extend the metaphor to the classroom, asking how do we remove the colonizing practices of classroom management that only allow the invasive behaviors to thrive and create the niches in which all individually unique and diverse children can thrive? How do we learn from the ecology of our classrooms through trial and error to build the unique dynamic that responds to the humans in our care?

Abolitionist Teaching for Joy and Empowerment in the Classroom

Decolonized classrooms could be informed by abolitionist teaching models and pedagogy that comes out of prison reform efforts and teaching about how to imagine a society without prisons. "Abolitionist education explicitly intends, through content and instructional methods, to work toward liberation from a system of neoliberalism, oppression, and mass imprisonment" (Whynacht, Arsenault, & Cooney, 2018). Bettina Love (2019) envisioned the transformation of schools and society to build freedom and joy for all. Some abolitionists have a rich spiritual tradition of the biblical depiction of freeing the Israelites from the pharaohs as a model of the freeing of the African slaves in the United States. Abolitionist educators provide visions of the promised land and creating schools and learning spaces that empower every child and adult to reach their full humanity, realize their gifts, and find their "calling" and potential.[1] Classrooms can be life-giving niches that provide the conditions for every child to flourish.

Culturally Sustaining Pedagogy

Building on sociocultural traditions that recognize the assets of communities, such as funds of knowledge (Gonzalez et al., 2005), biography-driven culturally responsive teaching (Herrera, 2010), Paris and Alim (2017) calls for teaching practices that value and affirm the traditions students bring from home, acknowledging the cultural wealth (CCW) framework (Yosso, 2005) that comes from communities. Teachers need to learn about the various cultural traditions that students bring with them to the classroom, including but not limited to communication styles, expectations of teachers and schooling, and interpersonal interactions across differences including gender, age, and authority. In multicultural classrooms, teachers can work with their students to make these traditions explicit and negotiate agreements for how students and teachers will interact in the classroom in response to who is present in the classroom.

CONCLUSION

> I've come to a frightening conclusion that I am the decisive element in the classroom. It's my personal approach that creates the climate. It's my daily mood that makes the weather. As a teacher, I possess a tremendous power to make a child's life miserable or joyous. I can be a tool of torture or an instrument of inspiration. I can humiliate or heal. In all situations, it is my response that decides whether a crisis will be escalated or de-escalated and a child humanized or dehumanized.
> —Haim Ginott, 1975

The teacher in a classroom has tremendous power in creating the learning environment that shapes young minds, identities, and sense of self through creating the group norms, dynamics, and values within the classroom. The assumptions, norms, beliefs, and expectations of teachers from one culture will be different from the cultures of some of their students. The first step in decolonizing one's classroom management is to become aware of one's own identity and culture as one of many ways of being in the world.

Schools are historical tools of the state to create a "civil" homogenous society that has required the erasure of the cultural heritage and language of many children. This history must be acknowledged and reckoned with to be able to move forward with the progressive vision of schools as tools of liberatory pedagogy and student empowerment. Critical examination of the epistemological and ontological origins of practices (Kincheloe, 2017), theories, and frameworks in education is needed as a foundation for understanding how to build culturally sustaining practices (Paris & Alim, 2014).

Teachers are responsible for building the models of a diverse, equitable, and inclusive society in their classrooms as the training ground for our future citizens. The potential and challenge of this undertaking cannot be underestimated. We need critical frameworks and guiding models to prepare them for this work.

NOTE

1. The religious language is used intentionally and explicitly in keeping with the guidance of the emerging FaithCrit framework developed by Drs. Larissa Malone and Quiana Lachaud (2022).

REFERENCES

Apple, M. (1979). *Ideology and curriculum*. Routledge.
Battiste, M. (2013). *Decolonizing education: Nourishing the learning spirit.* University of British Columbia, Purich Publishing.
Bell, D. A. (1980). Brown v. Board of Education and the interest-convergence dilemma. *Harvard Law Review, 93*(3), 518–533. https://doi.org/10.2307/1340546
Brayboy, B. (2005). Toward a tribal critical race theory in education. *Urban Review, 37*(5), 425–446. https://doi.org/10.1007/s11256-005-0018-y
Crenshaw, K., Gotanda, N., & Peller, G. (1996). *Critical race theory: The key writings that formed the movement*. New Press.
Crenshaw, K. W., Harris, L. C., Hosang, D. M., & Lipsitz, G. (2019). *Seeing race again: Countering colorblindness across the disciplines*. University of California Press.
Cross, T. (1997). Relational worldview model. *Pathways Practice Digest, 12*(4), 6–7. https://doi.org/10.1002/ajcp.12372
Cull, I., Hancock, R., McKeown, S., Pidgeon, M., and Vedan, A. (2018). Indigenous ways of knowing and being. In *Pulling together: A guide for front-line staff, student services, and advisors*. BCCampus. https://opentextbc.ca/indigenizationfrontlineworkers/chapter/indigenous-ways-of-knowing-and-being/
Delgado, R., & Stefancic, J. (2001). *Critical race theory: An introduction*. New York University Press.
Delpit, L. (1995). *Other people's children: Cultural conflict in the classroom*. Norton.
Domínguez, M. (2021). Cultivating epistemic disobedience: Exploring the possibilities of a decolonial practice-based teacher education. *Journal of Teacher Education, 72*(5), 551–563. https://doi.org/10.1177/0022487120978152
Freire, P. (1970). *Pedagogy of the oppressed*. Penguin Random House.
Ginott, H. G. (1975). *Teacher and child: A book for parents and teachers*. Macmillan.
Giroux, H. A. (1988). *Schooling and the struggle for public life: Critical pedagogy in the modern age*. University of Minnesota Press.
Greene, M. (2000). *Releasing the imagination: Essays on education, the arts, and social change*. Wiley.
Herrera, S. (2010). *Biography-driven culturally responsive teaching*. Teachers College Press.
hooks, b. (1994). *Teaching to transgress: Education as the practice of freedom*. Taylor & Francis Group.
Kimmerer, R. W. (2013). *Braiding sweetgrass: Indigenous wisdom, scientific knowledge, and the teachings of plants*. Milkweed Editions.

Kincheloe, J. L. (2017). A critical complex epistemology of practice. *Taboo: The Journal of Culture and Education, 10*(2). https://doi.org/10.31390/taboo.10.2.12

Kohlberg, L. (1984). *The psychology of moral development: The nature and validity of moral stages (Essays on moral development, vol. 2)*. Harper & Row.

Lorde, A. (1984). The master's tools will never dismantle the master's house (comments at the "The Personal and the Political Panel," Second Sex Conference, New York, September 29, 1979). In *Sister outsider* (pp. 110–113). Sister Visions Press. (Original work published 1979)

Love, B. (2019). *We want to do more than survive: Abolitionist teaching and the pursuit of educational freedom*. Beacon Press.

Malone, L., & Lachaud, Q. (2022). FaithCrit: Towards a framework of religio-spirituality in critical race theory. *Journal of Critical Race Inquiry, 9*(2), 93–103.

McCarter, S., Venkitasubramanian, K., & Bradshaw, K. (2020). Addressing the school-to-prison pipeline: Examining micro- and macro-level variables that affect school disengagement and subsequent felonies. *Journal of Social Service Research, 46*(3), 379–393. https://doi.org/10.1080/01488376.2019.1575323

Moll, L. C., Amanti, C., Neff, D., & Gonzalez, N. (1992). Funds of knowledge for teaching: Using a qualitative approach to connect homes and classrooms. *Theory into Practice, 31*(2), 132–141.

Paris, D., & Alim, H. S. (2014). What are we seeking to sustain through culturally sustaining pedagogy? A loving critique forward. *Harvard Educational Review, 84*(1), 85–100.

Paris, D., & Alim, H. S. (2017). *Culturally sustaining pedagogies: Teaching and learning for justice in a changing world*. Teachers College Press.

Piaget, J. (1936). *Origins of intelligence in the child*. Routledge & Kegan Paul.

Pratt, R. H. (1892/1973). *Americanizing the American Indians: Writings by the "friends of the Indian" 1880–1900*. Harvard University Press, 260–271.

Sanford, R. M., & Plumley, W. S. (2020). *River voices: Perspectives on the Presumpscot*. North Country Press.

Sarche, M. C., & Whitesell, N. R. (2012). Child development research in North American Native communities—looking back and moving forward: Introduction. *Child Development Perspectives, 6*(1), 42–48. https://doi.org/10.1111/j.1750-8606.2011.00218.x

S. Hrg. 112–848—Ending the school to prison pipeline. (2024, February 12). https://www.congress.gov/event/112th-congress/senate-event/LC1164/text

Tuck, E., & Yang, K. W. (2012). Decolonization is not a metaphor. *Decolonization: Indigeneity, Education & Society, 1*(1), 1–40.

Veracini, L. (2010). *Settler colonialism: A theoretical overview*. Palgrave Macmillan.

Vygotsky, L. S. (1978). *Mind in society: The development of higher psychological processes*. Harvard University Press. (Originally published in Russian in 1930)

Watson, K., & Jeppsen, S. (2021). Settler fragility: Four paradoxes of decolonizing research. *Revista de Comunicacao Dialogica, 4*(2), 78–109. https://doi.org/10.12957/rcd.2020.55392

Weinstein, C., Curran, M., & Tomlinson-Clarke, S. (2003). Culturally responsive classroom management: Awareness into action. *Theory into Practice, 42*(4), 269–276. https://doi.org/10.1207/s15430421tip4204_2

Whynacht, A., Arsenault, E., & Cooney, R. (2018). Abolitionist pedagogy in the neoliberal university: Notes on trauma-informed practice, collaboration, and confronting the impossible. *Social Justice, 45*(4), 141–162, 164. http://www.jstor.org/stable/1477388

Yosso, T. J. (2005). Whose culture has capital? A critical race theory discussion of community cultural wealth. *Race, Ethnicity and Education, 8*(1), 69–91. https://doi.org/10.1080/1361332052000341006

Ziai, A., Bendix, D., & Muller, F. (2020). Decolonizing knowledge orders, research methodology and the academia: An introduction. In D. Bendix, F. Muller, & A. Zial (Eds.), *Beyond the master's tools?: Decolonizing knowledge orders, research methods and teaching* (pp. 1–15). Rowman & Littlefield.

2

Colonialism, Assimilation, and Dominant Discourse

A Brief History of Classroom Management

Adam Schmitt

Classroom management, and the underlying societal concern of how to control children, looms large in the public imagination. What gets lost in popular discourse, though, is a critical understanding of how approaches to classroom management, as a part of the structural organization of schools, are culturally situated and therefore based upon assumptions rooted in dominant discourse. Before proceeding, it is important to note that my status as a straight, cisgender, white male inherently shapes the perspective I bring to my analysis. Public school is a space designed for and by people who look like me, and as such I was not a target of classroom management systems that seek to oppress marginalized groups.

In this chapter, I explore these assumptions and their impact by considering the historical context and larger philosophical movements that have shaped classroom management. Specifically, I argue that classroom management is, and has always been, part and parcel of how dominant discourse frames race, immigration status, and social class. Approaches to classroom management that have emerged in the past couple of decades seek to create a more just, learner-centered approach to classroom management. Although they recognize the impact of these dominant discourses, they are often still entangled in them and fall short of the promise they aim for.

PROVIDING CONTEXT

In his presidential address to the American Educational Studies Association, Butchart (1994) argued that classroom management hasn't been given much space in foundations literature because exploring issues related to it "suggest power and its historical abuses" and "insist that we face the contradictions and paradoxes of control and freedom" (p. 166). As Carson (1995) noted in his response to Butchart, though, "discipline cannot be understood in isolation from the larger framework of social issues and socialization processes. The classroom is a society in miniature, aiming toward a particular vision of humankind" (p. 214). To better understand Butchart's and Carson's concerns, I start by considering how the historical purposes of schooling and differing conceptions of childhood served as organizing principles of classroom management.

Purposes of Schooling

The architects of American public education have always been keenly aware of school's relationship to broader society. The purposes of education that have dominated reform discourse at any given time have been connected to lofty goals from the preparation of "good" citizens to maintain American democracy to the preparation of "good" workers to fulfill national economic needs to school as a lever for social mobility for individuals to rise above those who came before them (Labaree, 2011). However, public education was designed by and for white men and has, at different times, marginalized or outright barred white women, immigrants, and BIPOC individuals through exclusionary and assimilationist practices. As a result, what being a "good" citizen or a "good" worker means has always been filtered through unequal social expectations that simultaneously reflect and construct dominant hierarchies.

Writing about American public education in the Gilded Age and Progressive Era, Stratton (2016) argued that schools functioned as a "domestic colonial institution" (p. 3) that aimed to "reform and subordinate foreign and native-born children of color for future industrial, domestic, and agricultural work" (p. 4). Stratton's argument reveals the historical abuses of power and socialization processes that Butchart (1994) and Carson (1995) respectively highlight. The social, political, and economic context of the time shaped schooling in a way that embedded racial and class inequality in its very structure and predetermined the educational opportunities available to students based on that inequality. Although this process existed (and exists) above and beyond classroom management, it is an organizing framework that is important for understanding how management practices have been applied to different student populations over time.

Evidence of public schooling's role as a "domestic colonial institution" (Stratton, 2016, p. 3) is easy to come by. In 1819, Congress passed the Civilization Fund Act, aimed at "introducing . . . the habits and arts of civilization" to Indigenous people and gradually led to the establishment of the boarding school system (as cited in Fraser, 2019, p. 33). That system was based on the idea that Indigenous culture was doomed to die out and needed to be replaced with dominant white ideology surrounding religion, landownership, and family structure.

In the wake of the Civil War, newly emancipated African Americans clamored for education, and a variety of schools, formal and informal, sprouted up in the South from the emancipated themselves as well as missionary organizations working with the Freedmen's Bureau (Anderson, 1988). Gradually, however, Black education was co-opted by northern philanthropists and southern reformers who desired a well-ordered South where African Americans occupied the lowest rungs of labor and were discouraged from taking part in politics (Anderson, 1988). Therefore, industrial education, focused on manual labor and skill attainment, funded by northern philanthropic organizations, and committed to continuing the social, political, and economic oppression of African Americans became prevalent. Other racial and ethnic groups had similar experiences. National rhetoric may have stressed the importance of school in protecting democracy, but for Black and Indigenous Students its purpose was to teach a particular brand of Americanism that reinforced the dominant racial hierarchy.

Conceptions of Children

Although the underlying purposes of schooling shaped the educational experience, dominant conceptions of children played an important role in conceptualizing classroom management. The origin of public schooling in the United States is often connected back to religious schooling in colonial New England. In 1647, Massachusetts passed the Old Deluder Satan Law, which mandated the establishment of public schools to create scripturally literate children who could fend off the devil (as cited in Fraser, 2019). Puritan conceptions of children, born with sin, facilitated the use of corporal punishment in educational settings. Drawing from the biblical expression "spare the rod, spoil the child," early educators in colonial America, and later the United States, believed corporal punishment was necessary to literally beat the devil out of children (Bartman, 2002).

As the 1800s continued, however, there was a shift in how children were understood. Drawing from European reformers such as Pestalozzi and

Froebel, there was a new focus on children's natural curiosity and innate goodness (Reese, 2011) that carried over to the institution of schooling. Corporal punishment was still present, but classroom management shifted to a more proactive phase with focus placed on creating meaningful, engaging learning experiences that curtailed the need for active discipline (Ryan, 1994). Despite this shift, schooling still looked different depending on who you were. Middle-class white students might have had access to play and informal learning experiences, whereas manual labor dominated the schooling of African American, Indigenous, and immigrant working-class children.

METHODS OF MANAGEMENT

Methods of management have always been linked to overarching purposes of education and how children are socially conceptualized. In this section, I focus on primary methods of management that have often been used in the United States to extend a colonial approach to education.

Corporal Punishment

Corporal punishment is one image that springs to mind when people think about the history of classroom management, and indeed it has been consistently employed as a disciplinary practice in American schools since their inception (Ryan, 1994). In the early national period "most district and old-field schoolteachers as well as their urban counterparts used and defended physical punishments to keep order" (Kaestle, 1983, pp. 18–19). Corporal punishment was often seen as a necessity for keeping order in classrooms that could number 40–60 students of varying ages and where instruction was focused on memorization and recitation (Kaestle, 1983).

Corporal punishment was a key feature of how Black and Indigenous People experienced, or were dissuaded from, education. Although enslaved people sought and engaged in literacy practices during the antebellum period (Williams, 2009), physical violence (up to and including death) was a disciplinary practice meant to deter African Americans from learning to read and write. Corporal punishment was also a key management feature of the Indigenous boarding schools that emerged in the late 1800s and focused on dismantling Indigenous cultural identity. Boarding schools were run like military camps: students had their hair cut, were forced to wear military-like uniforms, and were banned from speaking their home languages. Official policy gradually banned the use of corporal punishment, but its use was common in practice (Adams, 2020). Child (1998) observed that "recalcitrant students were flogged, and most boarding schools had some form of jail on the premises" (p. 39). Corporal punishment was not common in Indigenous homes (Adams, 2020), so its use in boarding schools points to the perception of Indigenous children as savages in need of assimilation, as well as a complete disregard for the cultural practices of Indigenous communities.

Even though corporal punishment has been on the decline, the Supreme Court deemed it constitutional in its 1977 *Ingraham v. Wright* decision. As a result, corporal punishment remains legal in 19 states, with schools in Alabama, Arkansas, Mississippi, and Texas being the most frequent users (U.S. Department of Education Office for Civil Rights, 2023a). The specter of race looms large in the data related to corporal punishment, with Black students experiencing corporal punishment at slightly more than twice the rate of their enrollment and Indigenous students experiencing corporal punishment at slightly less than twice their rate of enrollment (U.S. Department of Education Office for Civil Rights, 2023a). In the 2017–2018 school year, Native American students in North Carolina accounted for 55% of corporal punishment cases while comprising just over 1% of the overall student population (U.S. Department of Education Office for Civil Rights, 2022). Even though the use of corporal punishment is in decline, its continued use in some states reflects dominant understandings of who should be punished and how, with some minoritized populations being subjected to it at higher rates, in keeping with historical trends that disproportionately targeted those groups.

Exclusionary Practices

Corporal punishment was a primary means of classroom management until the 1960s, when exclusionary practices, such as in-school and out-of-school suspensions, became more prevalent (Simson, 2014). Part of the appeal of corporal punishment was how visible it was to other students in the school, and the threat of violence was a means of keeping students in line. As school populations expanded, due to the baby boom, corporal punishment was relegated to more private spaces, such as the principal's office, and became less effective as a means of management (Insley, 2001). Instead of acting as a deterrent, the goal of exclusionary practices, such as suspension, was to simply remove problematic student and their influence, from the school (Insley, 2001). By the late 1990s, the vast majority of schools had zero-tolerance policies related to specific fears around drug and alcohol use and bringing weapons to school (Blumenson & Nilsen, 2002).

Much like corporal punishment, research shows that exclusionary practices have an outsized impact on students of color. In 2021–2022, Black boys comprised approximately 18% of expulsions and out-of-school suspensions despite only comprising 8% of the overall student population (U.S. Department of Education Office for Civil Rights, 2023b). In fact, Black boys were twice as likely as white boys to receive an out-of-school suspension or expulsion (U.S. Department of Education Office for Civil Rights, 2023b). Bacher-Hicks, Billings, and Deming (2021) demonstrate the reality of the school-to-prison pipeline. Their research shows that "young adolescents who attend schools with high suspension rates are substantially more likely to be arrested and jailed as adults" (para. 5). This finding applied to all students at the schools, regardless of whether they had personally been suspended and showed a larger impact for Black and Hispanic students. According to Blumenson and Nilsen (2002), these "policies are contributing to an uneducated underclass that just gets larger, more despairing, and more entrenched" (p. 76). Zero-tolerance policies signal the application of adult consequences to children that is meant to speak to the dominant desire for order but does not actually attain the results that are sought.

CONTEMPORARY CHANGES

Exclusionary practices still persist in schools, but in recent years the shift has been toward inclusionary approaches to classroom management. Contemporary approaches to classroom management seek to address the power dynamics and social context that concerned Butchart (1994) and Carson (1995). In general, they aim to correct the biases of other forms of classroom management, take a proactive approach to managing behavior, and avoid punitive measures that alienate students from the classroom and broader school communities.

One common feature of many contemporary approaches to classroom management has been a desire to correct the biases of approaches such as corporal punishment and exclusionary practices. These modern approaches can easily connect or are designed to work with asset-based pedagogical approaches such as culturally responsive pedagogy (Ladson-Billings, 1995) or culturally sustaining pedagogy (Paris, 2012). Culturally responsive classroom management (CRCM) is an example of an approach that stems from this literature. In CRCM, teachers

> recognize their biases and values. They reflect on how these influence their expectations for behavior and interactions with students. They recognize that the ultimate goal of classroom management is not to achieve compliance or control but to provide all students with equitable opportunities for learning. (Weinstein et al., 2004, p. 27)

CRCM is less about a prescriptive approach to classroom management that stresses specific strategies and more about the process of recognizing the power dynamics of culture to create space for all students.

Other classroom management strategies are more focused on creating structures that proactively help students navigate behavioral expectations of schools. Approaches such as positive behavioral intervention and supports (PBIS) focus on multitiered systems that begin with school-wide preventative measures and provide more individualized goal setting when needed. Social emotional learning (SEL) is an approach that highlights lessons related to issues such as managing emotions, conflict resolution, and listening (Jones et al., 2013). PBIS and SEL are not inherently focused on issues of decolonization, race, or oppression. If race is centered in how these approaches are understood and enacted, though, they can become important means for fostering spaces that, in the case of PBIS, can question the implicit biases of school policies (Center for PBIS, 2020) and in the case of SEL, foster a humanizing environment for Black students (Legette et al., 2022).

Finally, contemporary classroom management seeks to avoid punitive measures by restoring the students' place within the classroom and school community. Restorative justice practices, for example, seek to redefine the relationship between disciplinary practices, institutions, and the individual. Instead of focusing on the institutional rules that have been broken and the resulting consequence, restorative justice "entails giving back the harm or wrongdoing to the community most affected and enables a process for the community to address the harm through . . . *restitution, resolution,* and *reconciliation*" (Morrison & Vaandering, 2012, p. 140). Restorative justice, then, is not about exclusion but, rather, creating space to keep and encourage students' connections to one another. It is important to note, however, that contemporary approaches to classroom management are still bound to the dominant discourses of school and society. Therefore, it is imperative, as the following chapters in this volume argue, to consider the underlying goals of classroom management practices, their design, implementation, and impact to ensure that equity is centered and old problems are not just being enacted in new ways.

CONCLUSION

In closing, classroom management has always been an outgrowth of dominant colonial discourse that has sought to reinforce the American racial hierarchy and assimilate those who have deviated from dominant conceptions of American culture. It has also been nonlinear, with tensions existing between proponents of different models of classroom management over time. This process still exists today, as traditional disciplinary measures used to manage public school classrooms still unfairly target students of color. As this volume will show, however, hope can be seen in a reconfiguration of how classroom management is thought of, particularly when management moves from maintaining the status quo of institutional rules to focusing on the diverse cultural practices and needs of students.

REFERENCES

Adams, D. W. (2020). *Education for extinction: American Indians and the boarding school experience, 1875–1928*, revised and expanded. University Press of Kansas.

Anderson, J. D. (2010). *The education of Blacks in the South, 1860–1935*. University of North Carolina Press.

Bacher-Hicks, A., Billings, S., & Deming, D. (2021). Proving the school-to-prison pipeline. *Education Next, 21*(4).

Bartman, A. (2002). Spare the rod and spoil the child-corporal punishment in schools around the world. *Indiana International & Comparative Law Review, 13*, 283–315.

Blumenson, E., & Nilsen, E. S. (2002). How to construct an underclass, or how the war on drugs became a war on education. *Journal of Gender Race & Justice, 6*, 61–109.

Butchart, R. E. (1995). Discipline, dignity, and democracy: Reflections on the history of classroom management (AESA Presidential Address-1994). *Educational Studies, 26*(3), 165–184.

Carson, R. N. (1996). Reaction to presidential address of Ronald Butchart. *Educational Studies, 27*(3), 207–216.

Center on PBIS (2020). *A commitment to racial equity from the Center on PBIS*. https://www.pbis.org/announcements/resources-for-using-pbis-to-increase-racial-equity

Child, B. J. (1998). *Boarding school seasons: American Indian families, 1900–1940*. University of Nebraska Press.

Fraser, J. (2019). *The school in the United States: A documentary history*. Routledge.

Jones, S. M., & Bouffard, S. M. (2012). Social and emotional learning in schools: From programs to strategies. *Society for Research in Child Development, 26*(4), 1–22.

Insley, A. C. (2001). Suspending and expelling children from educational opportunity: Time to reevaluate zero tolerance policies. *American University Law Review, 50*(4), 1039–1074.

Kaestle, C. F. (1983). *Pillars of the republic: Common schools and American society, 1780–1860*, vol. 154. Macmillan.

Labaree, D. F. (2011). Consuming the public school. *Educational theory, 61*(4), 381–394.

Ladson-Billings, G. (1995). Toward a theory of culturally relevant pedagogy. *American Educational Research Journal, 32*(3), 465–491.

Legette, K. B., Rogers, L. O., & Warren, C. A. (2022). Humanizing student–teacher relationships for black children: Implications for teachers' social–emotional training. *Urban Education, 57*(2), 278–288.

Morrison, B. E., & Vaandering, D. (2012). Restorative justice: Pedagogy, praxis, and discipline. *Journal of School Violence, 11*(2), 138–155.

Paris, D. (2012). Culturally sustaining pedagogy: A needed change in stance, terminology, and practice. *Educational Researcher, 41*(3), 93–97.

Pratt, R. H. (1892). *Official report of the nineteenth annual conference of charities and correction.* https://historymatters.gmu.edu/d/4929/

Reese, W. J. (2001). The origins of progressive education. *History of Education Quarterly, 41*(1), 1–24.

Ryan, F. J. (1994). From rod to reason: Historical perspectives on corporal punishment in the public school, 1642–1994. *Educational Horizons, 72*(2), 70–77.

Simson, D. (2013). Exclusion, punishment, racism, and our schools: A critical race theory perspective on school discipline. *UCLA Law Review, 61*, 506–563.

Stratton, C. (2016). *Education for empire: American schools, race, and the paths of good citizenship.* University of California Press.

Tozer, S., Violas, P. C., & Senese, G. B. (2002). *School and society: Historical and contemporary perspectives* (4th ed.). McGraw-Hill.

U.S. Department of Education Office for Civil Rights (2022). 2017–2018 state and national tables. *Civil Rights Data Collection.* https://ocrdata.ed.gov/estimations/2017-2018

U.S. Department of Education Office for Civil Rights (2023a). Corporal punishment in public schools. https://ocrdata.ed.gov/assets/downloads/Corporal_Punishment_Part4.pdf

U.S. Department of Education Office for Civil Rights (2023b). Student discipline and school climate in U.S. public schools. *Civil Rights Data Collection.* https://www2.ed.gov/about/offices/list/ocr/docs/crdc-discipline-school-climate-report.pdf

Weinstein, C. S., Tomlinson-Clarke, S., & Curran, M. (2004). Toward a conception of culturally responsive classroom management. *Journal of Teacher Education, 55*(1), 25–38.

Williams, H. A. (2009). *Self-taught: African American education in slavery and freedom.* University of North Carolina Press.

3

Common and Preferred Practices, But Not Necessarily Best

Problematizing Classification of Best Practices in Educational Research

Ronald Cunningham

In 2014, I was part of a seven-person team of school building and district leaders tasked with opening a K–8 charter school. We were told that the opportunity would challenge us to align school policies with the best available research-based approaches to teaching and learning. The group was encouraged to actively seek out current *best practices* to guide our work. That commitment of employing best practices began when I walked into our new building and learned that all our workstations would be housed in one large room for several months as that was a highly effective means of promoting frequent collaboration opportunities. As the academic director, I was sharing a space with two principals, two deans, and two chief officers. I was in a position where the ramifications of the systems I created had the potential to shape instructional practices throughout an entire charter network all the while I was learning from a chief officer with more district-level experience.

While working on the master schedule, a question arose about recess. We were immediately engaged in a debate about the role of unstructured playtime. There was consensus that lower elementary ought to have recess, but disagreement arose when we began discussing upper elementary. Three members of the team agreed that recess was an opportunity for students to be physically active and practice peer-to-peer social skills. However, the chief academic officer reminded us that third- and fourth-grade recess had not been in place at the network's other charter schools. He communicated that recess at that age was not considered a best practice, and "the research" supported his statement. Though I fundamentally disagreed with his position, I did not readily have access to research of my own to dispute his claim.

Two realities should be considered here. First, the two chief officers, one white and one Black, had previously founded two charter networks. They made considerable profit from having opened those schools and built a name for themselves among educators in that region. Second, the principals, deans, and I were all Black educators and transplants from predominantly Black and Latino turnaround schools in Chicago, Nashville, Oakland, Cleveland, and Washington, D.C. We were all recruited to make research-based decisions. Yet in that instance, the chief academic officer created a school policy based purely on familiarity and personal preference. Further, he made no attempt to educate those of us he perceived as less knowledgeable. His actions created a set of conditions that forced us to submit out of respect for his authority, recognition of his superior expertise, or some combination of the two. His reference to a best practice that "highly effective" schools used trumped anything we might offer. The chief academic officer's behavior strongly suggested some degree of inexperience or even incompetence among the rest of us. It also communicated that he had knowledge of information we all ought to have known, and due to his superior knowledge, it was imperative that we defer to his judgment.

HISTORY AND DEFINITION OF BEST PRACTICES

As far back as the 19th century, attempts have been made to ground educational practices in evidence-based approaches (Reese, 2001). Beginning in the 1970s, there were attempts to make high-quality "programmatic models, exemplary service strategies, and innovative program designs" available to educational practitioners (Peters & Heron, 1993, p. 373). Our current understanding of best practices has its origin in special education research. The term is an extension of an earlier concept, the criterion of ultimate functioning, a framework offering direction for supporting students with severe disabilities (Brown et al., 1976), prompting recognition for a similar resource to address even broader educational needs.

By the 1980s, educational researchers had moved beyond simply embracing the concept of best practices and were actively working to clarify its use. One of the first references to best practices in educational research appeared in a study of early childhood special education (Vincent & Salisbury, 1980), followed by research ranging from consideration of instruction for exceptional students (Wallace et al., 1987) to early intervention programs (Hanson

& Lynch, 1989) and broader consideration of individuals with disabilities (McDonnell & Hardman, 1988). The educational reform movement of the later 20th century was also a significant development because it produced a series of federal policies and financial incentives designed to strengthen the connection between educational practices and research-based knowledge (Franciosi, 2004).

A best practice involves coordination of theory and evidence to ensure that decisions are driven by empirical evidence. It functions as acknowledgment that other practitioners have previously created activities, policies, or programmatic approaches capable of addressing current challenges (Peters & Heron, 1993; Capps et al., 2012). Rather than devote time and resources attempting to do something that has already been done successfully, a best practice leverages existing approaches as they have already demonstrated some capacity to author positive changes to student attitudes or academic behaviors under a particular set of conditions. At its core, a best practice rejects decision making based on traditions and personal judgment and favors evidence-based approaches that display a high level of effectiveness.

THE DANGERS OF MISUSE

Fairly consistent misuse of best practices is well-documented, and no evidence exists of broad movement toward responsible behavior in their use (Arendale, 2010; Peters & Heron, 1993; Kreamer et al., 2023). Using culturally responsive practices (CRP) is an example of this. The approach is grounded in concern for the whole student, motivated by a desire to empower vulnerable student populations, and actively draws on customs, characteristics, and perspectives to create tools for classroom instruction, satisfying the standard of an exemplary educational practice (Kozleski, 2010; Ford et al., 2014; Powell et al., 2016). Students of color have measurably less access to economic or political power and are more likely to deal with some form of overt or policy-based racial discrimination as part of their school experience (Blackwell, 2010; Scott et al., 2017). Students of color are also much more likely to be referred to special education than white students with identical characteristics, be enrolled in a school classified as low or underperforming, face suspension or expulsion, and, as a group, they have less access to meaningful school-based financial and curricular resources than white students (Suarez-Balcazar et al., 2003; Delpit, 2006; Gay, 2018, Stevens et al., 2018). They are less likely to be placed in gifted programs along with honors and advanced placements courses, suffer from low expectations from their teachers, and are overrepresented in remedial programs (Ford & Webb, 1994; Morris, 2001; Olszewski-Kubilius & Thomson, 2010).

Given these realities alongside the social function of schools and the history of physical, verbal, and psychological violence imposed on children of color in American schools, two realities emerge. First, fundamental values promoted through public education that speak to individual worth, what it means to be a "good" American citizen, have always centered white dominance and marginalized the values of people of color (Rivière, 2008; Carroll, 2014). This enforcement of understandings of ethnic and moral superiority on students of color directly contributes to educational inequity and is an inherently colonizing practice. Values promoted through public education in the United States prioritize advancement of political and economic agendas over any commitment to improving individual conditions (Spring, 2017). A best practice abandons its usefulness and functions as a harm when it promotes colonial hierarchical systems based on a series of assumptions about perceived limitations of a group of learners.

There is added concern when a practice promotes belief that only a particular group of educators is uniquely positioned to provide remedy to those perceived limitations (Anderson, 2013). Thus, rather than trust that best practices will naturally promote beneficial outcomes, we must ask best outcomes for whom, as misuse has the capacity to both harm the vulnerable populations they aim to serve and reify social norms grounded in colonizing values (Gorski, 2008).

FROM MISUSE TO EDUCATIONAL POLICY

The way in which many K–12 educators define and employ best practices is directly informed by Doug Lemov's *Teach Like a Champion* (TLAC, 2010), *Teach Like a Champion 2.0* (2015), and *Teach Like a Champion 3.0* (2021). Let's consider two examples of TLAC's most popular practices. In SLANT, students are required to sit up (S), lean forward (L), ask/answer questions (A), nod their heads (N), and track the speaker (T). It promotes the belief that if one does not maintain zealous eye contact with the person speaking, then the student is not engaged in learning. The practice focuses narrowly on what a student ought to look like and offers a clear classification of what it deems unacceptable body positions. However, the belief that eye contact with the person speaking is a reliable indicator of listening or learning is inconsistent with cultural traditions in several communities of color; further, the form of eye contact that the STAR/SLANT practice requires poses unrealistic expectations for a number of neurodivergent learners, most notably many with autism (Ashby & Woodfield, 2019). Finally, eye contact can be influenced by emotions. Insisting that a student maintain eye contact may be overwhelming for a student navigating an emotional response from events that occurred earlier that day (Stephani et al., 2019).

Another TLAC practice, Format Matters, provides guidance for how students should speak. An effective teacher, as defined by Lemov, rejects use of what is considered slang or incorrect grammar usage, choosing instead to correct tone and ensure that communication reflects "college language." This practice imposes strict guidance around language use and offers a no-excuse approach to any deviation. Yet, linguistic research recognizes that language is expressed differently among different cultures (Kramsch, 2014). Despite that, this practice relies on an understanding of what constitutes appropriate language for children of color, as defined by word choice and sound, that is based on white norms. Lemov's colonizing approach to education is essentially a behavior management toolkit that promotes a number of actions, misclassified as best practices, and several of those so-called best practices are directly at odds with proven scientific knowledge.

CONCLUSION

In the introduction I described a situation where I witnessed someone in a position of power make broad reference to a best practice without offering a detailed explanation to show how application of that behavior was appropriate in that setting. Sadly, that was neither the first nor the last time I encountered this behavior. There seem times when educators are prone to advocate so aggressively for a particular approach that they risk conflating *preferred* practices with *best* practices as a means of dismissing an opposing viewpoint and eliminating opportunity for thoughtful discussion. The concept of a best practice is weaponized when the individual using the term wields authority over others, is in a formal or informal role that involves some form of capacity building or coaching of others, uses the term for a self-serving purpose, or some combination of these three conditions. When this occurs, interactions seem less about attempts to identify the most beneficial course of action than an assertion of power grounded in privilege. Certainly, novice practitioners in any discipline must be aware of practices that have produced beneficial outcomes. However, we have seen what can happen when individuals in positions of authority capitalize on the ambiguity of the term along with the power activated by classifying a preferred behavior as a best, absent adherence to a clear set of standards outlined in the existing best practice framework.

In the face of harmful outcomes resulting from misuse of best practices, our current challenges are easily remedied. There is no need to redefine the concept as a body of work outlining a clear definition of best practices, complete with explanation of types of practices and emphasis on context already exists. Rather than redefine or come up with a new definition, we simply need to embrace the guidance provided through the existing definition and hold other educators accountable to ensure that they do the same.

REFERENCES

Anderson, A. (2013). Teach for America and the dangers of deficit thinking. *Critical Education, 4*(11). https://doi.org/10.14288/ce.v4i11.183936

Arendale, D. (2010). *What is a best education practice?* Unpublished manuscript. Department of curriculum and instruction, University of Minnesota, Minneapolis. https://www.arendale.org/best-education- practices.

Ashby, C., & Woodfield, C. (2019). Honoring, constructing and supporting neurodivergent communicators in inclusive classrooms. In *Promoting social inclusion: Co-creating environments that foster equity and belonging* (pp. 151–167). Emerald Publishing Limited.

Blackwell, D. M. (2010). Sidelines and separate spaces: Making education anti-racist for students of color. *Race Ethnicity and Education, 13*(4), 473–494. https://doi.org/10.1080/13613324.2010.492135

Brown, L., Nietupski, J., & Hamre-Nietupski, S. (1976). Criterion of ultimate functioning. In M. A. Thomas (Ed.), *Hey, don't forget about me!: Education's investment in the severely, profoundly, and multiply handicapped* (pp. 2–15). Council for Exceptional Children.

Capps, D. K., Crawford, B. A., & Constas, M. A. (2012). A review of empirical literature on inquiry professional development: Alignment with best practices and a critique of the findings. *Journal of Science Teacher Education, 23*(3), 291–318. https://doi.org/10.1007/s10972-012-9275-2

Carroll, S. (2014). The construction and perpetuation of whiteness. *Journal of Unschooling & Alternative Learning, 8*(15).

Delpit, L. (2006). *Other people's children: Cultural conflict in the classroom*. New Press.

Ford, B. A., Stuart, D. H., & Vakil, S. (2014). Culturally responsive teaching in the 21st century inclusive classroom. *Journal of the International Association of Special Education, 15*(2), 56–62.

Ford, D. Y., & Webb, K. S. (1994). Desegregation of gifted educational programs: The impact of Brown on underachieving children of color. *Journal of Negro Education, 63*(3), 358–375. https://doi.org/10.2307/2967187

Franciosi, R. J. (2004). *The rise and fall of American public schools: The political economy of public education in the twentieth century*. Bloomsbury Publishing USA.

Gay, G. (2018). *Culturally responsive teaching: Theory, research, and practice*. Teachers College Press.

Gorski, P. C. (2008). Good intentions are not enough: A decolonizing intercultural education. *Intercultural education, 19*(6), 515–525. https://doi.org/10.1080/14675980802568319

Hanson, M. J., & Lynch, E. W. (1995). *Early intervention: Implementing child and family services for infants and toddlers who are at risk or disabled.* PRO-ED Austin, TX.

Kozleski, E. B. (2010). Culturally responsive teaching matters! Online submission.

Kramsch, C. (2014). Language and culture. *AILA Review, 27*(1), 30–55.

Kreamer, L. M., & Albritton, B. H., Tonidandel, S., & Rogelberg, S. G. (2023). The use and misuse of organizational research methods "best practice" articles. *Organizational Research Methods, 26*(3), 387–408. https://doi.org/10.1177/10944281211060706

Lemov, D. (2010). *Teach like a champion: 49 techniques that put students on the path to college.* Jossey-Bass.

Lemov, D. (2015). *Teach like a champion 2.0: 62 techniques that put students on the path to college.* Jossey-Bass.

Lemov, D. (2021). *Teach like a champion 3.0: 63 techniques that put students on the path to college.* Wiley.

McDonnell, A., & Hardman, M. (1988). A synthesis of "best practice" guidelines for early childhood services. *Journal of the Division for Early Childhood, 12*(4), 328–341. https://doi.org/10.1177/105381518801200406

Morris, J. E. (2001). African American students and gifted education: The politics of race and culture. *Roeper Review, 24*(2), 59–62. https://doi.org/10.1080/02783190209554130

Olszewski-Kubilius, P., & Thomson, D. L. (2010). Gifted programming for poor or minority urban students: Issues and lessons learned. *Gifted Child Today, 33*(4), 58–64. https://doi.org/10.1177/107621751003300413

Peters, M. T., & Heron, T. E. (1993). When the best is not good enough: An examination of best practice. *Journal of Special Education, 26*(4), 371–385. https://doi.org/10.1177/002246699302600403

Powell, R., Cantreall, S. C., Malo-Juvera, V., & Correll, P. (2016). Operationalizing culturally responsive instruction: Preliminary findings of CRIOP research. *Teachers College Record, 118*(1), 1–46. https://doi.org/10.1177/016146811611800107

Reese, W. J. (2001). The origins of progressive education. *History of Education Quarterly, 41*(1), 1–24. http://www.jstor.org/stable/369477

Rivière, D. (2008). Whiteness in/and education. *Race Ethnicity and Education, 11*(4), 355–368. https://doi.org/10.1080/13613320802478838

Scott, J., Moses, M. S., Finnigan, K. S., Trujillo, T., & Jackson, D. D. (2017). Law and order in school and society: How discipline and policing policies harm students of color, and what we can do about it. National Education Policy Center.

Spring, J. (2017). *American education.* Routledge.

Stephani, T., Driller, K. K., Dimigen, O., & Sommer, W. (2020). Eye contact in active and passive viewing: Event-related brain potential evidence from a combined eye tracking and EEG study. *Neuropsychologia, 143*, 107478. https://doi.org/10.1016/j.neuropsychologia.2020.107478

Stevens, C., Liu, C. H., & Chen, J. A. (2018). Racial/ethnic disparities in US college students' experience: Discrimination as an impediment to academic performance.

Journal of American College Health, 66(7), 665–673. https://doi.org/10.1080/07448481.2018.1452745

Suarez-Balcazar, Y., Orellana-Damacela, L., Portillo, N., Rowan, J. M., & Andrews-Guillen, C. (2003). Experiences of differential treatment among college students of color. *Journal of Higher Education, 74*(4), 428–444. https://doi.org/10.1080/00221546.2003.11780855

Vincent, L. J., & Salisbury, C. G. (1980). *Program evaluation and curriculum development in early childhood/special education: Criteria of the next environment.* University of Wisconsin.

Wallace, G., Cohen, S. B., & Polloway, E. A. (1987). *Language arts: Teaching exceptional students.* Pro-Ed.

4

Under the Hood of a Well-Oiled Machine

Revealing Racism and Ableism Within Classroom Management Practices Through Disability Critical Race Theory (DisCrit)

April Coloma Boyce and Maggie R. Beneke

In schools, classrooms with efficient routines, organized environments, and high test scores are often described to "run like well-oiled machines." Although drawing a likeness between classrooms and machines may seem purely figurative, this comparison evokes a factory model of schooling. Brought about by 19th-century American industrialization (Leland & Kasten, 2002), the one-size-fits-all factory model of school emphasized specific behaviors and compliance with written and unwritten rules (e.g., respecting authority, following directions, reliability, and productivity). Today, a focus on classroom management still dominates teacher education programs and is often seen as necessary for learning (Migliarini & Annamma, 2020).

Despite their popularity, techniques of classroom management create racial-ability hierarchies, with children of color's *abilities* being hyper-surveilled for behavioral deficits, hyper-labeled for special education services, and hyper-punished through suspensions and expulsions (Annamma et al., 2021; Beneke et al., 2022). And although rigid approaches to classroom management have been critiqued for reproducing a factory model of education (Katz, 1971; Keenan, 2021), less work has troubled the ways they leverage ableism[1] and racism to do so.

In this chapter, we use disability critical race theory (DisCrit; Annamma et al., 2013) to specify the ways ableism and racism are inherent within current models of classroom management. We apply DisCrit through fictionalized vignettes (Caine et al., 2017), illustrating how seemingly neutral classroom management practices and discipline policies maintain racism and ableism in schools. Last, we offer implications for using DisCrit in practice as a way forward to reframe behaviors and classroom management. Throughout, we argue that instead of desiring classrooms that operate as well-oiled machines, we must disrupt classroom management models rooted in racism and ableism, breaking away from the mold of a cookie-cutter education and toward more liberatory approaches for children.

APPLYING DISCRIT TO CLASSROOM MANAGEMENT

We build and expand on previous work examining how ableism and racism intersect vis-à-vis classroom management in teacher education (Migliarini & Annamma, 2020), using DisCrit to reveal how children of color with and without disabilities are further marginalized by efforts to bring order to preK–12 classrooms. Bringing together perspectives from critical race theory (Bell, 1980; Delgado & Stefancic, 1998; Ladson-Billings & Tate, 1995) and disability studies in education (Baglieri et al., 2011, Ware, 2001), and extending the lineage of Black feminist theorizing surrounding intersectionality (Collins, 1990; Crenshaw, 1989; Lorde, 1984), DisCrit examines how ableism and racism intersect in schools and society (Annamma et al., 2013).

In this chapter we foreground two key principles of DisCrit. First, DisCrit illuminates how ableism is leveraged as a seemingly "neutral" tool to perpetuate racism, pathologizing children of color (Yancy, 2023). For instance, classroom management techniques such as positive behavioral interventions and supports (PBIS) and social-emotional learning curricula are often touted as beneficial for children, yet in reality they uphold ideals of "normative behavior" rooted in white, nondisabled ways of knowing and being (e.g., sitting crisscross applesauce in a group, working silently, making eye contact). We show how ableism and racism intersect in management techniques that position children of color as having behavioral challenges (Annamma, 2018; Love & Beneke, 2021; Waitoller & Annamma, 2017). Next, although race and ability/disability are socially constructed, DisCrit highlights the material and psychological impacts of being labeled outside of dominant societal norms (Annamma et al., 2022). Indeed, when children of color are labeled with behavioral deficits or disabilities, they are positioned as problems that require interventions to be "fixed," often leading to experiences of exclusion and segregation (Annamma et al., 2021; Kulkarni et al., 2022). We illustrate how pathologizing management processes leads to harmful lived consequences for children of color in preK–12 school settings.

CLASSROOM MANAGEMENT: MORE HARM THAN GOOD

In what follows, we draw on narrative methods of fictionalization to trouble conventional understandings of classroom management and imagine otherwise possibilities (Barone, 2001; Caine et al., 2017). We present the fictionalized classroom of Ms. Jones, a white, nondisabled first-grade teacher. We also introduce Henry—a curious, energetic six-year-old Black boy labeled "developmentally delayed" and described by his teachers and principal as having emotional and behavioral challenges. The interactions we describe between Ms. Jones and Henry are composite vignettes (Humphreys & Watson, 2009) representative of our experiences teaching and observing in U.S. public school classrooms over the past 15 years.

As former teachers and current teacher educators, we implicate ourselves in having carried out some of these same management techniques in our own practice. We understand the constraints placed on educators, who often deploy management practices to meet unrealistic and unsustainable schooling requirements. Thus, we are not interested in blaming teachers. Instead, we seek to reveal how, despite best intentions, educators regularly engage in classroom management practices rooted in racism and ableism. As James Baldwin (1962) famously stated, "[N]othing can be changed until it is faced." We expose the ways ableism and racism intersect in classroom management practices as a first step toward supporting teachers in transforming them.

Rewarding Compliance and Punishing Deviance

Ms. Jones walks into her first-grade classroom that she spent all summer preparing. On the walls are colorful posters with words she hopes to instill in her students: "you are welcome here," "believe in the power of yet," "sprinkle kindness like confetti." Ms. Jones believes that classroom management is foundational to academic learning. She sets up desks in groups of four to strengthen peer relationships and sets out two baskets of crayons for each group to promote taking turns and sharing. The district's new social-emotional learning curriculum includes a daily check-in to improve classroom management, so at each desk she places a check-in worksheet, with four "feeling" faces for children to choose from and space to write why they feel that way.

As children enter the classroom, Ms. Jones greets them with a smile. She instructs children to sit and work on their check-in sheets. After 10 minutes, Ms. Jones sings out, "one, two, three, eyes on me!" Several children sing back, "one, two, eyes on you." Pleased that most children have learned the attention-getter so quickly, she holds up a bell and continues, "When you hear this bell, it's time to put your crayons in the baskets and your baskets in the middle of the table. When your group has materials put away, that means you're all ready and will earn a table point for the prize box on Friday!" Ms. Jones rings the bell. Scanning the room, she sees a table with two green baskets at the center. Ms. Jones collects the papers and shouts, "The green table is ready; nice work! You earned a table point!" She continues around the room and stops at the blue table. "Great job; blue table has earned a point!" She scans the remaining tables. "Yellow table is almost clear, but I still see friends at the red table who aren't ready." She places her hand on Henry's desk. He doesn't notice and continues drawing on his paper. Henry's tablemate, Tristan, shakes their head disapprovingly. "Now we won't get a point." Another child, Krista sighs, turns to Mr. K (the instructional aide), and suggests, "Henry needs your help."

Despite her best intentions, Ms. Jones's classroom management practices reward compliance and create competition rather than cultivate a strong community. The problematic nature of group contingencies (i.e., table points) is shrouded under goals of teamwork and cooperation. When children are promised rewards contingent on their peers, children exhibiting behaviors deemed as "inappropriate" in the classroom are singled out for their noncompliance, further marking them as outliers in their community. The expectation of being responsible for group rewards creates hierarchies and competition to gain access to privileges and social status. This harkens back to the factory model, sorting workers by their ability to meet white, nondisabled standards. Individuals who could comply with normative expectations were rewarded for maintaining the status quo. In schooling, the one-size-fits-all approach further marginalizes children of color with and without disabilities. Tristan and Krista express disapproving statements aimed at Henry, implicitly labeling him as inconsiderate and incapable, thus pushing him to the bottom of the social ladder. As seen among Ms. Jones's students, the pressure to meet classroom expectations reproduces social stratification by both race and ability (Sleeter, 2015).

Training Children to Adhere to Normative Behavioral Standards

Ms. Jones calls out, "Green table! Thanks for putting things away quickly—you may tuck your chairs in and join me for group time." Children at the green table tuck in their chairs and sit crisscross on the green row of the rug. Ms. Jones continues dismissing the other tables while Mr. K supports Henry's transition with visual reminders and a sticker chart. If Henry earns all his stars by following directions, he gets five minutes of iPad time at the end of the day. Henry is motivated—he puts away his crayons and walks toward the rug.

Classroom management practices such as the group and individual rewards Ms. Jones doles out prioritize normative behavioral standards. Behaviorist theories suggest that token economies (e.g., sticker charts) can increase achievement and improve children's behavior (Kazdin, 1975; Nevin, Johnson, & Johnson, 1982; Main & Munro, 1977), but critical scholars have pointed out that methods such as these aim to "train" children's compliance, coercing them to follow directions rooted in white supremacy (Jones & Okun, 2001) and ableist behavioral expectations (Beneke et al., 2022). These practices implicitly devalue behaviors deemed nonnormative (i.e., hyperactivity, stimming). They also allow preK–12 general educators to deflect their responsibility to build meaningful relationships with children, and instructional aides or paraprofessionals are often left to train children's compliance to the sound of bells or the promise of treats (Kohn, 1993). Education is more than demanding conformity; these strategies must be reconsidered to shift from controlling behaviors to cultivating relationships (Keenan, 2021).

Revising Children's Words to Fulfill the Adult Gaze

> Ms. Jones sits at the front of the rug. In a quiet voice, she sings, "Eyes are watching, ears are listening, voices quiet, body calm. This is how we listen at circle time." The class is quiet. Ms. Jones continues, "Today, we're working on our classroom charter. A charter is what we use to make sure we all know how to care for our community. First, let's talk about how we want to feel." On a posterboard, she writes, "In this class we want to feel . . . " She continues, "How do you want to feel in our class? Raise a quiet hand if you would like to share." Ms. Jones writes the words as children share: calm, respected, safe. She notices Henry bouncing on his knees with his hand in the air. "Henry, thanks for raising your hand! Sit with a calm body, and I'll call on you." Henry sits and shouts, "Silly!" Ms. Jones responds, "Hmm, silly? Do you mean like having fun?" Henry nods his head. "Great idea! What about if we add 'joyful'?" Henry gives a dissatisfied look but mutters, "Sure."

Henry and Ms. Jones's interaction illustrates a practice all too common in classrooms: revising children's thoughts to fulfill the adult gaze (Templeton & Vellanki, 2022). Although Ms. Jones attempted to listen to children's ideas for the charter, she did not fully accept Henry's word choice and revised it to fit her own agenda. In addition, Ms. Jones deemed silliness as antithetical to learning, despite the ways play and humor are meaningful to both children and adults making meaning (Banas et al., 2011). Even as they attempt to follow children's lead, educators are frequently challenged by barriers including curricular constraints and limited time (Wessel-Powell et al., 2019; Yoon & Templeton, 2019). This means that they often default to shaping and shifting children's words and ideas to guide conversations and ultimately decide what gets put on classroom charters and displayed on walls.

The adult gaze also creates a hierarchy among students. Children whose statements are revised or redirected are publicly marked as inadequate. When educators correct some children more than others, ideologies of normalcy are constructed, and children internalize messages about who is deemed smart and good (or not) (Beneke & Cheatham, 2021; Broderick & Leonardo, 2016; Leonardo & Broderick, 2011). Because children of color are most often targets of pathologization, educators must consider ways to decenter the adult gaze to disrupt patterns of racism and ableism in the classroom.

Social-Emotional "Competence" and Discarding the Weakest Link

> After group time, Ms. Jones announces, "I'm looking for calm and quiet bodies to line up for recess." She scans the room, looking at children sitting on their carpet squares mimicking the teacher with their fingers pressed to their lips. As Ms. Jones begins to call on children, she shoots an irritated look at Henry who is humming loudly in the back row. One by one, children walk past Henry, who soon realizes that his peers are leaving. He bolts to the line. Ms. Jones stands in his path and reminds him, "Only quiet voices get to line up. Please sit back down!" Mr. K escorts him back to his carpet square and holds up his star chart to remind Henry of his reward.
>
> Later during math work time, Ms. Jones turns attention to the red table. Henry is sitting on the floor, drumming his pencil on the table legs while his classmates sit at their desks with plastic cubes and worksheets. Exasperated, Ms. Jones takes a deep breath. "We take care of our classmates and our materials. That drumming is too distracting for your friends, and you might break the pencil." She helps Henry back to his chair and reminds him to get back to work. "I'm hungry and I'm tired. This is too hard; I can't do it!" Henry exclaims. Ms. Jones points to the poster on the wall: "Remember growth mind-set! You can't do it YET." She gives him a gentle pat on the back, smiles, and walks away. Henry grunts, crumples his worksheet, and continues drumming. Ms. Jones turns back with furrowed brows. "Henry, it looks like you're feeling angry. Please go take a break in the hallway."

In Ms. Jones's classroom, children who are "calm and quiet" are first to access opportunities and privileges. Racism and ableism co-construct such ideals of social-emotional competence, which are then weaponized to police children's bodies and minds (Kaler-Jones, 2020). In schools, self-regulation is frequently promoted for the sole purpose of focusing and producing more academic work (versus a consideration of the child's well-being). Indeed, a "calm" and "focused" body is commonly used in classroom charters, yet these behavioral expectations are narrowly defined (Beneke et al., 2022). And although character education is frequently integrated to encourage children's development toward social-emotional competence, when educators introduce topics such as "growth mind-set," they may inadvertently ignore or disregard broader issues that may be at play in children's lives (e.g., socioeconomic disparities driven by centuries of systemic racism) (Yeh et al., 2023).

Finally, prioritizing compliance with ideals of social-emotional competence—or rather, encouraging children to mask behaviors deemed nonnormative—means that children's inability to "follow directions" typically results in punishment (Beneke et al., 2022; Shalaby, 2021). Ms. Jones deemed Henry's behavior as disruptive to his classmates to justify his removal from the classroom. Although educators may suggest that removing a disruptive child from the classroom will benefit the "greater good," this sends a message to all children that certain bodies and minds are disposable.

CONCLUSION

When children are positioned as "problems" vis-à-vis classroom management in preK–12 classrooms, schools and society are absolved of the responsibility to support certain children or transform the systems contributing to the child's pathologization (Janzen, 2019). Although scholars have highlighted the pervasiveness of whiteness in dominant approaches to classroom management (McManus, 2022), DisCrit offers a critical lens for explicating how ableism functions to ensure that classrooms run like a "well-oiled machine," instantiating racial hierarchies through so-called neutral classroom management techniques. Naming the oppressive ideologies undergirding these techniques creates space to imagine alternatives, including in teacher education (both preservice and in-service). That is, DisCrit can operate as a lever for praxis, supporting teacher educators, administrators, and preK–12 teachers themselves to resist dehumanizing processes of compliance and control, making space for multiply marginalized children to authentically thrive.

NOTES

1. Talila Lewis (2022) defines ableism as "A system of assigning value to people's bodies and minds based on societally constructed ideas of normalcy, productivity, desirability, intelligence, excellence, and fitness" (n.p.).

REFERENCES

Annamma, S. A. (2018). Mapping consequential geographies in the carceral state: Education journey mapping as a qualitative method with girls of color with dis/abilities. *Qualitative Inquiry, 24*(1), 20–34. https://doi.org/10.1177/1077800417728962

Annamma, S., Connor, D., & Ferri, B. (2013). Dis/ability critical race studies (DisCrit): Theorizing at the intersections of race and dis/ability. *Race, Ethnicity and Education, 16*(1), 1–31. https://doi.org/10.1080/13613324.2012.730511

Annamma, S. A., Ferri, B. A., & Connor, D. J. (Eds.). (2022). *DisCrit expanded: Reverberations, ruptures, and inquiries.* Teachers College Press.

Annamma, S. A., Morgan, J., & Brown, K. (2021). A DisCrit abolitionist imaginary: CRT, DisCrit, and the abolition of youth prisons. In *Handbook of critical race theory in education* (pp. 236–248). Taylor and Francis. https://doi.org/10.4324/9781351032223-20

Baglieri, S., Valle, J. W., Connor, D. J., & Gallagher, D. J. (2011). Disability studies in education: The need for a plurality of perspectives on disability. *Remedial and Special Education, 32*(4), 267–278. https://doi.org/10.1177/0741932510362200

Baldwin, J. (1962, January 14). As much truth as one can bear. *New York Times.* https://www.nytimes.com/1962/01/14/archives/as-much-truth-as-one-can-bear-to-speak-out-about-the-world-as-it-is.html

Banas, J. A., Dunbar, N., Rodriguez, D., & Liu, S. J. (2011). A review of humor in educational settings: Four decades of research. *Communication Education, 60*(1), 115–144. https://doi.org/10.1080/03634523.2010.496867

Barone, T. (2001). Pragmatizing the imaginary: A response to a fictionalized case study of teaching. *Harvard Educational Review, 71*(4), 734–742. https://doi.org/10.17763/haer.71.4.254711411187p4m8

Bell, D. A. (1980). Brown v. board of education and the interest-convergence dilemma. *Harvard Law Review, 93*(3), 518–533. https://doi.org/10.2307/1340546

Beneke, M. R., & Cheatham, G. A. (2020). Teacher candidates talking (but not talking) about dis/ability and race in preschool. *Journal of Literacy Research, 52*(3), 245–268. https://doi.org/10.1177/1086296X20939561

Beneke, M. R., Machado, E., & Taitingfong, J. (2022a). DisCrit literacies: Early childhood teachers critically reading school as text and imagining an otherwise. *Reading Research Quarterly, 57*(4), 1237–1257. https://doi.org/10.1002/rrq.466

Beneke, M. R., Machado, E., & Taitingfong, J. (2022). *Dismantling carceral logics in the urban early literacy classroom: Towards liberatory literacy pedagogies with/for multiply marginalized young children.* Urban Education. https://doi.org/10.1177/00420859221091235.

Caine, V., Murphy, M. S., Estefan, A., Clandinin, D. J., Steeves, P., & Huber, J. (2017). Exploring the purposes of fictionalization in narrative inquiry. *Qualitative Inquiry, 23*(3), 215–221. https://doi.org/10.1177/1077800416643997

Collins, P. H. (1990). Black feminist thought in the matrix of domination. In *Black feminist thought: Knowledge, consciousness, and the politics of empowerment* (pp. 221–238). Routledge.

Crenshaw, K. (2013). Demarginalizing the intersection of race and sex: A black feminist critique of antidiscrimination doctrine, feminist theory and antiracist politics. In K. Masche (Ed.), *Feminist legal theories* (pp. 23–51). Routledge. https://chicagounbound.uchicago.edu/uclf/vol1989/iss1/8

Delgado, R., & Stefancic, J. (1998). Critical race theory: Past, present, and future. *Current Legal Problems, 51*(1), 467–491. https://doi.org/10.1093/clp/51.1.467

Humphreys, M., & Watson, T. (2009). Ethnographic practices: From "writing up ethnographic research" to "ethnographic writing." In S. Ybema, D. Yanow, & H. Wels (Eds.), *Organizational ethnography: Studying the complexities of everyday life* (pp. 40–55). Sage.

Jones, K., & Okun, T. (2001). White supremacy culture. *Dismantling racism: A workbook for social change*. https://www.cwsworkshop.org/PARC_site_B/dr-culture.html

Jones, R. T., & Kazdin, A. E. (1975). Programming response maintenance after withdrawing token reinforcement *Behavior Therapy, 6*(2), 153–164. https://doi.org/10.1016/S0005-7894(75)80136-5

Katz, M. B. (1971). *Class, bureaucracy, and schools: The illusion of educational change in America.* Praeger. https://doi.org/10.1080/00131727309339245

Keenan, H. B. (2021). Building classroom communities: A pedagogical reflection and syllabus excerpt. In Education for liberation network & critical resistance editorial collective, *Lessons in liberation: An abolitionist toolkit for educators* (pp. 156–169). AK Press.

Kohn, A. (1993). *Punished by rewards.* Houghton Mifflin.

Kulkarni, S. S., Kim, S., & Powell, T. (2022). Playing together: A call for multiple stakeholders to reduce exclusionary and harsh discipline for young BICOC with disabilities. *Perspectives on Early Childhood Psychology and Education, 6*(1), 251–278. https://doi.org/10.58948/2834–8257.1008

Ladson-Billings, G., & Tate, W. F. (1995). Toward a critical race theory of education. *Teachers College Record, 97*(1), 47–68. https://doi.org/10.1177/016146819509700104

Leland, C. H., & Kasten, W. C. (2002). Literacy education for the 21st century: It's time to close the factory. *Reading & Writing Quarterly, 18*(1), 5–15. https://doi.org/10.1080/105735602753386315

Leonardo, Z., & Broderick, A. A. (2011). Smartness as property: A critical exploration of intersections between whiteness and disability studies. *Teachers College Record, 113*(10), 2206–2232. https://doi.org/10.1177/016146811111301008

Lorde, A. (1984). *Sister outsider.* Crossing Press.

Love, H. R., & Beneke, M. R. (2021). Pursuing justice-driven inclusive education research: Disability critical race theory (DisCrit) in early childhood. *Topics in Early Childhood Special Education, 41*(1), 31–44. https://doi.org/10.1177/0271121421990833

Main, G. C., & Munro, B. C. (1977). A token reinforcement program in a public junior high school. *Journal of Applied Behavior Analysis, 1*(1), 93–94. https://doi.org/10.1901/jaba.1977.10–93

Mcmanus, M. E. (2022). "Breathe and be ready to learn": The issue with social-emotional learning programs as classroom management. *Perspectives on Early Childhood Psychology and Education, 6*(1), 6. https://doi.org/10.58948/2834-8257.1006

Migliarini, V., & Annamma, S. A. (2020). Classroom and behavior management: (Re)conceptualization through disability critical race theory. *Handbook on promoting social justice in education*, 1511–1532. Springer. https://doi.org/10.1007/978-3-319-74078-2_95-2

Nevin, A., Johnson, D. W., & Johnson, R. (1982). Effects of group and individual contingencies on academic performance and social relations of special needs students. *Journal of Social Psychology, 116*(1), 41–59. https://doi.org/10.1080/00224545.1982.9924394

Sleeter, C. (2015). Multicultural education vs. factory model schooling. In H. P. Baptiste, A. Ryan, B. Artaujo, & R. Fuhon-Sells (Eds.), *Multicultural education: A renewed paradigm of transformation and call to action* (pp. 115–136). Caddo Gap Press.

Templeton, T. N., & Vellanki, V. (2022). Decentering the adult gaze: Young children's photographs as provocations for place-making. *Language Arts, 99*(4), 227–240. https://doi.org/10.58680/la202231740

Waitoller, F. R., & Annamma, S. A. (2017). Taking a spatial turn in inclusive education: Seeking justice at the intersections of multiple markers of difference. In M. Tejero Hughes & E. Talbott (Eds.), *The Wiley handbook of diversity in special education* (pp. 23–44). Wiley. https://doi.org/10.1002/9781118768778.ch2

Ware, L. (2001). Writing, identity, and the other: Dare we do disability studies? *Journal of Teacher Education, 52*(2), 107–123. https://doi.org/10.1177/0022487101052002003

Wessel-Powell, C., Buchholz, B. A., & Brownell, C. J. (2019). Polic(y)ing time and curriculum: How teachers critically negotiate restrictive policies. *English Teaching: Practice & Critique, 18*(2), 170–187. http://dx.doi.org/10.1108/ETPC-12-2018-0116

Yancy, G. (2023, April 11). Let's confront ideas of "normality"—they are rooted in racism and ableism. *Truthout*. https://truthout.org/articles/lets-confront-ideas-of-normality-they-are-rooted-in-racism-and-ableism/

Yoon, H. S., & Templeton, T. N. (2019). The practice of listening to children: The challenges of hearing children out in an adult-regulated world. *Harvard Educational Review, 89*(1), 55–73. https://doi.org/10.17763/1943-5045-89.1.55

5

Building Belonging in Classroom Learning Communities

Erika McDowell

Belonging is defined as experiencing appreciation, validation, acceptance, and fair treatment within an environment (Cobb & Krownapple, 2019). Implementation strategies to decolonize classrooms should center on understanding and building relationships with the folx in the community to sustain and cultivate belonging within classroom environments. No one solution exists that will transform schools to impact disparities in educational opportunities and outcomes (Bal et al., 2016). Interventions are great efforts, yet none combat the colonization of classroom environments, consciously or unconsciously. Educators continue to try to combine evidence-based approaches but still fall short in creating classroom environments where everyone belongs.

To address these significant issues, we must center a love ethic and adapt the way we teach to cultivate belonging and shift what is harmful in our classrooms. As I reflect on my practice, when I have flown and driven to different schools, districts, conferences, offices, hotels, and houses of worship, I have come to the stark realization that understanding belonging starts with the individual, and one belongs to oneself first. A lack of love pedagogy in educational environments begins with the educator. We can radically accept and change what is not working when we understand that real transformative change starts and is sustained at an interpersonal level. The global educational community is not OK, and belonging is the next step to dismantling and rethinking current practices, individually and collectively.

Decolonization, belonging, and community must be centered on responding to and building liberating environments and strengthening the bonds of community. Bell (2005) states,

We must recognize and acknowledge (at least to ourselves) that our actions are not likely to lead to transcendent change and, despite our best efforts, may be of more help to the system we despise than to the victims of that system we are trying to help. (p. 192)

Let's suppose actions and practices are critical in helping learners. In this case, we must use strategic tools to assist educators to ensure that classrooms are equitable, full of love, centered in evidence-based practice, and understanding of the history of community and education. The purpose of this chapter is to explore decolonizing classrooms through love, community, and belonging. This is inclusive of building a framework to cultivate belonging and building relationships with community through love pedagogy. Strategies to actualize belonging in community and practices can give educators a starting point in decolonizing our classrooms and our work.

BUILDING A FRAMEWORK OF BELONGING

According to the National Assessment of Educational Progress (NAEP, 2023), "Frameworks define the subject-specific content and thinking skills needed by students to deal with the complex issues they encounter in and out of the classroom." Frameworks define the work and thinking skills, shared in a manner where school partners and participants are included in safe environments and create a world in which all can thrive. One could argue that frameworks are a little like a recipe. Let's look at classroom environments as a recipe. It stands to reason that one must adapt their work for *all* for a recipe to be received and not cause harm physically. We must build a framework of belonging based on relationships with equity and community at the center to liberate and not harm our learners.

Imagine that a school is hosting a gathering, and the community is culturally and linguistically diverse. Before inviting various members of the community, educators must ponder the inclusive measures that should be taken so the gathering can center belonging. For example, the invitations may be translated into different languages spoken in the community, accommodations may be provided, or certain community members may need to be honored. This starts with a review of who is part of the larger school community that impacts the classroom environments in a school and must be done mindfully by the educators beforehand. Why do most invitations to social events ask questions about food preferences? The planner needs a certain amount of data to make decisions about food preparation based on the recipients who are attending. A school can adapt the "recipe" to make the necessary adjustments so that the event is a safe experience.

Educators must be committed to using cultural and linguistic data points and understanding the history of our work as practitioners to shift our approach to a *with* mind-set rather than a fixed mind-set. The practice of cultivating belonging helps educators become good at seeing people authentically, but it first starts with educators richly connecting with the community they are in service to and work in. No learner should have to lean into the dominant culture of a classroom simply because nothing is wrong with the culture the learner hails from. Instead, educators need to ask themselves, "What are we going to do to change so everybody feels good here?" Educators also have a responsibility to work on building community, which entails listening to the local community where the school environment lives, making space for the community to be involved and belonged to learners' education journeys, and allowing the community to be active participants in decolonizing classrooms with the community.

Dr. Ronald Whitaker's H.E.L.P. framework (Misner, 2021) provides strategies to build belonging to ensure that every learner is safe and whole in a learning environment. The H.E.L.P framework

- acknowledges the history of racism and racist acts in educational spaces and society (DuBois, 1903; Horsford, 2011; West, 1995);
- analyzes the difference between equality and equity (Gorski, 2019);
- argues that love is an essential element to a student's sense of belonging (Glaude, 2016; Hill & Bartol, 2016; Strayhorn, 2012); and
- accentuates the importance of employing cultural pedagogical and school leadership practices and programming (Gay, 2002; Khalifah, 2018; Ladson-Billings, 1995; Paris, 2012).

Leveraging this framework to start the process of decolonizing our classrooms will build communities of resistance that commit to the whole child and the work of decolonization. Using and sustaining this framework could dramatically shift classroom practices for the freedom and liberation of all community members by centering the belonging of learners, with participation with the community they live in.

UNPACKING HISTORICAL CULTURE

Defining culture has been difficult and done differently depending on the legal, political, and educational perspectives of those involved (Sugai et al., 2012). If belonging is a goal, and building relationships is key, an exploration and understanding of a learner's culture is necessary. Multiple research studies have attempted to tackle defining culture in their work (Fallon et al., 2012;

Sugai et al., 2012; Vincent et al., 2009). This work has stemmed from the need to understand the diversity of student backgrounds in schools. Critical race pedagogy notes that race informs the culture of schools (Ledesma & Calderón, 2015), and teachers are encouraged to use cultural referents in pedagogy (Ladson-Billings, 1995).

From Knoster's (2018) viewpoint, culturally competent approaches are needed and must be emphasized in endeavors to reach diverse students. Thus, practically defining culture can limit cultural misunderstanding (Sugai et al., 2012). Natesan et al. (2011) note that understanding the instructional and education of African American students is a challenge for teachers. Schools might develop structures of support built around the outcomes of students and push student success that works regardless of cultural background (Vincent et al., 2011). Understanding culture and context can be a crucial lever in decolonizing schools' classroom climates.

BUILD RELATIONSHIPS IN COMMUNITY AS THE FOUNDATION OF LOVE

Classroom cultures in schools can be improved by considering the context, learning history, and culture of families, students, community members, and staff (Sugai et al., 2012). Building and refining classroom environments must take into consideration the cultural and linguistic dynamics of all stakeholders. This starts with building relationships where culture is valued, and love is centered. To attain a decolonized classroom, centering belonging begins with a school's entire community. Otherwise, non-inclusive and non-welcoming climates, where certain families, students, and staff members do not belong, will be inherent in our school system (Cobb & Krownapple, 2019).

Being in partnership with community members, defined as any person who supports the whole child on her educational journey, within the school allows for positions of authority to decolonize classrooms *with* people instead of *to* or *for* the collective (Cobb & Krownapple, 2019). Partnering with community members recognizes that everyone who touches schools comes with something to offer. Educators, who are products of our educational system, must realize that the work truly starts with them and start to dig deep into the cultural communities in their classrooms, inclusive of the educator's own. Educators must also decolonize any tool or evidence-based strategy used with learners. This step is critical to prevent harm to the community being served and to cultivate a way to discuss and grow in competency alongside the community. A tool is only as good as its user. If we start to think about all the tools and strategies used in the classroom, we must also start to look at the user and recipient of them. Recipients are inclusive of our learners and the communities in which they dwell. The goal of teaching is to help our students thrive, which includes recognizing that community members know students in different capacities. Teachers, staff, parents, administrators, the local grocer, salon owners, and even barbers are all a part of the process. It is imperative that belonging is centered and leveraged in creating community, with love and belonging, within schools.

The idea of community must be unpacked and its connections to belonging and decolonization made plain. Reflecting on various cultural communities, we can recognize that we work with others, outside of the school environment, to inform educational spaces. Mr. McDowell, my grandparent, realized early on that we are all a part of a collective agreement related to community and relationships.

> [The] role of a barber in a neighborhood or community? It's been a business throughout the ages; It's a very important place in a neighborhood. Like years ago: first the home, the church, and the school. Then when it comes down to the neighborhood: the grocery store, the barber, and all like that, the butcher. They all fall in line making up the community. (McDowell & Levitas, 1994)

He made an astute and useful point about community. Educators have a role in becoming competent, and this work must start *with* educators. The educator has a responsibility to support what is happening in the larger environment in which learners reside. Educators can start to leverage this power by remembering their own cultural communities. Differences need to be seen as necessary polarities in which our creativity can spark dialogue; only then does the necessity for interdependency become nonthreatening. Only within that interdependency of these different strengths (and communities), acknowledged and equal, can the power to seek new ways of being in the world generate, as well as the courage and sustenance to act where there are no charters (Lorde, 2007). We can use the tools and strategies to center belonging and charter a decolonized framework for our classrooms, in which difference of thought and lived experience, especially our own, is seen as a strength.

STRATEGIES TO ACTUALIZE BELONGING

School leaders must understand the need to recruit and retain culturally responsive educators prepared to work with students of color (Khalifa et al., 2016). Hiring and sustaining a culturally responsive staff to enhance school-wide measures will ensure more equitable practices and outcomes and cultivate belonging. The efforts of a school-based administrative team are instrumental in making classrooms successful and liberating, yet this success must be sustained by policy and systematic efforts on the district level. Effective leader development becomes a critical part of the process of retaining and recruiting the best teachers for students who have been marginalized (Khalifa et al., 2016). Bal and colleagues (2016) emphasize the need for school districts to examine disciplinary practices and transform the current system producing racial disparities. Districts can allocate more funding for personnel in classrooms to help teachers implement evidence-based interventions. Thus, plans should be reviewed periodically with the entire school community to ensure that the student population is reflected in its practice.

Also, achievement and discipline gaps are unlikely to be eliminated without a focus on a change in student relationships (Anyon et al., 2016). As the student population in schools has become more diverse, the teaching field remains mostly white and female (Natesan et al., 2011; Will, 2020). While increasing staff, a focus on improving efforts to diversify the teaching population in communities is key.

A focus on training and support for culturally responsive approaches is necessary to improve classroom, disciplinary, and teaching practices to home in on creating environments where learners can feel a strong sense of belonging. Districts and schools must give sufficient time to professional development concerning culturally responsive approaches and classroom management (Skiba & Losen, 2015). Also, districts must provide staff with examples of culturally relevant teaching in both theory and practice (Ladson-Billings, 1995). It is essential for this work to be long term and include engaging in dialogue that mandates teachers be aware of the needs of minority students (Whitford et al., 2016).

IN COMMUNITY

Decolonizing classrooms is a community effort. Valdivia (2002) shares that bell hooks found solace, comfort, and liberation through the written word. They note that she began to develop her keen sense and theory of justice and privilege as a young girl watching both her father and her brother enjoy disproportionate authority and control in family and community matters as well as learning from her grandfather's more just ways. There should be urgency to provide each learner with opportunities to learn from all parts of their community, inclusive of their own. Families and community members can use their roles in the school community as tools of liberation and not colonization.

Because the liberation of classrooms is bound up between and within communities, we have no other choice but to bind together to curate belonging in classrooms and school communities. It must be centered on belonging so all folx can feel validated and appreciated. Educators, who are also considered community members for learners, are bound together in this work. At first glance, this decolonization of classrooms may seem painful in process, yet to do the work we must be in relationship with people in the larger school community to help give every learner what she needs to be successful. We have to figure out when we feel that pain in the implementation process, call on your community, and we promise that H.E.L.P. (history, equity, love, and practices) will be used as a framework to start these conversations in community to liberate classroom environments. (Misner, 2021).

PEDAGOGICAL PRACTICES

In the book *We Want to Do More Than Survive: Abolitionist Teaching and the Pursuit of Educational Freedom*, Dr. Love (2019) shares: "Pedagogy, regardless of its name, is useless without teachers dedicated to challenging systemic oppression with intersectional social justice." Educators can prepare for the work of creating classrooms, centered in belonging, by reflecting on the current pedagogy used in classrooms to teach. Students need spaces to critique and name injustice to help them develop the agency to build a better world. As long as oppression is in the world, young people need pedagogy that nurtures critical thinking (Muhammad, 2020). Educators must reflect on the pedagogical stances taken in a classroom. What comes from this reflection can be the beginning of creating a decolonized framework for classrooms by adapting a classroom framework that centers learners.

Many educators have been faithful to the work of educating learners, yet more needs to be done. Active engagement with communities and schools would open conversations with educators and students of color (Hines-Datiri, 2015). For there to be a collective impact on school communities, educators must embrace social justice and become inclusive in their teaching. This step will start the work of all learners feeling centered and a part of their classroom environment. Educators are the greatest and dearest tool we have in dismantling systems of oppression, and school communities must provide a space for them to walk into a season of learning that centers our most beloved.

REFERENCES

Anyon, Y., Zhang, D., & Hazel, C. (2016). Race, exclusionary discipline, and connectedness to adults in secondary schools. *American Journal of Community Psychology, 57*(3–4), 342–352. https://doi.org/10.1002/ajcp.12061

Bal, A., Schrader, E. M., Afacan, K., & Mawene, D. (2016). Using learning labs for culturally responsive positive behavioral interventions and supports. *Intervention in School and Clinic, 52*(2), 122–128. https://doi.org/10.1177/1053451216636057

Bell, D. A. (2005). *Silent covenants: Brown v. Board of education and the unfulfilled hopes for racial reform.* Oxford University Press.

Cobb, F., & Krownapple, J. (2019). *Belonging through a culture of dignity: The keys to successful equity implementation.* Mimi & Todd Press.

Du Bois, W. E. B. (1903). *The souls of Black folk* (B. H. Edwards, Ed.). Oxford University Press.

Fallon, L. M., O'Keeffe, B. V., & Sugai, G. (2012). Consideration of culture and context in school-wide positive behavior support: A review of current literature. *Journal of Positive Behavior Interventions, 14*(4), 209–219. https://doi.org/10.1177/1098300712442242

Glaude, E. S. (2016). *Democracy in Black: How race still enslaves the American soul.* Crown.

Gorski, P. (2019). Avoiding racial equity detours. *Educational Leadership, 76*(6), 56–61.

Hill, N. S., & Bartol, K. M. (2016). Empowering leadership and effective collaboration in geographically dispersed teams. *Personnel Psychology, 69*(1), 159–198. https://doi.org/10.1111/peps.12108

Hines-Datiri, D. (2015). When police intervene: Race, gender, and discipline of Black male students at an urban high school. *Journal of Cases in Educational Leadership, 18*(2), 122–133. https://doi.org/10.1177/1555458915584676

Horsford, S. D. (2011). Vestiges of desegregation: Superintendent perspectives on educational inequality and (dis)integration in the post–civil rights era. *Urban Education, 46*(1), 34–54. https://doi.org/10.1177/0042085910391596

Khalifa, M. A. (2018). *Culturally responsive school leadership.* Harvard Education Press.

Khalifa, M. A., Gooden, M. A., & Davis, J. E. (2016). Culturally responsive school leadership: A synthesis of the literature. *Review of Educational Research, 86*(4), 1272–1311.

Knoster, T. (2018). Commentary: Evolution of positive behavior support and future directions. *Journal of Positive Behavior Interventions, 20*(1), 23–26. https://doi.org/10.1177/1098300717735056

Ladson-Billings, G. (1995). But that's just good teaching! The case for culturally relevant pedagogy. *Theory into Practice, 34*(3), 159–165. https://doi.org/10.1080/00405849509543675

Ledesma, M. C., & Calderón, D. (2015). Critical race theory in education: A review of past literature and a look to the future. *Qualitative Inquiry, 21*(3), 206–222. https://doi.org/10.1177/1077800414557825

Lorde, A. (2007). *Sister outsider: Essays and speeches*, revised edition. Crossing Press.

Love, B. (2019). *We want to do more than survive: Abolitionist teaching and the pursuit of educational freedom*, 1st edition. Beacon Press.

McDowell, R. L., & Levitas, S. (1994). Sometimes even the barber has been a place where men could come and pour out their troubles to. [Audio] Retrieved from the Library of Congress, https://www.loc.gov/item/afcwip002842/.

Misner, S. (2021, January 15). The critical HELP framework by Dr. Ronald W. Whitaker, II. MCIU Learning Network. https://learn.mciu.org/the-critical-help-framework-by-dr-ronald-w-whitaker-ii/

Muhammad, G. (2020). *Cultivating genius: An equity framework for culturally and historically responsive literacy.* Scholastic.

Natesan, P., Webb-Hasan, G. C., Carter, N. P., & Walter, P. (2011). Validity of the cultural awareness and beliefs inventory of urban teachers: A parallel mixed methods study. *International Journal of Multiple Research Approaches, 5*(2), 238–253. https://doi.org/10.5172/mra.2011.5.2.238

National Assessment of Educational Progress. (May 9, 2023). Assessment frameworks. https://nces.ed.gov/nationsreportcard/assessments/frameworks.aspx#:~:text=Frameworks%20define%20the%20subject%2Dspecific,they%20meet%20current%20educational%20requirements

Paris, D. (2012). Culturally sustaining pedagogy: A needed change in stance, terminology, and practice. *Educational Researcher, 41*(3), 93–97. https://doi.org/10.3102/0013189X12441244

Skiba, R. J., & Losen, D. J. (2015). From reaction to prevention: Turning the page on school discipline. *American Educator, 39*(4), 4.

Strayhorn, T. L. (2012). *College students' sense of belonging: A key to educational success for all student*s, 1st edition. Routledge. https://doi.org/10.4324/9780203118924

Sugai, G., O'Keeffe, B. V., & Fallon, L. M. (2012). A contextual consideration of culture and school-wide positive behavior support. *Journal of Positive Behavior Interventions, 14*(4), 197–208. https://doi.org/10.1177/1098300711426334

Valdivia, A. N. (2002). bell hooks: Ethics from the margins. *Qualitative Inquiry, 8*(4), 429–447. https://doi.org/10.1177/10778004008004003

Vincent, C., Cartledge, G., May, S., & Tobin, T. (2009). *Do elementary schools that document reductions in overall office referrals document reductions across all student races and ethnicities?* Center on Positive Behavioral Interventions and Support.

West, C. (1995). *Jews and Blacks: Let the healing begin.* Putnam.

Will, M. (2020, November 19). *Still mostly white and female: New federal data on the teaching profession. Education Week.* https://www.edweek.org/leadership/still-mostly-white-and-female-new-federal-data-on-the-teaching-profession/2020/0

Whitford, D. K., Katsiyannis, A., & Counts, J. (2016). Discriminatory discipline: Trends and issues. *NASSP Bulletin, 100*(2), 117–135. doi:10.1177/0192636516677340

6

Decolonizing Classroom Relationships

Dina Strasser

It is a truism that all effective classrooms are rooted in positive relationships and that teachers occupy a powerful role in developing and nurturing those relationships. Teachers are presented with a bewildering range of approaches to the crucial work of building relationships: from nitty-gritty lists of procedures to overarching psychological theories, from rule-driven authoritarianism to student-centered self-management.

It is tempting for time-strapped educators to seek universally applicable, silver bullet solutions to this challenge. However, despite the recent proliferation of multicultural, socioemotional, and antiracist initiatives and approaches in schools, there is still not enough acknowledgment that *cultural assumptions are embedded in all approaches to building relationships.* No practice or classroom community is culturally impartial: culture is the soil in which human community is rooted, and classrooms cannot be removed or divested from it. The question for teachers to answer, then, is not "What are the foolproof 'best practices' to creating positive relationships in my classroom?" but rather, "How do the cultural choices I individually make in my classroom support the growth and health of the specific child in front of me?"

I am a white, middle class, cis-hetero woman: a person looking at me would see someone who is literally the statistical mean of American teachers. Where I exceed the mean is in the length of my tenure in schools: I've been an educator now for more than 20 years. Altogether, as we shall discuss in this paper, this means that I represent not only the teacher who perhaps most needs to ask hard questions about teachers' relationships in schools but also a teacher who can attempt to provide guidance on the answers.

To that end I will draw on my experience and scholarship to first interrogate what we mean when we say "classroom relationship." I'll then suggest that rather than relying on preset relationship-building techniques to decolonize a classroom, teachers should gain a wider knowledge of the cultural identifiers of all the stakeholders in their classroom relationships—and then act tangibly on that specific knowledge.

WHAT IS A "CLASSROOM RELATIONSHIP"?

When we speak casually of classroom relationships, they are primarily between two people: the teacher and the student. In a nuanced conversation about educational decolonization, however, classroom relationships are multidirectional and irreducibly complex: an ecosystem. This ecosystem encompasses not only specific people (parents, the nurse, the principal, the superintendent) and institutions (the school, the district, the neighborhood, the city), but also multiple cultural identifiers for these stakeholders, such as religious beliefs, weight, and age. Indeed, the National Association of Independent Schools (2023) currently lists 17 identifiers on its website.

Four cultural identifiers have most consistently impacted my classroom relationships.

1: Classroom relationships are informed by social values. What *is* the job of a teacher? This answer has shifted and changed and is dependent upon who, where, and when I answer this question. As a Fulbright English Teaching Assistant in Korea in 1994, I was as revered as doctors and lawyers are in the United States, even free (and often encouraged) to administer corporal punishment to students. In contrast, as a public-school teacher almost 30 years later, I can be a source of deep trepidation for students and families who may or may not be documented residents—or for my politically conservative students and families, who can look suspiciously on any governmental influence in their lives. Conflict about a teacher's role in education, in particular, has a special impact on classroom relationships; a potent example is our society's response to the growing voices of gender diversity among our young people (Rankin & Beemyn, 2012). In this past year alone, in my small, rural school district, I've worked with four students who are openly using alternative names or pronouns as early as fifth grade—indeed, students sometimes deliberately experiment with gender labels at school rather than at home (Baker, 2023). This raises critical questions for decolonizing educators about the role of the teacher within the intersection of gendered home expectations, school codes of conduct, and state law, such as those recently passed against school-supportive measures for transgender students (Paris, 2023). These intersections also include the habitual social values of older educators such as me, who grew up three generations ago with a rigidly dualistic set of gender expectations.

2: Classroom relationships are informed by race. It is important to recognize race as a social construct that has no biological basis (Gannon, 2016). Regardless, racism is a pervasive, destructive, and embedded idea in our country, and teachers must contend with it. In particular, white teachers, who as of 2021 made up 80% of our public teaching force (National Center for Education Statistics, 2023), need to ensure that their perceptions of students of color are not racially compromised. Dr. Lisa Delpit (2006) exposed how Black students' frustrated expectations are often misinterpreted by white teachers as opposition and defiance, and that Black teachers' perspectives on what their Black students need are downplayed and ignored by their white colleagues. Delpit's invaluable critiques seemed to sting white progressive educators especially, and researchers theorize that we are the hardest nuts to crack when it comes to recognizing our own racial biases (Kendi, 2016; Love, 2020).

I experienced this firsthand as a professional development facilitator for a national school reform model, leading a two-day teacher workshop on classroom management in Tennessee. Most of the participants were Black while my co-lead and I were white. When I repeated one of my favorite management sentiments—"The student who meets you on the street should see the same person who teaches her every day"—one of the breakout groups burst into kind but incredulous laughter. "I don't agree with that at all," one of the teachers stated. "When I go out dancing and have a few beers, you're telling me *that's* the same person I need to be in my classroom?" What followed was one of the most personally formative discussions I've had on classroom relationships, where we dove deeply into what Delpit (2006) has identified as expectations of teachers by Black students: "teachers are expected to show that they care about their students by controlling their students; exhibiting personal power; [and] establishing meaningful interpersonal relationships" (p. 133). To me, "meaningful interpersonal relationships" with students meant that there should be no dividing line between how I acted in the classroom and how I acted outside it. To adopt a traditional top-down teacher role, I felt, would run dangerously close to establishment-supporting fakery. From the Black participants, however, I learned that a well-defined, authoritative role as a Black teacher was not only expected by Black students—and arguably *better for B*lack students (Easton-Brooks, 2019)—but it was in no way inauthentic just because it happened to look different from other social contexts the teachers might find themselves in. My "progressive lens" (Philip, 2011) had distorted the unique strengths of the teachers of color in front of me. I learned a lot that day.

3: Classroom relationships are informed by socioeconomic class. Curricula centered explicitly on social and emotional learning (SEL) has become de rigueur in many schools in the United States. The Collaborative for Academic, Social, and Emotional Learning (CASEL) has advocated for this kind of instruction since 1994 (CASEL, 2023). A well-intentioned assumption might be that SEL curricula would automatically support a decolonized classroom, because SEL is by its own definition about learning to create and maintain healthy relationships. However, although there are strong arguments for fostering this kind of learning in schools in general (Jones & Doolittle, 2017), it may surprise teachers—as it did me—to consider how implementing these skills may reflect a problematic, class-based set of emotional priorities for our students.

If you asked my eighth-grade student Katarina about SEL circles, she would roll her eyes. She and her peers are occasionally pulled from my English as a New Language (ENL) classroom to attend an SEL circle, and I noticed that, more and more, they were leaving with real reluctance. Katarina told me why. "I have a *lot* to say in circle," she said. "I have a lot of thoughts in my head. But I'm not gonna share them. I don't trust anyone there."

Katarina mistrusts for many reasons, but at least part of her intuition about her circle has to do with conflict and resistance interpreted as personal or cultural deficits instead of as simple expressions of a student's reality. Specifically, SEL can include an emphasis on the concepts of happiness, joy, and an absence of conflict and resistance that Clio Stearns believes is "hegemonic positivity" (2016), rooted in neoliberal notions of class. A similar class-based critique has been advanced on teaching the specific SEL skill of grit, or resilience, in schools (Mehta, 2015). Much of our public discourse, policies, and practices require individual students to exhibit "grit" and resiliency (Gorski, 2016; Love, 2019) to surmount the unjust circumstances they find themselves in rather than redress the inequities that create the challenges. Young people are sensitive and intuitive; they know quickly when something feels hypocritical to them. If there is a mismatch between the relationship values that SEL espouses (e.g., "this is a safe space") and what it implements (e.g., "conflict and resistance are not tolerated"), students will react to that mismatch with confusion and cynicism. As a result, SEL techniques, when implemented superficially or with not enough care toward SEL socioeconomic messaging, will not help develop the kind of trust that is the foundation of decolonized classrooms. In fact, in a terrible irony, they may even damage that trust.

4: Classroom relationships are informed by power. In an inegalitarian society, all cultural identifiers such as social values, class, and race ultimately reproduce societal hierarchies: they indicate who possesses hierarchical power

(Harris, 1993). These unbalanced power dynamics are invariably enacted in classrooms, from to white working-class students subjected to severe exclusion and punishment when they exhibit mild resistance in the classroom (Freie & Eppley, 2014), to the ground-level ways teachers can police student bodies through how students sit and raise their hands (Foucault, 1995). The most obvious and important power difference in a classroom is that of the teacher over the students. Even in the most democratically organized classroom, there's no way around the fact that teachers are leaders of students: guiding and directing both the content being taught and the activities through which content is conveyed. This can present very specific challenges in terms of power: "white women have assumed positions of power that enable them to reproduce the servant-served paradigm in a radically different context" (hooks, 1994, p. 103). As Matias, Walker, and del Hierro elaborate, "This is especially true within a field like education, whereby a majority of K–12 teachers, teacher candidates, teachers obtaining a master's degree in education, professors of education, collaborating teachers and administrators are all white, and particularly, middle class white females" (2019).

Deconstructing inegalitarian relationships of power and building relationships of equity and justice in their place is the heart of all decolonization. The central question of decolonized classroom relationships, then, is not *whether* a teacher has power—but *how* justly, wisely, and compassionately the teacher wields and shares that power.

CULTURAL QUESTIONS FOR TEACHERS TO CONSIDER

Rather than adopting a set of relationship-building "best practices" that falsely position themselves as commonsense and culturally neutral, educators would do better to rigorously investigate answers to a series of critical questions about the cultural identifiers in play in their classroom. Ideally, a teacher is conducting this inquiry of all the stakeholders in the classroom relationship—*especially* herself. Yolanda Sealey-Ruiz presents a loving path through this difficult work called *The Archeology of Self* (Mentor & Sealey-Ruiz, 2021).

For the sake of brevity, however, the following is a sample of the questions a teacher can fruitfully ask about her next equally important stakeholders: students.

Teachers should remember that, like anything else they do, this information-seeking approach holds cultural assumptions about trust, privacy, and the societal role of government/public institutions that will need to be navigated within the unique ecosystems of their classrooms.

Table 6.1. Sample Questions for Students.

Social Values	What is the purpose of education?
	What is more important than education?
	What is the role of a teacher in the classroom?
	How are students motivated?
	How and when should students be disciplined and/or punished?
Race/Ethnicity	What is the racial/ethnic makeup of my classroom?
	What languages are spoken at home?
	Are my students immigrants, or were they born to immigrant parents?
	What ethnic traditions, customs, and celebrations are important in my classroom?
	What race/ethnicities in my students differ from the dominant culture?
Class	What is the socioeconomic makeup of my classroom?
	Which of my students qualify for the federal free and reduced lunch programs?
	Do any of my students work outside of school? Are any of them responsible for contributing to family income?
	Are any of my students responsible for caretaking siblings, or other household responsibilities, to assist parents or guardians who work?
	How might my students/families' socioeconomic status differ from the dominant culture?
Gender	What is the gender makeup of my classroom?
	How do my students conceive of gender and gender roles?
	How do students conceive of their *own* gender or gender roles?
	How do the home cultures of my students conceive of gender or gender roles?
	How might students'/families' conceptions of gender differ from the dominant culture?

WHERE DO WE GO FROM HERE?

For me, the work of Dr. Martha Nussbaum is a good place to begin building on Dr. Ruiz's "archeology of self." Dr. Nussbaum names three fundamental human capacities:

1. "critical examination of oneself and one's traditions";
2. "an ability to see themselves not simply as citizens of some local region or group but also, and above all, as human beings bound to all other human beings by ties of recognition and concern"; and
3. "narrative imagination"—that is, the ability to imagine another person's perspective accurately and feel compassion for him. (Nussbaum, 1998, 2011)

Compare Nussbaum, however, to the educational philosophy of Dr. Benjamin Mays, an American civil rights giant and the sixth president of

Morehouse College: "Generally speaking, education is designed to train the mind to think clearly, logically and constructively; to train the heart to feel understandingly and sympathetically the aspirations, the sufferings, and the injustices of mankind; and to strengthen the will to act in the interest of the common good" (Mays, 2003).

The deep affinity between Dr. Mays's and Dr. Nussbaum's statements, written in unrelated contexts more than 60 years apart, takes my breath away. Yet a critical difference between them transforms merely well-intentioned teachers into decolonizers: Dr. Mays emphasizes *action* as well as capacity.

Let me make this final proposal, then: to build decolonized relationships, teachers can work jointly with their students to co-organize their classroom toward the mutual goals of thinking clearly, feeling compassionately, and acting concretely as citizens—not only in the world as it is, but toward the world as it could be.

REFERENCES

Baker, K. J. M. (2023, January 22). When students change gender identity, and parents don't know. *New York Times.* https://www.nytimes.com/2023/01/22/us/gender-identity-students-parents.html

Collaborative for Academic, Social, and Emotional Learning. (2023, November 25). *Our history.* https://casel.org/about-us/our-history

Delpit, L. (Ed.). (2006). *Other people's children: Cultural conflict in the classroom*, 2nd edition. New Press.

Easton-Brooks, D. (2019). *Ethnic matching: Academic success of students of color*. Rowman & Littlefield.

Foucault, M. (1995). *Discipline and punish: The birth of the prison*. Vintage.

Freie, C., and Eppley, K. (2014). Putting Foucault to work: Understanding power in a rural school. *Peabody Journal of Education, 89*(5), 652–669. https://doi.org/10.1080/0161956X.2014.958908

Gannon, M. (2016). Race is a social construct, scientists argue. *Scientific American, 5*, 1–11.

Gorski, Paul C. (2016). Poverty and the ideological imperative: A call to unhook from deficit and grit ideology and to strive for structural ideology in teacher education. *Journal of Education for Teaching, 42*(4), 378–386. https://doi.org/10.1080/02607476.2016.1215546

Harris, C. I. (1993). Whiteness as property. *Harvard Law Review, 106*(8), 1707–1791. https://doi.org/10.2307/1341787

hooks, b. (1994). *Teaching to transgress: Education as the practice of freedom*, 1st edition. Routledge. https://doi.org/10.4324/9780203700280

Jones, S. M., & Doolittle, E. J. (2017). Social and emotional learning: Introducing the issue. *Future of Children, 27*(1), 3–11.

Kendi, I. X. (2016). *Stamped from the beginning: The definitive history of racist ideas in America*. Nation Books.

Love, B. L. (2019). "Grit is in our DNA": Why teaching grit is inherently anti-Black. *Education Week, 38*, 21–32.

Love, B. L. (2020, February 6). White teachers need anti-racist therapy. *Education Week*. https://www.edweek.org/teaching-learning/opinion-white-teachers-need-anti-racist-therapy/2020/02

Matias, C., Walker, D., & del Hierro, M. (2019). Tales from the ivory tower: Women of color's resistance to whiteness in academia. *Taboo: The Journal of Culture and Education, 18*(1). https://doi.org/10.31390/taboo.18.1.04

Mays, B. E. (2003). *Born to rebel: An autobiography*. University of Georgia Press.

Mehta, J. (2015, April 27). The problem with grit. *Education Week*. https://www.edweek.org/education/opinion-the-problem-with-grit/2015/04

Mentor, M., & Sealey-Ruiz, Y. (2021). Doing the deep work of antiracist pedagogy: Toward self-excavation for equitable classroom teaching: Teacher educators of antiracist pedagogies must begin by asking ourselves the question: How do issues of race, class, religion, and sexual orientation live within us? *Language Arts, 99*(1), 19.

National Association of Independent Schools. (2023, July 25). *Sample cultural identifiers*. https://www.nais.org/articles/pages/sample-cultural-identifiers/

National Center for Education Statistics. (2023). Characteristics of Public School Teachers. *Condition of Education*. U.S. Department of Education, Institute of Education Sciences. Retrieved July 25, 2023, from https://nces.ed.gov/programs/coe/indicator/clr

Nussbaum, M. C. (1998). *Cultivating humanity*. Harvard University Press.

Nussbaum, M. C. (2011). *Creating capabilities: The human development approach*. Harvard University Press.

Paris, F. (2023, June 5). See the states that have passed laws directed at young trans people. *New York Times*. https://www.nytimes.com/2023/06/05/upshot/trans-laws-republicans-states.html

Philip, T. M. (2011). Moving beyond our progressive lenses: Recognizing and building on the strengths of teachers of color. *Journal of Teacher Education, 62*(4), 356–366. https://doi.org/10.1177/0022487111409414

Rankin, S., & Beemyn, G. (2012). Beyond a binary: The lives of gender-nonconforming youth. *About Campus, 17*(4), 2–10. https://doi.org/10.1002/abc.21086

Stearns, C. (2016). Responsive classroom?: A critique of a social emotional learning program. *Critical Studies in Education, 57*(3), 330–341. https://doi.org/10.1080/17508487.2015.1076493

7

Centering Humanity, Love, and Connection in Classroom Management

Erica Holyoke

It is impossible to teach without the courage to love, without the courage to try a thousand times before giving in. In short, it is impossible to teach without a forged, invented, and well-thought-out capacity to love. (Freire, 2005, p. 5)

LOVE IN CLASSROOM MANAGEMENT

Many educators proclaim that they teach because they *love all their students*. Although this notion may be grounded in care, care is not the same as being loved (hooks, 2018). To center love in teaching, it needs to be humanizing and revolutionary "because it upends the traditional hierarchy of student-teacher relationships . . . with teachers expressing deep vulnerability as we try to be better, by, with, and for our students" (Torres, 2021, p. 187).

Authentic love, not to be confused with superficial love, drives actions, interactions, and pedagogies leading toward liberation and freedom. This love is referred to in various terms across literature, including critical love (Freire, 2000; Brooks, 2017), revolutionary love (e.g., Barcelos, 2021; hooks, 2018; Johnson et al., 2019; Kaur, 2020; Lanas & Zembylas, 2015; Torres, 2021; Wynter-Hoyte et al., 2021), pedagogical love (e.g., Caraballo & Soleimany, 2019; Wang et al., 2022), humanizing love (e.g., Matias & Allen, 2013), and radical love (e.g., Robinson-Morris, 2019; Stachowiak, 2016). These forms are transformative in resisting the status quo and promoting anti-oppressive teaching and learning. In classroom management, superficial love perpetuates systems that control movement, thought, and ideas, asking students to conform to specific ways of being or risk exclusion (Morris, 2016). Love in classrooms must be rooted in emancipation to resist racist, biased, and inequitable foundations of which U.S. education was created.

Inquiring into language and practices in the name of love allows for critique, hope, and action (Freire, 2000). Kimmerer explains that "language is the dwelling place of ideas . . . it is a prism through which to see the world" (2013, p. 258). As such, this chapter critiques shallow and superficial forms of so-called love focused on care or kindness and encourages a shift to an understanding and enactment of love rooted in connections, liberation, and trust (Barcelos, 2021; Brooks, 2017; hooks, 2018). As the status quo of classroom management exists to replicate colonizing practices (Casey et al., 2013), it is critical to co-construct narratives in which actions of love are aligned with liberation. Decolonizing classroom management through love means ceasing practices of control and teaching love as a way of being. Further, love as liberation creates space for individuals to be fully human and values the "innate dignity of all human life and also actively creates practices that reunites and rehumanizes" (Brooks, 2017, p. 108).

Shallow forms of love are often performative without substantive action directly and indirectly sanctioning harmful behaviors, such as zero-tolerance policies, falsely promoted for the benefit of students. This enactment results in a "fake love" (Johnson et al., 2019) drawing on neoliberal views of multiculturalism without recognizing systemic oppression and marginalization (Carey et al., 2018; Johnson et al., 2019). Specific to classroom management, shallow notions of loving all children ignore children's cultural and linguistic strengths. They erase multiple forms of marginalization, especially children who identify as Latine, Indigenous, Black, disabled, or with fluid gender identities, be it curricular, emotional, exclusion, or physical.

I am a white, female, cisgendered educator, and I have been drawn to acting through love as praxis and simultaneously recognizing my privilege, power, and complicity in oppression and colonization. Love has been a guide, and I strive to align my actions, language, and teaching to love that is emancipatory. We love (hooks, 2018) and practice in community (Shalaby, 2017). As such, in the remainder of the chapter, I turn to collaborations with educators and children in which we inquired into enactments of revolutionary love. These collaborations occurred through teacher education methods courses as well as work with in-service educators through research projects and mentoring through antiracist educator groups.

A CURRICULUM OF LOVE

Classroom management must be seen as a curriculum (Shalaby, 2020) to be decolonized to honor the humanity of each child and the group while explicitly teaching authentic love. Classroom management, as conformity, even when executed with care, requires children to reduce themselves into the school culture and agenda (Shalaby, 2017; 2020). Love must be both the defiance of using systems that inflict harm to children and result in liberation where children co-construct the classroom from their whole and full selves. We must envision a curriculum of classroom community building rooted in authentic love as a model for how educators negotiate tensions within neoliberal systems.

All classrooms and communities are unique, and practices of love must be crafted to the relations of that context. Table 7.1 offers a categorization of tenets of authentic love in schools, along with questions to guide educators in enacting a classroom management curriculum of love.

Enacting love, as an act of resistance (e.g., hooks, 2018; Johnson et al., 2019) promotes anti-oppressive experiences in the classroom. The seven tenets and guiding questions in table 7.1 are intended to serve as an anchor for educators to self-assess and create curriculums of love in place of traditional classroom management. To close the chapter, I share three ways to illustrate, with examples, how a curriculum of love manifests in classroom contexts.

LOVING PRAXIS: "IT PROTECTS US"

Loving praxis means embodying love as emancipatory and aligning actions to beliefs. Choosing love allows people to move toward freedom and embrace the personhood of others (Freire, 2000; hooks, 2018). Thus, when considering classroom management through a lens of love, it encapsulates what is done in the classroom and beyond in decolonizing existing structures. Questioning power in policies, systems, and behaviors is a starting place for this work. When collaborating with educators, they often begin by exploring the implications of micro-decisions in the classroom, asking questions such as "What does it communicate when I am in a chair [above] children?" or "What am I messaging when I am the gatekeeper for when and how children respond to questions?" Loving praxis means approaching classroom management through a critique and questioning what is.

Table 7.1. Categorization of Tenets of Authentic Love in Schools.

Tenet of Love	Summary	Questions to Ask
Inquiry of Oneself and the World	This provides opportunities for educators to reflect on experiences and beliefs within an education system that privileges whiteness, whether harm or complicity (Torres, 2021).	How do my experiences enable, empower, or hinder me from engaging in practices of love that are liberating?
Building Community in Community	This offers opportunities to position oneself as a member of, rather than the sole leader of, a community (Shalaby, 2017).	How does love allow us to be shared participants in building and sustaining community?
Committing to Love with Children	This focus ensures a humanizing (Brooks, 2017) approach where children, their emotions, needs, experiences, and expressions are paramount (Holyoke, in press).	How can I amplify the needs and voices of children?
Committing to Love as Advocacy	A priority is building critical consciousness and opportunities to decolonize school habits, systems, and spaces (Darder, 2017; Freire, 2000).	How can I work as an advocate through love? Where are opportunities for children to build critical consciousness?
Centering Authentic Relationships	This is a focus on relationships that are empowering, liberating, and genuine (Johnson et al., 2019).	How are relationships founded on trust? In what ways am I showing love to children for who they are, not who I hope them to be?
Embracing Discomfort	Beyond vulnerability and self-inquiry, this is about being in challenging moments and prioritizing dignity for everyone; prioritizing care over punishment and complexities over binaries (Lanas & Zembylas, 2015).	When tensions arise, how do I respond and from love? How do I seek out root causes rather than respond to behaviors?
Living Love as Praxis	Individuals see themselves within a collective, and love as a way of being rather than singular actions or responses (Hannegan-Martinez, 2020; Shalaby, 2017).	How do I question, reflect, and ask myself how actions are grounded in school and classroom transformation? How do I show myself authentic love? Encourage authentic love between children/adolescents?

An Example of Loving Praxis

I turn to a kindergarten child, Darnell,[1] to illustrate loving praxis. Darnell, a curious and joyful Black boy, thrived in his kindergarten community but was often reprimanded and excluded in other contexts (i.e., specials, lunch, etc.). In the classroom, he was loved and seen for who he was, not who he *should* be by someone else's measures or expectations. The teacher's focus was creating space for Darnell to thrive in collaboration with others rather than controlling his actions. Darnell often explored his experiences through writing. One day he drew a picture paralleling protection for fictitious characters in his drawing to the community in his kindergarten classroom, announcing that the community [the teacher and peers] "protects us." This speaks to the realities of schools inflicting harm on children to feel the need for protection and urgency for embodying love.

It is a responsibility to build a culture of love with children. Ms. Ryan, Darnell's teacher, took actionable steps to center children in the curriculum (Winn et al., 2019), the physical space, and seeking solutions (Holyoke, 2024). She enacted many behaviors and teaching moves but used reflections like those in table 1 to guide her decision making and measure her successes. Beyond her work with children, Ms. Ryan also positioned herself as an advocate beyond her teaching to build structures in the school that supported Darnell and other children to expand fully who they are and not be excluded.

Although this provides a movement toward love, negotiations are required. When engaging in loving praxis, I propose that systems and structures must be revised and re-created from a place of love. This means reconsidering power dynamics behind decisions that exert control over another (namely, children). Decolonizing classroom management structures is collaborative and a movement from fake love *for* children to relationships and community *with* children.

LOVE AND DISCIPLINE: "IT'S EVERYONE'S POWERFUL WORDS"

A discipline of love is not about punishment but, rather, about vulnerability (Torres, 2021), authentic dialogue (Freire, 2000; Darder, 2017), and practicing ways of being together. It is about dismantling harmful, racist, and dehumanizing structures that exist and replacing them with connection. Negotiating discipline through love means questioning why there are unjust practices, such as what Darnell faced while creating anew. The ideas of being love are expansive, and "when we are loving, we openly and honestly express care, affection, responsibility, respect, commitment, and trust." (hooks, 2018,

p. 45). To build a discipline of love means practicing definitions, thoughts, and actions of love through a humanizing stance.

An Example of Love and Discipline

In another classroom, I explored the idea of community with a diverse group of first graders. I share an excerpt of their conceptualizations. The dialogue focuses on discipline as a collaborative learning experience to build habits and communal responses in love.

> Erica (researcher): What does community mean in your classroom?
>
> Jordan: You agree, add on, or *respectfully* disagree.
>
> James: I agree with Jordan.
>
> Erica: Can you tell me more about that?
>
> Jordan: Yeah, because you help them. You give them more information, and community and connection are the same.
>
> Dylan: It's like a family!
>
> Jordan: And community and connection are the same. We decided that. And we do that.
>
> Jacob: It's all being here . . . it's being connected.
>
> [. . .]
>
> Jacob: We get to hear people's thoughts.
>
> Dylan: It's everyone's powerful words.

The children created a vision and pedagogy of love where each person and idea holds power, importance, and place in the classroom. Related to this, Al-Mahmood and colleagues (2020) examine love through acts of witnessing, which is about "deliberate attendance to people, seeing and taking notice of that which they believe is meaningful" (p. 83). Applying what the children noted to challenging behaviors or tensions in a classroom, we can examine the power of each person's reality, experiences, and words. It is not about being right but making things right together through witnessing, listening, and embracing humanizing experiences.

This example illustrates how children consider loving one another and practicing love together. They see humanity and the value of each person's stories. And, when conflict arose, they approached it through love; expressing their feelings and knowing they would be seen. Accountability was important, but judgment and punishment were not. The ways educators negotiate this type of learning through building a discipline of love means resisting systems that degrade and dehumanize children and challenges that arise within and beyond classrooms. It also means establishing collaborative foundations of how members in the classroom, including adults, are held responsible so that each person is fully valued to embody love.

MULTIDIMENSIONAL LOVE: "ALL YOU NEED IS LOVE"

Revolutionary love in the classroom is multidirectional between oneself, all individuals, and each individual and collective to the world. When educators embody love, we can more deeply love and lead. Self-love is a critical part of the layers of love. Authentic acts of love for oneself, others, and the world serve as resistance to systems privileging outcomes rather than people.

An Example of Multidimensional Love

Self-love means vulnerability, appreciation, and accountability in classroom management. For educators, this vulnerability is often about decolonizing actions and beliefs or healing from harm caused in school. Elena, a Latina preservice teacher, reflected on this as she built her vision of classroom management through a "commitment to centering love." She said, "We talk about growth mindsets toward students and even teaching them to have [these] mindsets themselves, but I often forget to have a growth mindset for myself." She held space for love with children and herself in the classroom.

When viewing self-love and multidirectional love, relationships must be focused on liberation, trust, and humanity. It is about merging individual needs and wants and working to achieve the community's needs. Multidirectional love means flexibly building classroom communities and responsibilities with contributions from each person. However, without self-love and the important ways that reclaim the educator's identities and knowledge, it can be hard to model and encourage this type of relational love with students for themselves and one another.

CONCLUSION

The opening quote from Freire provides an imperative of operating from a place of love. He continues, "If I do not love the world—if I do not love life—if I do not love people—I cannot enter into dialogue" (2005, p. 90). The transformative love explored in this chapter amplifies the humanity of individuals and classroom communities. It requires dialogic work to prioritize freedom for individuals while striving to disrupt, decolonize, and create systems to honor children.

hooks and others explore the need for love as a critical and necessary component of education. Love must be an action, a choice, and praxis for leading decisions in one's life and teaching. The needed authentic love extends beyond simple or superficial views and becomes a love that promotes liberation in schools and the world. Boggs (2012), an activist, author, and philosopher, notes, "Love isn't about what we did yesterday; it's about what we do today and tomorrow and the day after" (p. 70). As we collectively envision liberating love in classrooms, we actively decolonize learning and resist scripts of control and imaging and enact something new.

NOTE

1. All names in this chapter are pseudonyms to protect the privacy of each child and teacher.

REFERENCES

Al-Mahmood, R., Papalia, G., Barry, S., Nguyet Nguyen, M., Roemhild, J., Meehan-Andrews, T., & Louie, J. (2020). Love acts and revolutionary praxis: Challenging the neoliberal university through a teaching scholars development program. *Higher Education Research & Development, 39*(1), 81–98. https://doi.org/10.1080/07294360.2019.1666803

Barcelos, A. M. F. (2021). Revolutionary love and peace in the construction of an English teacher's professional identity. In R. L. Oxford, M. M. Olivero, M. Harrison, & T. Gregersen (Eds.), *Peacebuilding in language education* (pp. 96–109). Multilingual Matters.

Brooks, D. N. (2017). (Re)conceptualizing love: Moving towards a critical theory of love in education for social justice. *Journal of Critical Thought and Praxis, 6*(3), 102–114. https://doi.org/10.31274/jctp-180810-87

Boggs, G. L., & Kurashige, S. (2012). *The next American revolution: Sustainable activism for the twenty-first century*. University of California Press.

Caraballo, L., & Soleimany, S. (2019). In the name of (pedagogical) love: A conceptual framework for transformative teaching grounded in critical youth research. *Urban Review, 51*, 81–100. https://doi.org/10.1007/s11256-018-0486-5

Casey, Z. A., Lozenski, B. D., & McManimon, S. K. (2013). From neoliberal policy to neoliberal pedagogy: Racializing and historicizing classroom management. *Journal of Pedagogy, 4*(1), 36–58. https://doi.org/10.2478/jped-2013-0003

Carey, R., Yee, L., & DeMatthews, D. (2018). Power, penalty, and critical praxis: Employing intersectionality in educator practices to achieve school equity. *Educational Forum, 82*(1), 111–130. https://doi.org/10.1080/00131725.2018.1381793.

Darder, A. (2017). *Reinventing Paulo Freire: A pedagogy of love*. Taylor & Francis.

Freire, P. (2000). P*edagogy of the oppressed*. Continuum.

Freire, P. (2005). *Teachers as cultural workers: Letters to those who dare teach*. Routledge.

Hannegan-Martinez, S. (2020). *Literacies of love: Trauma, healing, and pedagogical shifts in an English classroom*. University of California–Los Angeles.

Holyoke, E. (2024). Relational literacies and restorative justice: "We're part of something bigger, and as big as the collective." *Reading Horizons: A Journal of Literacy and Language Arts, 63*(1), 62–89.

hooks, b. (2018). *All about love: New visions*. Harper.

Johnson, L. L., Bryan, N., & Boutte, G. (2019). Show us the love: Revolutionary teaching in (un)critical times. *Urban Review, 51*, 46–64. https://doi.org/10.1007/s11256-018-0488-3

Kaur, V. (2020). *See no stranger: A memoir and manifesto of revolutionary love*. One World.

Kimmerer, R. (2013). *Braiding sweetgrass: Indigenous wisdom, scientific knowledge and the teachings of plants*. Milkweed Editions.

Lanas, M., & Zembylas, M. (2015). Revolutionary love at work in an Arctic school with conflicts. *Teaching Education, 26*(3), 272–287. https://doi.org/10.1080/10476210.2014.996744

Matias, C. E., & Allen, R. L. (2013). Loving whiteness to death: Sadomasochism, emotionality, and the possibility of humanizing love. *Berkeley Review of Education, 4*(2), 285–309. https://doi.org/10.5070/B84110066

Morris, M. (2016). *Pushout: The criminalization of Black girls in schools*. New Press.

Robinson-Morris, D. W. (2019). Radical love, (r)evolutionary becoming: Creating an ethic of love in the realm of education through Buddhism and Ubuntu. *Urban Review, 51*, 26–45. https://doi.org/10.1007/s11256-018-0479-4

Shalaby, C. (2017). *Troublemakers: Lessons in freedom from young children at school*. New Press.

Shalaby, C. (2020). Classroom management as a curriculum of care. *Educational Leadership, 78*(3), 40–45.

Stachowiak, D. (2016, November 16). Living, breathing, and teaching with radical love: What it means, what you need, and where to start. *Educator Collaborative Community*. https://community.theeducatorcollaborative.com/living-breathing-and-teaching-with-radical-love-what-it-means-what-you-need-and-where-to-start/

Torres, F. L. (2021). Reflection and action: Revolutionary love and the possibility for more equitable literacy classrooms. *Language Arts, 98*(4), 179–188. https://doi.org/10.58680/la202131153

Wang, Y., Derakhshan, A., & Pan, Z. (2022). Positioning an agenda on a loving pedagogy in second language acquisition: Conceptualization, practice, and research. *Frontiers in Psychology, 13*, 1–7. https://doi.org/10.3389/fpsyg.2022.894190

Winn, M. T., Graham, H., & Alfred, R. R. (2019). *Restorative justice in the English language arts classroom.* National Council for Teachers of English.

Wynter-Hoyte, K., Braden, E., Myers, M., & Sanjuana, C., & Thornton, N. (2022). *Revolutionary love: Creating a culturally inclusive classroom.* Scholastic.

8

From Interest Convergence in PBIS to Co-Generative Praxis

Matthew Green and Jade Calais

Although the framework of Positive Behavioral Interventions and Supports (PBIS) provides a nod to equity, without an explicit focus on race or a mandate for co-generative spaces to develop policies and interventions, PBIS is what Gregory et al. (2017) term an "implement and hope" intervention, or an intervention that positively impacts a general group with a presupposition that this intervention will lead to equitable outcomes for other subgroups. Interventions that don't explicitly account for race will do little to resolve the racial discipline gap for Black and Brown students or decolonize classroom management. Perhaps, then, the greatest failure of PBIS is the failure to critically reflect on the harmful effects of how the program is often implemented.

Over the past two decades, Louisiana has been the incarceration capital of the United States and has often incarcerated more people as a state than nations of similar size. Louisiana also ranks third in the United States in percentage of students suspended from school and second in percentage of students expelled (NCES, 2018). Further, poor students, Black and Latine students, and students in special education are often suspended at higher rates than other students (Barrett et al., 2017; Skiba et al., 2002). Race, poverty, and gender interplay with school discipline to make schools ancillary to the juvenile justice system (Morris & Perry, 2017). Exclusionary discipline contributes to the school-to-prison nexus, a metaphor that illuminates the complex, interconnected relationship between schools and prisons (Okilwa et al., 2017).

As authors, we write this chapter as two educators living in south Louisiana but from different positionality. I, author 1, am white, cisgendered, and male, born and raised in the U.S. South attending public schools shaped by both segregation and desegregation, a former third-grade teacher, and currently an assistant professor of education in Louisiana. My positionality informs and continually shapes how I come to understand educational phenomena, school discipline, whiteness, and conduct education research and advocacy. I, author 2, am a Black, Christian, heterosexual, cisgender, middle-class woman who was born and raised in Louisiana. My positionality is highly influenced by the marginalities I experience and have witnessed as a Black female leader in the K–12 school system. Further, I am often aware that I occupy an interesting perch, critiquing a system that I work in while simultaneously mothering children, my biological children and students, through this same system.

On May 1, 2009, the Southern Poverty Law Center (SPLC), in conjunction with a dozen partners, released a report outlining a pathway for the State of Louisiana and educators to create effective discipline for student success with the goal of reducing student and teacher dropout. Within this report were myriad possibilities for reducing school suspensions, discipline disproportionalities, and providing educators with alternatives to exclusionary, and oftentimes carceral, practices. A year later, this report led to the creation of Act 136, which added a provision into Louisiana law adopting PBIS as part of the state's "Model Master Discipline Plan" for supporting student behavior and discipline (Louisiana Believes, 2023). Following Act 136, PBIS was legislated statewide as the "model" solution for reducing school suspensions and discipline disproportionalities in an effort to disrupt the school-to-prison nexus.

The trend of PBIS being used as a remedy to excessive school suspensions and disproportionate school discipline outcomes has become the norm nationally (Bornstein, 2017b). More than 10 years after the introduction of PBIS as a "model" for school discipline practices in Louisiana, racial, socioeconomic, and ableist disparities remain. The "model" and system aimed at alleviating and disrupting the school-to-prison nexus has in fact reproduced many of the same disparate outcomes.

PBIS has been implemented in schools across all 50 states, the District of Columbia, and Puerto Rico (OSEP Technical Assistance Center on Positive Behavioral Interventions and Supports, 2020) as an alternative to traditional discipline practices in schools. PBIS, a multi-tiered system used to prevent disciplinary problems, features three progressive tiers (McDaniel et al., 2017; OSEP Technical Assistance Center on Positive Behavioral Interventions and Supports, 2020). The PBIS framework is lauded as a program that supports all students' social-emotional, academic, and behavioral outcomes (Center on Positive Behavioral Interventions & Supports, 2023a).

Equity, systems, data, practices, and outcomes have been outlined as key elements of the framework (see figure 8.1). Although equity overlaps the

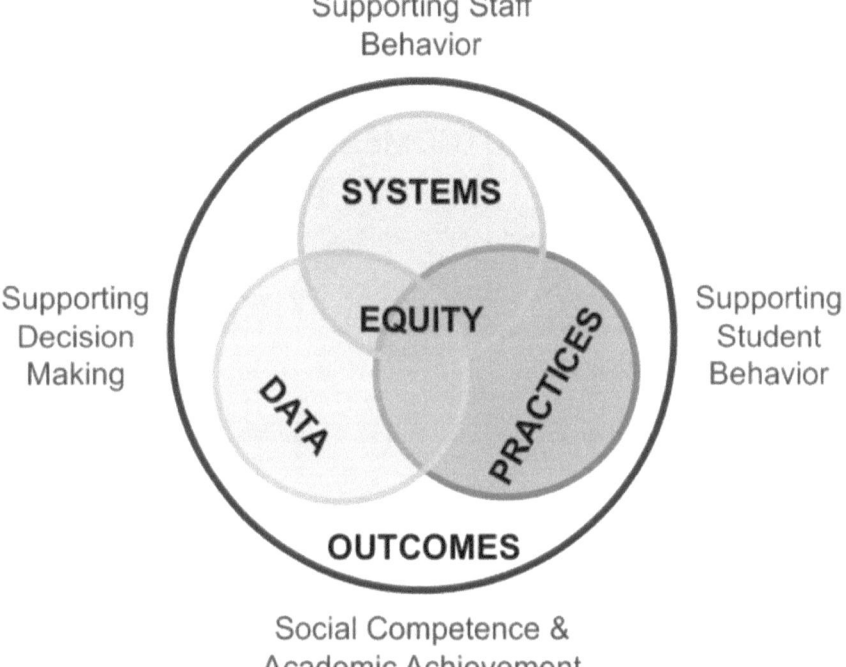

Figure 8.1. Five Elements of PBIS. Center on Positive Behavioral Interventions & Supports. (2023a). What is PBIS? https://www.pbis.org/pbis/what-is-pbis

other four elements in the framework, it is the only element that has not been delineated as a critical feature of PBIS (see figure 8.2).

The "practices" element of PBIS is the feature that is most heavily emphasized by educators within schools. Within the PBIS framework, "practice" specifies that a team

1. creates a shared vision for behavior support and responses,
2. outlines three to five positive expectations and explicitly teaches these, and
3. encourages "contextually appropriate behavior" (Center on Positive Behavioral Interventions & Supports, 2023b) through a system of rewards.

These steps represent a key aspect of PBIS in which educators determine norms and standards of behavior they expect within the classroom and school wide. When collecting and evaluating data, the framework does call for a consideration of "the local culture and context throughout the decision-making process" to establish equitable outcomes for students and staff.

Figure 8.2. PBIS Foundational Elements.
Note: Center on Positive Behavioral Interventions & Supports. (2023b). School-wide. https://www.pbis.org/topics/school-wide

INTEREST CONVERGENCE AND WHITENESS AS PROPERTY

One reason for this, we argue, is that PBIS represents a means of *interest convergence* and *whiteness as property*, two core tenets of critical race theory as articulated by Bell (1976), Harris (1993), and Ladson-Billings and Tate (1995). Together these elements function to negate any remedies or racial disproportionality in school discipline and uphold racial hierarchies. Bell (1976) identifies the concept of interest convergence as racial progress occurring only when it also benefits the interests of the white populace and in the maintenance of white racial hierarchy and norms. Milner (2013) and Ladson-Billings and Tate (1995) point out that the tenet of whiteness as property is integral to interest convergence insofar as pedagogy, curriculum, schools, classroom management, and discipline all represent a form of "property" to be controlled and wielded within the U.S. education system. Even the name "classroom management" identifies that control and ownership is central to the endeavor. This control exists on a binary loss-gain relationship;

it stipulates that giving a remedy to one group (such as remedying discipline disproportionalities) would mean another group losing something (Milner, 2013). As Milner et al. (2008) state,

> A critical race theory perspective would suggest that the ability, will, and fortitude of White people to negotiate and make difficult decisions in providing more equitable policies and practices might mean that they lose something of great importance to them, including their propensity to control others, and their ability to reproduce and maintain their self-interests—which can be viewed as the status quo. (p. 345)

Critical race theory provides us with a useful framework in working to decolonize classroom management because as an analytic tool it can explain how and why PBIS has functioned to reproduce the discipline outcomes it was introduced to remedy.

PBIS as Interest Convergence and Whiteness as Property

Without an understanding of racial socialization, perception, and a focus on race, PBIS results in white socialization. PBIS is a tool that, when employed incorrectly, passively indoctrinates students into white, middle-class norms. Across the United States, about 80% of public-school educators and principals are white (Irwin et al., 2023; Schaeffer, 2021; USDOE, 2016), and as many as 40% of schools may not employ a single teacher of color (Hansen & Quintero, 2018). This fact becomes key when looking at PBIS through an interest convergence and whiteness as property lens. Tier 1 PBIS teams should consist of school personnel in addition to family and student representation (Center on PBIS, 2023c). Yet, these teams are primarily comprised of school administrators and classroom educators.

Through its implementation and in asking educators and schools to identify classroom norms, PBIS ends up systematizing and formalizing the maintenance of white norms and protocols of participation (Gay, 2002), and reinforcing racist schooling practices (Bornstein, 2017a). Instead of empowering students, PBIS is often used as an enforcement system of white socialization and coercion (Williams & Land, 2006). PBIS does not take into account the identity of PBIS team members and how they might unconsciously, or even consciously, define and evaluate behaviors through racial filters (Bornstein, 2017a, 2017b).

Hegemonic structures privilege white identity, resulting in a white standard of normativity. Tatum (2017) argues that this leads to a veiled white socialization in which white students or educators have not had to consider their white identity or think about the implications of being white. As Gay (2002) outlines protocols of participation and speech patterns that can vary racially, ethnically, and culturally. These differences can include speech volume, call-and-response patterns, and whether students and educators engage in a passive receptive style of communication or an active participatory one. When PBIS norms are created in a way that reproduces hegemonic white normative structures, PBIS highlights both how the interest of educators converges to maintain their control of classroom discipline (whiteness as property) and maintains disproportionalities and existing racial hierarchies.

These racial filters have been identified repeatedly through research in how educators respond to Black boys as young as kindergarten as threatening (Todd et al., 2016), how implicit bias affect how educators surveil and expel Black boys in particular (Gilliam et al., 2016), how race factors into educators' perceptions of Black students as angrier than white peers (Halberstadt et al., 2022), and how Black boys are often seen as older and less innocent than white peers (Goff et al., 2014).

Family and Community Involvement

As Tyre and Feuerborn (2021) note, too often schools implementing PBIS do not do deep reflections on perceptions of behavior and discipline, a key aspect of creating norms and standards of behavior. In addition, educators' perception of parental involvement is often greater than how parents see their own involvement, where parents often feel left out of the PBIS implementation process (Rose et al., 2023). Further, school staff make assumptions and often believe that providing parents and families with information about PBIS is the equivalent of parent and family involvement in the PBIS implementation process (Rose et al., 2023; Witte et al., 2021).

These common issues with PBIS implementation create scenarios nationwide in which majority white educators are solely responsible for determining the standards for classroom behaviors and what defines "behaviorally acceptable" without family, parent, or community involvement. Although PBIS guidebooks indicate a space for community, parent, and caregiver approval and student input, these practices rarely go as far as balancing decision-making power in classrooms and schools. Although this may be a distinction between what is supposed to happen in theory and what happens in practice, PBIS in practice often occurs insularly (Rose et al., 2023; Witte et al., 2021).

This imbalance between white education personnel and students and families of color is amplified in school discipline because evaluations of student behavior are highly contextualized and evaluated through cultural experiences and lenses (Smith, 2018). As a result, students are being socialized into largely white normative ways of being, their behavior is evaluated through a white gaze, and PBIS decision making functions through interest convergence of white educators and their ownership of classroom discipline, instructional, and curricular practices (Skiba & Peterson, 2003).

Problematizing whiteness in education, Matias and Newlove (2017) argue that to attain freedom we must eradicate tyrannies, such as whiteness, that are embedded in our semiotics and epistemologies. Implicated in this probe is making visible the ways in which interest convergence and whiteness as property pervades policies and practices within schools. PBIS discourse is shrouded by norms that are so prevalent that they are accepted unquestioningly. These policies perpetuate whiteness as the standard, privileging white viewpoints of behavior, language, and attitudes. The assumed racial neutrality in PBIS must be challenged in addition to the color-evasive nature in which it is often implemented.

Co-generative Praxis

We have been called to (re)think, (re)imagine, (re)envision, (re)define, to (re)humanize. Re- implies doing what has already been done—again. Much of what we aim to do again, as designated by the prefix re-, would be fixed if instead of doing it again, we did things jointly. What would happen if co-, as a prefix and a construct, guided our educational futures? What would happen if we co-build educational spaces, if we co-develop schools, if we co-define possibilities, if we co-humanize students, or if we co-create visions?

To develop a conceptual path forward in decolonizing classroom management, we borrow from Chris Emdin's (2008) concept of *co-generative dialogue* and Freire's (1970) concept of *praxis* to propose the concept of *co-generative praxis* where educational spaces are co-constructed and co-developed with families and communities. Emdin (2008) defines co-generative dialogues as "conversations in which people come together to discuss a social field where they have had—and will continue to have—a shared experience" (p. 774). Emdin (2008) notes that these conversations are designed to turn classrooms and curriculum into cosmopolitan spaces of shared power, shared teaching, and mutual responsibility. Freire (1970) defines praxis as "reflection and action towards the world in order to transform it" (p. 51). The Freire Institute states that the concept of praxis

> is not enough for people to come together in dialogue in order to gain knowledge of their social reality. They must act together upon their environment in order critically to reflect upon their reality and so transform it through further action and critical reflection.

As identified by Milner (2008), to move away from interest convergence and whiteness as property in school discipline there is a need for collective interests in eliminating racial inequities in education. Co-generative praxis calls for the inclusion of typically excluded stakeholders and the recognition that collective interests must outweigh personal interests of maintaining the racialized status quo of who owns "educational property."

A key difference between PBIS practices and co-generative praxis approach is that although PBIS asks for community input in the creation of classroom discipline practices, co-generative praxis see parents,' families,' and community's role co-building educational spaces, co-developing schools, co-defining possibilities, and co-humanizing students as central, not merely as check-in. In this sense we see co-generative praxis as a solution for the interest convergence and whiteness as property issues that exist in many schools across the United States.

Models of Co-Generative Practice

One example of co-generative praxis includes efforts by Village of Wisdom (2021, 2023) in Durham, North Carolina. Village of Wisdom works with families and schools to create culturally and racially affirming educational curriculum, practices, and spaces. To do this, Village of Wisdom centers the knowledge and experiences of parents, families, and students to cocreate and co-lead how classroom practices are shaped through the creation of culturally affirming instructional environments, which are built between educators and parent-researchers (Barrie et al., 2021; Village of Wisdom, 2021, 2023). To cocreate these environments, schools, students, and parents partner in what we would call co-generative praxis—reflecting and acting on education environments to cocreate community approved instructional and discipline practices.

Another group working to create co-generative praxis as a means of decolonizing classroom management is Friends and Families of Louisiana Incarcerated Children (FFLIC). FFLIC is a grassroots organization headquartered in New Orleans with multiple chapters in cities across Louisiana. This group works to disrupt the school-to-prison nexus by supporting those closest to it—justice-impacted families and students. FFLIC's mission is "to create a better life for all of Louisiana's youth, especially those involved in or targeted by the juvenile justice system" (FFLIC, n.d.). Further, FFLIC embodies co-generative praxis because it identifies the pivotal role of families and communities in creating systemic change. Their mission statement explains:

> We believe the people most affected by the systems are the ones who have to transform the systems. We believe that we are the experts on what our

communities need. Solidarity and collective action are our most powerful tools in the struggle for self-determination and justice for our children and families. (FFLIC, n.d.)

In its efforts to build grassroot capacity, FFLIC works with families and communities to advocate at school disciplinary hearings for students, become a liaison with schools to ensure family, parent, and community input, and advocates to educational leaders to adopt more restorative, human-centered approaches to discipline policies and practices. Both Village of Wisdom and FFLIC are examples of organizations engaging in co-generative praxis to disrupt the school-to-prison nexus and counter the function of interest convergence and whiteness as property in schools.

In their framework for eliminating inequities in school discipline, Gregory et al. (2017) outline principles for prevention and intervention that will facilitate a culturally responsive approach to discipline. This framework moves beyond focusing on students, as subjects in which discipline is enacted upon, and advocates for the inclusion of student and family voice, moving away from the vertical, one-way relationships that typically characterize school-family relationships to more horizontal, reciprocal co-relationships that rely less on a hierarchical exchange. Any intervention for school discipline that will result in more equitable outcomes and aims to decolonize classroom management must shift from a school-centric foci and voice toward a co-constructed voice between families, students, and schools. One concrete step in that direction is to ensure that on school and district levels, families of minoritized students impacted by the discipline gap be included on advisory boards and leadership teams to co-draft, co-review, and co-recommend policies. This will provide a formal space for Black and Brown families to co-facilitate change within the school system.

REFERENCES

Barrett, N., McEachin, A., Mills, J. N., & Valant, J. (2017). *Disparities in student discipline by race and family income.* Education Research Alliance NOLA. https://educationresearchalliancenola.org/ files/publications/010418-Barrett-McEachin-Mills-Valant-Disparities-in-Student-Discipline-by- Race-and-Family-Income.pdf

Barrie, R., Mays, R., McLaughlin, C., Page, D., Porter, N., & Majors, A. (2021). *A dreams assessment: The dreams of Black parents, Black students, and teachers during COVID and beyond.* Village of Wisdom. https://www.villageofwisdom.org/research

Bell, D. A. (1976). Serving two masters: Integration ideals and client interests in school desegregation litigation. *Yale Law Journal, 85*(4), 470–516.

Bornstein, J. (2017a). Entanglements of discipline, behavioral intervention, race, and disability. *Journal of Cases in Educational Leadership, 20*(2), 131–144. https://doi.org/10.1177/1555458917696810

Bornstein, J. (2017b). Can PBIS build justice rather than merely restore order? In N. Okilwa, M. Khalifa, & F. Briscoe (Eds.), *The school to prison pipeline: The role of culture and discipline in school* (pp. 135–168). Emerald Publishing.

Center on Positive Behavioral Interventions & Supports. (2023a). *What is PBIS?* https://www.pbis.org/pbis/what-is-pbis

Center on Positive Behavioral Interventions & Supports. (2023b). *School-wide.* https://www.pbis.org/topics/school-wide

Center on Positive Behavioral Interventions & Supports. (2023c). *What is tier 1 support?* https://www.pbis.org/pbis/tier-1

Emdin, C. (2008). The three C's for urban science education. *Phi Delta Kappan, 89*(10), 772–775.

Friends and Families of Louisiana Incarcerated Children (FFLIC) (n.d.). Friends and Families of Louisiana Incarcerated Children Mission and Vision. https://www.fflic.org/about-us/mission-vision/

Freire, P. (1970). *Pedagogy of the oppressed.* Seabury Press.

Freire Institute (n.d.). Concepts used by Paulo Freire. https://www.freire.org/paulo-freire/concepts-used-by-paulo-freire

Gay, G. (2002). Preparing for culturally responsive teaching. *Journal of Teacher Education, 53*(2), 106–116. https://doi.org/10.1177/0022487102053002003

Gilliam, W. S., Maupin, A. N., Reyes, C. R., Accavitti, M., & Shic, F. (2016). *Do early educators' implicit biases regarding sex and race relate to behavior expectations and recommendations of preschool expulsions and suspensions?* Yale University Child Study Center, 1–16.

Goff, P. A., Jackson, M. C., Di Leone, B. A. L., Culotta, C. M., & DiTomasso, N. A. (2014). The essence of innocence: Consequences of dehumanizing Black children. *Journal of Personality and Social Psychology, 106*(4), 526. https://doi.org/10.1037/a0035663

Gregory, A., Skiba, R. J., & Mediratta, K. (2017). Eliminating disparities in school discipline: A framework for intervention. *Review of Research in Education, (41)*1, 253–278. https://doi.org/10.3102/0091732X17690499

Halberstadt, A. G., Cooke, A. N., Garner, P. W., Hughes, S. A., Oertwig, D., & Neupert, S. D. (2022). Racialized emotion recognition accuracy and anger bias of children's faces. *Emotion, 22*(3), 403. https://doi.org/10.1037/emo0000756

Hansen, M., & Quintero, D. (2018) *Teachers in the US are even more segregated than students.* Brookings. https://www.brookings.edu/articles/teachers-in-the-us-are-even-more-segregated-than-students/

Harris, C. I. (1993). Whiteness as property. *Harvard Law Review, 106*(8), 1707–1791. https://doi.org/10.2307/1341787

Irwin, V., Wang, K., Tezil, T., Zhang, J., Filbey, A., Jung, J., Bullock Mann, F., & Parker, S. (2023). *Report on the condition of education 2023.* (NCES 2023–144). U.S. Department of Education. Washington, DC: National Center for Education Statistics. https://nces.ed.gov/pubsearch/pubsinfo.asp?pubid=2023144

Ladson-Billings, G., & Tate, W. F. (1995). Toward a critical race theory of education. *Teachers College Record, 97*(1), 47–68. https://doi.org/10.1177/016146819509700104

Louisiana Believes. (2023). *Positive Behavior Intervention Support (PBIS)*. https://www.louisianabelieves.com/resources/family-support-toolbox/positive-behavior-intervention-support-(pbis)

Matias, C. E., & Newlove, P. M. (2017). The illusion of freedom: Tyranny, whiteness, and the state of US society. *Equity & Excellence in Education, 50*(3), 316–330. https://doi.org/10.1080/10665684.2017.1336951

McDaniel, S., Kim, S., & Guyotte, W. (2017). Perceptions of implementing positive behavior interventions and supports in high-need school contexts through the voice of local stakeholders. *Journal of At-Risk Students, 20*(2), 35–44.

Milner, R., Pearman, F., & McGee, E. O. (2013). Critical race theory, interest convergence, and teacher education. In M. Lynn & A. D. Dixson, (Eds.), *Handbook of critical race theory in education* (pp. 359–374). Routledge.

Morris, E. W., & Perry, B. L. (2017). Girls behaving badly? Race, gender, and subjective evaluation in the discipline of African American girls. *Sociology of Education, 90(2)*, 127–148. https://doi.org/10.1177/0038040717694876

NCES. (2018). *Percentage of students suspended and expelled from public elementary and secondary schools, by sex, race/ethnicity, and state: 2017–18*. U.S. Department of Education. Institute of Education Sciences, National Center for Education Statistics. https://nces.ed.gov/programs/digest/d21/tables/dt21_233.40.asp?current=yes

Okilwa, N. S., Khalifa, M., and Briscoe, F. M. (2017). Introduction and overview, *The school to prison pipeline: The role of culture and discipline in school* (*advances in race and ethnicity in education*, vol. 4), (pp. 1–13). Emerald Publishing, Bingley https://doi.org/10.1108/S2051-231720160000004002

OSEP Technical Assistance Center on Positive Behavioral Interventions and Supports. (2020). *Positive behavioral interventions & supports.* https://www.pbis.org/

Rose, M., Mooney, M., Johnston, C., & Parada, R. H. (2023). Parent involvement in positive behaviour intervention and supports in Australia: Teacher and parent/caregiver perspectives. *Australian Educational Researcher*. https://doi.org/10.1007/s13384-022-00595-4

Schaeffer, K. (2021). *America's public school teachers are far less racially and ethnically diverse than their students.* Pew Research Center. https://www.pewresearch.org/short-reads/2021/12/10/americas-public-school-teachers-are-far-less-racially-and-ethnically-diverse-than-their-students/#:~:text=In%20schools%20where%20at%20least,97%25)%20also%20were%20White.

Skiba, R. J., Michael, R. S., Nardo, A. C., & Peterson, R. L. (2002). The color of discipline: Sources of racial and gender disproportionality in school punishment. *Urban Review, 34*(4): 317–342. https://doi.org/10.1023/A:1021320817372

Skiba, R., & Peterson, R. (2003). Teaching the social curriculum: School discipline as instruction. *Preventing School Failure: Alternative Education for Children and Youth, 47*(2), 66–73. https://doi.org/10.1080/10459880309604432

Smith, A. (2018). *Capturing the narrative: Campus administrators' understanding of cultural mismatch and discipline in the school* (Unpublished doctoral dissertation). Texas A&M University–Commerce.

Southern Poverty Law Center. (2009). Effective discipline for student success: Reducing student and teacher dropout rates in Louisiana. *Louisiana School-to-Prison Reform Coalition.* https://www.splcenter.org/sites/default/files/d6_legacy_files/downloads/LA_Reducing_Student_Dropout.pdf

Tatum, B. D. (2017). *Why are all the Black kids sitting together in the cafeteria: And other conversations about race.* Basic Books.

Todd, A. R., Thiem, K. C., & Neel, R. (2016). Does seeing faces of young Black boys facilitate the identification of threatening stimuli? *Psychological Science, 27*(3), 384–393. https://doi.org/10.1177/0956797615624492

Tyre, A. D., & Feuerborn, L. L. (2021). Ten common misses in PBIS implementation. *Beyond Behavior, 30*(1), 41–50. https://doi.org/10.1177/1074295621996874

United States Department of Education (USDOE). (2016). *The state of racial diversity in the educator workforce.* https://www2.ed.gov/rschstat/eval/highered/racial-diversity/state-racial-diversity-workforce.pdf

Village of Wisdom. (2021). *Keep dreaming: Summary report.* https://www.villageofwisdom.org/research

Village of Wisdom. (2023). *Dream big: Centering Black parent wisdom in designing culturally affirming and liberatory toolkits.* https://www.villageofwisdom.org/_files/ugd/0ac1ac_156214e337a442c1ad18c9ed38580a58.pdf

Williams, D., & Land, R. (2006). The legitimation of Black subordination: The impact of colorblind ideology on African American education. *Journal of Negro Education, 75(4),* 579–588.

Witte, A., Singleton, F., Smith, T., & Hershfeldt, P. (2021, June). *Enhancing family-school collaboration with diverse families.* Center on PBIS, University of Oregon. www.pbis.org/resource/enhancing-family-school-collaboration-with-diverse-families

9

Reimagining Classroom Management

A Humanizing Social and Emotional Framework

Brandie Oliver, Brooke Harris Garad, Brian Dinkins, Danielle Madrazo, and Katie Brooks

In an increasingly diverse and interconnected world, the importance of fostering inclusive and culturally sustaining learning environments is critical (Hammond, 2014; Paris, 2012). Traditional classroom management practices, often deeply rooted in colonial ideologies, have perpetuated oppressive power dynamics and cultural hierarchies within educational spaces, resulting in academic opportunity gaps and disproportionate disciplinary actions for BIPOC (Black, Indigenous, and people of color) students (Brantlinger & Danforth, 2013; Casey et al., 2013). More recent models for classroom management have integrated social and emotional learning (SEL) to shift from a punitive disciplinary stance to more student- and adult-centered approaches (Oliver & Berger, 2020). Although SEL is not inherently colonial, the ways in which it is implemented often perpetuate oppressive power dynamics and cultural hierarchies (DeMartino et al., 2022; Mayes et al., 2022).

We propose that without integrating SEL with race-equity work, restorative community practices, and culturally and linguistically sustaining approaches, these efforts will continue to perpetuate inequities, especially for BIPOC students. Ultimately, we hope to extend our learning from and with K–12 students, families, community members, administrators, teachers, preservice teachers, and teacher educators about the knowledge, skills, and dispositions necessary to create inclusive, supportive, culturally, and linguistically sustaining environments.

A HUMANIZING SOCIAL AND EMOTIONAL LEARNING FRAMEWORK

A humanizing social and emotional learning framework is an educational approach that attends to both academic and nonacademic aspects of students' development, making it contextual and relevant to their lived experiences. This approach begins with educators and seeks to deconstruct classroom management practices that often perpetuate oppressive power dynamics. Traditional SEL approaches focus on addressing individual student behavior rather than understanding and naming the systemic conditions that have influenced the school and learning community.

A humanizing approach to SEL attends to the social and emotional needs of students by building on their cultural assets, developing strong relationships, and empowering students through a co-learning process. The subsequent visual (figure 9.1) highlights essential elements of an approach to SEL that begins with educators, centers communities, and seeks to humanize and empower students. The first pillar of this approach is *culturally and linguistically responsive practices*, which honors and leverages the diverse cultural and linguistic backgrounds of students. The next pillar outlines *community-centered approaches* that recognize the importance of community engagement, input, and partnership in shaping educational practices. Within a humanizing SEL framework, we build upon research and knowledge as we include *restorative practices* as the third pillar, to emphasize the importance of repairing harm and restoring relationships rather than using punitive measures. Finally, we use *critical self-reflection* to engage in the ongoing assessment and evolution of practices based on introspective insights as the final pillar.

SEL practices resonate with diverse cultural values; SEL aims to build upon existing strengths through empowerment and agency and views all learners through a strength-based lens.

 Relationships at the core of addressing social and emotional issues; conflict and misbehavior addressed using empathic communication and critical discourse aiming to build skills and repair harm.

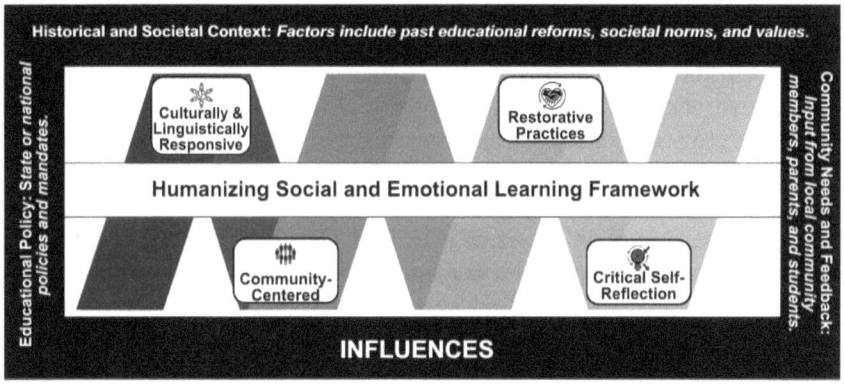

 Community-centered SEL curriculum; responsive to needs, values, and priorities of community; community co-constructs content & skill development.

 All educators participate in ongoing assessment and continual analysis of data to inform areas of growth and learning; evolution of practices based on introspective insights.

Throughout this chapter, we will continue to discuss the primary components of a humanizing SEL framework, further describing how it can be implemented and why we need this new approach. We will address the historical and societal contexts that have shaped our approach and focus on the importance of centering community in this work. Although we acknowledge the influence of state and/or national educational policies and mandates related to SEL within our framework, this chapter will focus instead on how and why to weave humanizing SEL practices within each of the four pillars.

A BRIEF HISTORY OF SOCIAL AND EMOTIONAL LEARNING

Social and emotional learning (SEL), also known as character education, 21st-century skills, noncognitive skills, soft skills, and college and career readiness skills among others, seeks to prepare all students to manage the inevitable challenges, stress, and uncertainties that often arise in everyday life as well as to attain personal and postsecondary success. The Collaborative for Academic, Social, and Emotional Learning (CASEL) defines SEL as the process through which students gain and effectively apply the knowledge, attitudes, and skills necessary to understand and manage emotions, set and achieve positive goals, feel and express empathy for others, develop and maintain positive relationships, and make responsible decisions (CASEL, 2018; CASEL, n.d.). These are the five core intrapersonal, interpersonal, and cognitive competencies that most SEL programs use.

Despite good intentions, many schools have applied SEL programs, policies, and practices that employ emotional and behavioral control strategies, reinforcing the idea that there is a "correct" way of behaving and feeling. In doing so, these SEL programs reinforce individualist values, beliefs, and practices; promote dominant culture norms; fail to address power dynamics in society; neglect addressing equity and social justice; minimize student voice, empowerment, and agency; and dedicate little attention to disrupting the implicit and explicit biases of educators (Jagers et al., 2019). Adopting a one-size-fits-all SEL program perpetuates discourses of control and power that minimize student voice and agency (McManus, 2022) and view historically marginalized groups through a deficit-based outlook. In contrast, schools could implement an SEL framework that aims to transform the school community and seeks to disrupt systems of power, oppression, and privilege.

CRITICALLY EXAMINING CULTURAL ASSUMPTIONS EMBEDDED WITHIN SEL

The journey toward humanizing SEL policies and practices in schools necessitates an essential but often overlooked process: the critical examination of cultural assumptions inherent within traditional SEL frameworks (CASEL, 2020). This critical examination requires deconstructing traditional approaches to SEL, which have frequently been shaped by monocultural perspectives that often marginalize diverse learners (Jagers et al., 2019; Williams & Jager, 2022). Further, such deconstruction demands an exploration of the embedded power dynamics that have been historically perpetuated in education systems (Williams & Jager, 2022). Educators should consider what types of behavioral classroom management strategies are commonly used in K–12 education and how these strategies might perpetuate power and control and minimize student voice and empowerment. In identifying and reflecting on these strategies, educators should ask themselves how they can disrupt traditional approaches in their context.

In most U.S. public schools, the racial and ethnic makeup of the students is not reflected among the teachers. White teachers have consistently dominated the workforce, significantly outnumbering both BIPOC educators and students for decades (Schaeffer, 2021). Given the racial makeup of the teachers and school leaders, it should not be surprising that scholars continue to argue that dominant school culture reflects white, middle-class values (Delpit, 2006; Harris Garad, 2013). The same has been said of SEL. While seeking to support students in the development of school and life skills, SEL often reifies whiteness by focusing on student deficits and mandating what they need to be successful. By addressing these power dynamics and cultural assumptions, educators and policy makers can refine their understanding of SEL and ensure that its policies and applications are both culturally and linguistically inclusive and sustaining. The ensuing discussion will delve into this critical process of deconstruction and offer a framework for developing more equitable and responsive SEL practices.

CASTING A VISION FOR A HUMANIZING APPROACH TO SEL

We cannot achieve what we cannot envision. Humanizing SEL focuses on a critical consciousness that deconstructs existing hierarchies of power, challenges behavioristic teaching and classroom management practices, and promotes humanistic, equitable, and just learning communities. This type of SEL approach is flexible, developmentally and culturally responsive, and aligns with community needs (Oliver & Berger, 2020).

Simmons (2021) states, "SEL faces the risk of becoming White supremacy with a hug," (p. 31) demonstrating how behavioral expectations in schools are rooted in white cultural assumptions and bigotry. Unfortunately, the fraught world Simmons describes can be found both within schools and outside them—and SEL, without a humanizing and empowering approach, is hardly enough. In schools where traditionally Black hairstyles are policed and punished (Byrd & Tharps, 2014), students' linguistic practices and home languages are diminished (Flores & Rosa, 2015), and the curriculum is whitewashed and ahistorical (Brown, 2017), students have little recourse for expressing their frustration with what amounts to school-sanctioned race- and identity-based bullying. When students express indignation over the injustices found in society and sustained in schools, we cannot offer standardized strategies or one-size-fits-all curricula that often problematize the students instead of the unjust systems themselves.

Let us examine, for example, the effectiveness of mindful breathing before a test. Is this SEL strategy still effective if a student is testing for a teacher who consistently underestimates their potential? We must consider that SEL strategies should not be the same for all students when the sources of stress are different. Although we can certainly use SEL strategies with all students, we must also give students the tools to name, circumvent, and dismantle the barriers to their own success and engage in critical self-reflection ourselves.

A humanizing SEL framework builds on the work of scholars who have called for synthesizing transformative SEL and an abolitionist teaching framework (DeMartino et al., 2022) and approaching SEL with an antiracist, justice-oriented lens (Mayes et al., 2022). We affirm these contributions to the field while reiterating the need for race-conscious, restorative, equity- and community-oriented approaches to SEL that sustain the cultural and linguistic practices of BIPOC K–12 students and families.

COMMUNITY-CENTERED SEL SYSTEMS AND PRACTICES

Research collected to help educators understand the value and importance of community and family engagement indicates that many different definitions of community can be found in a multitude of print and online texts (Henderson & Mapp, 2002). For the purposes of envisioning a humanizing approach to SEL, it is the collective vision, definition, and agreed upon characteristics of a community that ultimately matter. Margaret Wheatley says, "There is no power for change greater than a community discovering what it cares about" (2002, p. 55). When considering the implementation of community-centered SEL systems and practices, we must start by identifying the common values, beliefs, and needs of all stakeholders (e.g., students, families, educators, community members, policy makers) within the community.

COMMUNITY AS COLLECTIVE COLLABORATION, NOT A SYSTEM OF OPPRESSION

History has taught us that the institution of education can exhibit patterns of oppression from school leadership by leveraging their privilege and power to press their beliefs and values onto the communities they serve (Delpit, 1988). To disrupt this pattern, it is essential to develop meaningful relationships where all stakeholders routinely work together toward systemic change. Research has shown that when bringing together communities of students from nontraditional backgrounds, their voices offer rich, diverse perspectives and knowledge applicable for improved educational opportunities (Yosso, 2005). Integrating the systems that include voices from all stakeholders throughout the school year provides opportunity for accountability and shared decision making that reflect the ideas, beliefs, and values of the collective community. Examples include holding listening sessions, implementing regular student and family surveys, conducting home visits, forming a community council, and examining data from an equity lens.

SEL that is community-centered promotes intentional partnerships that bridge learning both in and out of school. Too often, SEL implementation lacks solidarity, and the communication is solely from school to home (Yeonjae et al., 2021). Using a community-centered approach helps remove silos and brings together diverse perspectives, knowledge, and voices to co-construct goals, action plans, policies, and practices that not only show up in schools but are integrated throughout the community. Examples include community healing circles, SEL embedded in after-school programs, library story time, hospital wellness programming, or community stakeholders advocating for policy change due to their investment in this work. A community-centered approach is comprehensive, helping to ensure that SEL is authentic and meaningful within all domains of a student's life.

RESTORATIVE PRACTICES WITHIN HUMANIZING SEL

Restorative practices is a framework that uses a relational approach to addressing harm and conflict, emphasizing the importance of repairing relationships rather than simply punishing undesirable behavior. At the heart of this approach is building strong relationships and creating community by viewing student behavior from a lens of inclusion over exclusion, strengths over deficits, belonging over fitting in, and accountability over punishment. It is impossible to repair a relationship if one never existed. Restorative actions seek to address the underlying causes of conflicts and behaviors to foster empathy, accountability, and community building (Zakszeski & Rutherford, 2021). Whereas traditional approaches emphasize punishment, restorative approaches focus on accountability and repairing harm. Through collaborative conversations with stakeholders (including the student), applicable SEL skills can be identified to support a student's growth development to prevent future harm. A peacemaking circle is an example of a restorative practice whereby students involved in a conflict come together to discuss harm, feelings, and methods for resolution (Pavelka, 2013). Through these circles, students can express their perspectives, hear from those impacted by their actions, and collaboratively devise strategies to prevent future issues.

Both restorative practices and SEL initiatives are integral to the humanizing approach to classroom management. SEL equips students with the emotional intelligence and communication skills necessary to navigate restorative conversations. Alone, SEL practices can inadvertently place the obligation on marginalized students to regulate their reactions to systemic dehumanization, reminiscent of Noguera's (2009) observations about identity choices in response to oppressive environments. Restorative practices in conjunction with SEL offers a more profound approach to understanding and rectifying these underlying systemic inequities that lead to misunderstanding, conflict, and exclusion. Integrating both approaches has the potential to ensure not only that students have the SEL skills necessary to develop, strengthen, and restore the relationships in their lives, but also that they demonstrate emotional resilience to address and resolve conflicts effectively.

CRITICAL SELF-REFLECTION FOR HUMANIZING SEL

Transitioning from traditional SEL paradigms to community-centered, culturally and linguistically sustaining SEL policies and practices can be a daunting task (CASEL, 2020). Despite the potential challenges, educators can begin the transformative journey of developing humanizing SEL systems and practices by using critical self-reflection to examine

- existing SEL policies and practices in your school and classroom;
- your beliefs about classroom and behavior management; and
- your relationships with students, families, and the community.

To ensure the academic success of all students, educators should further use critical self-reflection practices in their examination of power dynamics, school culture, bias, student expectations, and curriculum choices.

The transformative journey toward relationship-rich, community-centered, culturally and linguistically sustaining SEL often hinges on significant changes in educators' beliefs and practices (Jagers et al., 2019). This journey involves a conscientious shift from traditional models to approaches that meaningfully integrate the cultural and linguistic assets and perspectives of diverse families and communities (García & Guerra, 2004). To make this shift, educators must go beyond deficit perspectives that assume that culture, language, and experience are barriers to be overcome rather than personal and community assets (Brooks & Adams, 2015; Harris Garad, 2021). The transformative journey to humanizing SEL involves learning from and with these communities to co-construct SEL principles, perspectives, and practices that integrate insights from different cultures. This ongoing transformative journey necessitates a consistent commitment to self-reflection and growth as educators strive to create SEL environments that are not just supportive and inclusive, but also sustain the rich cultures of their students. Critically self-reflective practices to support this transformation could include reflecting on SEL scholarship written by BIPOC researchers and practitioners (Kendi, 2023); decentering oneself from diversity, equity, and inclusion (DEI) discussions and listening to diverse perspectives with more intentionality and reflectivity (Dinkins, 2021; Milner, 2010); reflecting on personal beliefs and biases through critical journaling and discussion (Brooks et al., 2018); engaging in participatory research with BIPOC students and communities to learn more about equity/access issues and to develop stronger relationships (Farley et al., 2017)'; being open and responsive to feedback received from others involving belonging, equity, diversity, and inclusion (BEDI) issues and experiences (Andrews et al., 2019; Kandel-Cisco); and reimagining what kinds of data we collect, value, and use in making decisions.

CONCLUSION

Traditional classroom management practices and approaches to SEL have played a role in perpetuating the inequities that shape the educational experiences of so many students, particularly within BIPOC communities, in the United States today. Bolstered by a vision for equitable and just learning opportunities for all, a humanizing SEL framework seeks to be transformative for students, educators, and communities by disrupting the legacies of coloniality and the systems of power, oppression, and privilege we find in schools of every kind. We propose a framework rooted in race equity work, informed by restorative practices, responsive to the culturally and linguistically diverse communities we serve, and collaboratively realized by K–12 students, families, community members, administrators, teachers, preservice teachers, and teacher educators. With this chapter and our discussion of the relevant contexts for and primary components of a humanizing SEL framework, it is critical that all educators engage in the process of envisioning, articulating, and realizing more equitable, just, and humanizing approaches to social-emotional learning for the benefit of ourselves, our students, and the communities we serve.

REFERENCES

Andrews, D. J. C., Brown, T., Castillo, B. M., Jackson, D., & Vellanki, V. (2019). Beyond damage-centered teacher education: Humanizing pedagogy for teacher educators and preservice teachers. *Teachers College Record, 121*(6), 1–28. https://doi.org/10.1177/016146811912100605

Brantlinger, E., & Danforth, S. (2013). Critical theory perspective on social class, race, gender, and classroom management. In E. T. Emmer & E. J. Sabornie (Eds.), *Handbook of classroom management* (pp. 167–190). Routledge.

Brooks, K., & Adams, S. R. (2015). Developing agency for advocacy: Collaborative inquiry-focused school change projects as transformative learning for practicing teachers. *New Educator, 11*(4), 292–308. https://doi.org/10.1080/1547688X.2015.1087758

Brooks, K., Adams, S., & Kandel-Cisco, B. (2018). Looking within: Teacher critical self-reflection on language and cultural integration in middle level schools. In P. Howell, S. Faulkner, J. Jones, & J. Carpenter (Eds.), *Preparing middle level educators for 21st century schools: Enduring beliefs, changing times, evolving practices.* Information Age Publishing.

Brown, K. D. (2017). Why we can't wait: Advancing racial literacy and a critical sociocultural knowledge of race for teaching and curriculum. *Race, Gender & Class, 24*(1–2), 81–96. https://www.jstor.org/stable/26529237

Byrd, A., & Tharps, L. (2014). *Hair story: Untangling the roots of Black hair in America.* Macmillan.

Casey, Z. A., Lozenski, B. D., & McManimon, S. K. (2013). From neoliberal policy to neoliberal pedagogy: Racializing and historicizing classroom management. *Journal of Pedagogy, 4*(1), 36–58. https://doi.org/10.2478/jped-2013-0003

Delpit, L. (1988). The silenced dialogue: Power and pedagogy in educating other people's children. *Harvard Educational Review, 53*(3), 280–298.

Delpit, L. (2006). *Other people's children: Cultural conflict in the classroom.* New Press.

DeMartino, L., Fetman, L., Tucker-White, D., & Brown, A. (2022). From freedom dreams to realities: Adopting transformative abolitionist social emotional learning (TASEL) in schools. *Theory into Practice, 61*(2), 156–167. https://doi.org/10.1080/00405841.2022.2036062

Dinkins, B. C. (2021). *An investigation of teachers' emotional intelligence and the relationship between the behaviors of African American male students in urban schools.* Ball State University.

Farley, L., Brooks, K., & Pope, K. (2017). Engaging students in praxis using photovoice research. *Multicultural Education, 24*(2), 49–55.

Flores, N., & Rosa, J. (2015). Undoing appropriateness: Raciolinguistic ideologies and language diversity in education. *Harvard Educational Review, 85*(2), 149–171.

Hammond, Z. (2014). *Culturally responsive teaching and the brain: Promoting authentic engagement and rigor among culturally and linguistically diverse students.* Corwin Press.

Harris Garad, B. (2013). Spiritually centered caring: An approach for teaching and reaching Black students in suburbia. In C. B. Dillard & C. L. E. Okpalaoka (Eds.), *Engaging culture, race and spirituality: New visions* (pp. 66–80). Peter Lang.

Harris Garad, B. (2021). "We came together on the idea of being 'foreign'": Teacher narratives for the teaching of immigrant and refugee youth. *British Educational Research Journal, 47*(4), 942–958. https://doi.org/10.1002/berj.3717

Henderson, A. T., & Mapp, K. L. (2002). *A new wave of evidence: The impact of school, family, and community connections on student achievement.* Annual Synthesis.

Jagers, R. J., Rivas-Drake, D., & Williams, B. (2019). Transformative social and emotional learning (SEL): Toward SEL in service of educational equity and excellence.

Educational Psychologist, 54(3), 162–184. https://doi.org/10.1080/00461520.2019.1623032

Kandel-Cisco, B., Brooks, K., & Bhathena, C. (2020). From the mouths of experts: Relationship building advice from immigrant and refugee families. *Multicultural Education, 27*(3/4), 45–47. https://files.eric.ed.gov/fulltext/EJ1280468.pdf

Kendi, I. X. (2023). *How to be an antiracist.* One World.

Mayes, R. D., Pianta, R., Oglesby, A., & Zyromskl, B. (2022). Principles of antiracist social emotional justice learning. *Theory into Practice, 61*(2), 178–187. https://doi.org/10.1080/00405841.2022.2036063

Milner, H. R. (2010). What does teacher education have to do with teaching?: Implications for diversity studies. *Journal of Teacher Education, 61*(1–2), 118–131. https://doi.org/10.1177/0022487109347670

Noguera, P. A. (2009). *The trouble with Black boys: . . . And other reflections on race, equity, and the future of public education.* Wiley.

Oliver, B. M., & Berger, C. T. (2020). Indiana social-emotional learning competencies: A neurodevelopmental, culturally responsive framework. *Professional School Counseling, 23*(1_part_3). https://doi.org/10.1177/2156759X20904486

Paris, D. (2012). Culturally sustaining pedagogy: A needed change in stance, terminology, and practice. *Educational Researcher, 41*(3), 93–97. https://doi.org/10.3102/0013189X12441244

Schaeffer, K. (2021). Among many US children, reading for fun has become less common, federal data shows. *Pew Research Center, 12.*

Simmons, D. (2021) Why SEL alone isn't enough. *Educational Leadership, 78*(6), 30–34. https://eric.ed.gov/?id=EJ1288370

Wheatley, M. J. (2002). *Turning to one another: Simple conversations to restore hope to the future.* Berrett-Koehler.

Williams, B. V., & Jagers, R. J. (2022). Transformative social and emotional learning: Work notes on an action research agenda. *Urban Education, 57*(2), 191–197. https://doi.org/10.1177/0042085920933340

Yeonjae L., Ramsey, B., & Rubalcaba, C. (2021, September 27). *Heeding the call for change: Centering equity in social & emotional learning.* Education First. https://www.education-first.com/library/publication/centering-equity-in-sel/

Yosso, T. J. (2005). Whose culture has capital? A critical race theory discussion of community cultural wealth. *Race Ethnicity and Education, 8*(1), 69–91. https://doi.org/10.1080/1361332052000341006

Zakszeski, B., & Rutherford, L. (2021). Mind the gap: A systematic review of research on restorative practices in schools. *School Psychology Review, 50*(2–3), 371–387. https://doi.org/10.1080/2372966X.2020.1852056

10

Decolonizing Mindfulness
Centering Liberation and Connection

Patricia Benitez Hemans

The use of mindfulness in schools has gained mainstream acceptance, due in part to its potential to reduce teacher and student stress and assist in behavior and classroom management (Albrecht et al., 2012; Long et al., 2018; Roeser et al., 2012). Much of the discourse on uses of mindfulness in schools has focused on the psychological and therapeutic aspects of the practice, focusing on the decrease of individual stress to produce resilient, attentive, and more productive teachers and students (Low, 2019). Although the health and well-being of educators and students is certainly a concern, contemporary uses of mindfulness tend to enforce the naturalization of stress and abstract it from its social context (Forbes, 2019): the focus is solely on how individuals cope with a stressful environment and adjust their behaviors, rather than addressing the root causes of stress and behavior issues that present themselves in schooling.

However, some scholars (Ergas, 2019; Forbes, 2016; Orr, 2002) call for a more radical form for the use of mindfulness in schools to disrupt systems of oppression that disadvantage and systematically harm marginalized students and communities. These scholars have critiqued the unmooring of mindfulness in schools from its inception as a spiritual practice with its own ethical framework. Instead of serving neoliberal and colonial objectives as the use of mindfulness in schools typically does, we are urged to decolonize mindfulness (Yellow Bird et al., 2020) to serve liberatory goals aligned with its historical origins.

WHAT IS MINDFULNESS?

Many consider mindfulness as originating from Buddhism 2,500 years ago (Janesick, 2015), though many Indigenous cultures have their own forms of spiritual mindfulness practices (Yellow Bird, 2013). Thích Nhất Hạnh, a famed Buddhist monk known for engaging in issues of justice, described mindfulness as "the practice of being fully present and alive, body and mind united. Mindfulness is the energy that helps us to know what is going on in the present moment" (Nhất Hạnh, 2020, para. 3). A mindfulness practice entails meditation of the present moment, paying mindful attention to the body, feelings, mind, and objects of the mind (Nhất Hạnh, 1998). Within the Buddhist tradition, mindfulness is taught within an ethical context that acknowledges the interconnectedness (or "inter-being") of all living beings, the truth that all beings experience suffering, and an ethical code of conduct (sīla) that compels practitioners to end the causation of suffering for all (Nhất Hạnh, 1998).

Today, mindfulness is a booming industry, thanks to the work of Jon Kabat-Zinn, who developed mindfulness-based stress reduction in 1979. The secularized use of mindfulness in the United States is seen as a universal practical and interventional method (Kabat-Zinn, 2003) due to extensive research on adults within mental health care, medicine, and wellness settings (see Goldberg et al., 2022). Nonclinical and nontherapeutic methods have also shown promising results with teachers and students in school settings—namely, the decrease in perception of stress and burnout, leading to teacher resilience, retention, and greater productivity (Roeser et al., 2012). This increase in occupational health and well-being may serve as a foundation for more effective classroom management, positive interpersonal climate, and positive teacher-student relationships, engendering students to feel a greater sense of belonging, an increase in motivation and engagement with learning, and fewer disciplinary referrals (Hoyt, 2016).

MINDFULNESS AND BEHAVIOR/ CLASSROOM MANAGEMENT

Though the aforementioned studies point to a more positive classroom climate when mindfulness is used in classrooms, the focus nonetheless is on behavior management tied to compliance and productivity, a symptom of the neoliberalization of schools, which Indigenous scholars argue is an extension of colonialism (Tuck, 2013). Mindfulness meditation becomes a "technology of the (neoliberal) self," transmitting the self-responsibilizing impulse to those practicing mindfulness (Reveley, 2016), whether they be educators or students.

For example, one study on third-grade students paired mindfulness with traditional classroom management strategies and found mindfulness to be successful in enhancing most of its student participants' engagement with "on-task behavior" (engaging with teacher-led classroom activities) and following classroom rules (such as raising hands to speak, staying seated, and keeping eyes on one's own work) (Kasson & Wilson, 2017). This study is typical of much of the literature on mindfulness in schools that, although garnering support for the use of mindfulness in schools for managing behavior, fails to critique the social context in which mindfulness is used. Much information is absent on the backgrounds of the student participants, explanation of what makes student behavior desirable or undesirable, as well as consideration of possible systemic reasons for student behavior. The study also lacks a critical examination of the onto-epistemological assumptions inherent in how mindfulness is being operationalized. As a pedagogical practice, this particular use of mindfulness supports the Eurocentric individualistic approach to learning and being that supports hierarchical relationships in the classroom, as well as centers productivity.

Neoliberalism as an extension of coloniality can also be seen in the way one's well-being and health are framed as solely a personal responsibility abstracted from environmental factors (Forbes, 2019; Reveley, 2016). A study by Long et al. (2018) on the efficacy of mindfulness versus traditional behavior management strategies at an alternative school reinforces the self-responsiblizing of students' well-being. The researchers found that those in the mindfulness group displayed more "positive" and "appropriate" behaviors after the intervention; however, they also saw an iatrogenic effect on students' well-being. This finding is not unique to this study, but it does acknowledge the social ecological factors of students who traditionally attend alternative schools. It is a rare acknowledgment in student mindfulness studies of the impact of students' social context on their behavior and well-being, which is a step in the direction of criticality.

However, mindfulness is still being centered as the individual student's intervention on their own well-being, and the findings from this study suggest that individual mindfulness practices are not the correct—or at least, not the sole—tool to enhance the well-being of students experiencing systemic harms. I will go so far as to say that it is irresponsible of educators and researchers to keep furthering mindfulness studies and practices that treat systemic issues (such as factors that affect student well-being and behavior) solely as individuals' problems. Mindfulness studies focusing on how well teachers and students cope with stress, increase production, and modulate behavior and emotion (Albrecht et al., 2012; Hoyt, 2016; Roeser et al., 2012) normalize neoliberal values of individualism and self-management, further reinforcing colonial logics and systems.

MINDFULNESS AND DECOLONIZATION

These two mindfulness studies are discussed not to show their exceptionalism among the literature on mindfulness in schools; they were selected to show the typical nature of mindfulness interventions that lack critical analysis of the social context, as well as the assumptions of what mindfulness is to be used for. Though the school mindfulness literature is full of these studies, framing mindfulness practices in schools within a liberatory paradigm—and, specifically, a decolonizing framework—can transform how it is used for classroom and behavior management. Within the United States, uses of mindfulness should be analyzed by the interconnected violences of settler colonialism (Andreotti et al., 2015) and must acknowledge the self-determination and sovereignty of Indigenous Peoples. Instead of using mindfulness to further colonial and neoliberal values, educators should be trained to use mindfulness to resist neoliberalism and coloniality, turning mindfulness from a "technology of the (neoliberal) self" (Reveley, 2016) into a "technology of resistance" (Rocheleau, 2007; Scott, 1990) to colonialism.

Decolonization can be defined as, "the intelligent, calculated and active resistance to the forces of colonialism that perpetuate the subjugation and/or exploitation of our minds, bodies and lands" (Wilson & Yellow Bird, 2005, p. 2). In the United States, at this point in history, decolonization operates within a paradigm of settler colonialism, which sees colonization as a structure rather than an event (Wolfe, 2006). This structure seeks to destroy and disappear Indigenous Peoples to claim supremacy over their lands for the purpose of excessive production to support capitalism, which is further upheld by the subjugation and forced labor of others (Tuck & Yang, 2012). By establishing settler sovereignty over land, Indigenous relationships with land are disrupted, resulting in ongoing violence against Indigenous Peoples, their worldviews, and ways of being.

Thus, decolonization should not be conflated with social justice or even other critical framings, but rather, must be explicit in its ties to Indigenous futurities and liberation. Though it must be careful to avoid this conflation, it is also a useful analytical tool because decolonization demands a complex analysis of settler entanglements with white supremacy, patriarchy, capitalism, and human supremacy (Spring, 2016). Decolonization as an analytic reveals how these entanglements help uphold settler colonialism to the detriment of both Indigenous and non-Indigenous liberation, and prompts the dreaming and creating of a truly inclusive society and education system (Battiste, 2013).

The current movement to decolonize mindfulness (as well as to decolonize yoga) mainly centers on stopping the commodification and appropriation of the practices (Blu Wakpa, 2018; Yellow Bird et al., 2020). What Indigenous scholars of these movements acknowledge is the need to decolonize place as well as practice and person: any decolonizing efforts taking place on Turtle Island must make sure efforts are about rematriating Indigenous life and land as well as centering the wellness of communities rather than individuals (Blu Wakpa, 2018; Yellow Bird et al., 2020). As Yellow Bird et al. (2020) surmise, a "decolonized mindfulness" must be envisioned and enacted that "not only create[s] liberation from the meditation cushion, but will bring a more radical, activist mindfulness to all participants who seek positive, loving, and radical change." In other words, decolonizing a *practice* and a *person* must be inextricably concerned with decolonizing a specific *place*.

DECOLONIZING MINDFULNESS: TOWARD LIBERATION AND CONNECTION

In the past decade, critical scholars have been using mindfulness paired with critical, feminist, and anti-oppressive pedagogies to explore liberatory goals. In these classrooms, mindfulness has been used as a "disruptive classroom practice" (Helmer, 2014), to find rest in and learn from discomfort (Berila, 2016; Hyde, 2013), to disrupt epistemological dominance of mind over body (Berila, 2016; Rendón, 2009), and to heal the split of mind/body/spirit (Cariaga, 2019; Wong, 2018). Decolonizing scholars expand upon these works, extending the practice of mindfulness for the use of decolonization explicitly from settler colonial structures and logics. Four examples of mindfulness being used explicitly from a decolonizing perspective follow.

Developing critical consciousness that includes understanding the mechanizations of settler colonialism serves as an important step in the process of decolonization. Michael Yellow Bird, a member of the MHA Nation (Mandan, Hidatsa, and Arikara), created the method of *neurodecolonization*, which uses mindfulness to shape consciousness to heal from the effects of colonization and unlearn internalized oppression (Yellow Bird, 2013). His is the only work that fuses mindfulness and neuroscience from an explicit decolonizing perspective and is a great contribution to decolonization on an internal level. However, a "deep embodiment of critical consciousness" must be applied in consistent action to resist neoliberal and settler colonial narratives in schools, their policies, and their curricula (Pewewardy et al., 2022, p.

6). The following are ways that mindfulness can be embodied in educational settings to work toward decolonizing schooling as a practice as well as place.

Within the context of decolonization, Anishnabe Midekway and Nehiy/naw Cree scholar Alannah Young Leon describes how mind, body, and spirit cannot be separated from land and how an embodied pedagogy she cocreated with Denise Nadeau can help support and maintain this interconnectedness. "All our relations'" pedagogy promotes the use of mindfulness to support presence building; and other embodied practices such as guided imagery, music, drawing, and movement are used to enhance and express connections with others, including animals, stories, memories, and places (Leon & Nadeau, 2018). This helps counter the intentional placelessness of Eurocentric schooling, which relies on the disembodiment from land and place to further global capitalism's extraction of human and natural resources (Greenwood, 2009).

In another study on the effectiveness of mindfulness within a "Spirituality and Critical Social Work" course, Yuk-Lin Renita Wong uses mindfulness to heal the mind/body split of Eurocentric consciousness. Taught within a decolonizing framework, mindfulness activities are used to help address the spiritual and emotional harm of colonization, focusing on "inter-being": the awareness that what is within us and what is outside of us is not separate, but interconnected—inseparable from all living beings, "we 'inter-are'" (Nhất Hạnh, 1991, pp. 95–96). After the course, students reported that by integrating the wholeness of their being through mindfulness, they reconnected with their identities that had been hidden and split by colonization, grounded themselves in their bodies, and reflected on what it means to be interconnected with all other living beings, which impacted their work as social workers (Wong, 2018).

Last, in my own study with P–20 critical educators enrolled in a "Mindfulness for Critical Educators" course, educator coresearchers are taught mindfulness practices within the framework of decolonization, embodiment, and empowerment. Coresearchers create an action project where they explore how mindfulness can be used toward decolonizing goals in their own educational settings. Some educator coresearchers had come into the course wary of how mindfulness had been appropriated for the purpose of behavior control in the classroom and were cautious regarding their intentions for using mindfulness with students. In the end, they used mindfulness toward developing their critical consciousness of decolonization. They also centered relationships and connections with self/students/others (including land and nature) and supported students' relationships with themselves and with others (Hemans, 2023). In addition, as the daughter of Filipino immigrants who settled on unceded Kumeyaay territory (the area colonized as San Diego) facilitating this workshop series to others who also did not identify as

Indigenous, we used mindfulness to navigate and learn from the discomfort of being in the social location of settlers interested in decolonization.

FROM "CLASSROOM MANAGEMENT" TO "CLASSROOM COMMUNITY"

What the examples in the previous section have in common is that the primary goals for the uses of mindfulness are to connect with self, connect with others, and heal the fractures and disconnections caused by colonization. Unlike the intervention-based literature on mindfulness in schools that tends to focus on classroom and behavior management, as well as the self-responsbilization of well-being and health, these studies instead focus on strengthening relationships. To strengthen relationships is to support the ecological vision of humanity as a part of the natural world (Battiste, 2013), which the editors of this book mention in chapter 1. The focus on relationships and our interconnectedness may serve as a way to resist settler colonialism in schools, "[honoring] and [nourishing] a respect for diversity rather than hierarchy and normative preferences" (Battiste, 2013, p. 114). Although this falls short of the ultimate goal of decolonization—the rematriation of land to her original people—the pedagogical, epistemological, and ontological shifts in the classroom brought on by these liberatory uses of mindfulness may help to bring us closer to this goal.

By decolonizing mindfulness from its ties to classroom management, instead focusing on strengthening the classroom community (as other authors in this book mention), the practice aligns itself more closely with its historical foundations: acknowledging our "inter-being" and how suffering for one means suffering for all. Our liberation is inextricably tied to one another, and mindfulness should be used in the service of communities, not individuals.

REFERENCES

Albrecht, N. J., Albrecht, P. M., & Cohen, M. (2012). Mindfully teaching in the classroom: A literature review. *Australian Journal of Teacher Education, 37*(12), 1–14. http://dx.doi.org/10.14221/ajte.2012v37n12.2

Andreotti, V. O., Stein, S., Ahenakew, C., & Hunt, D. (2015). Mapping interpretations of decolonization in the context of higher education. *Decolonization: Indigeneity, Education & Society, 4*(1), 21–40.

Battiste, M. (2013). *Decolonizing education: Nourishing the learning spirit*. Purich.

Berila, B. (2016). *Integrating mindfulness into anti-oppression pedagogy: Social justice in higher education*. Routledge.

Blu Wakpa, T. (2018). Decolonizing yoga? and (un)settling social justice. *Race and Yoga, 3*(1), i–xix. https://doi.org/10.5070/R331042080

Cariaga, S. (2019). Towards self-recovery: Cultivating love with young women of color through pedagogies of bodymindspirit. *Urban Review, 51*(4), 101–122. https://doi.org/10.1007/s11256-018-0482-9

Ergas, O. (2019). Mindfulness in, as and of education: Three roles of mindfulness in education. *Journal of Philosophy of Education, 53*(2), 340–358. https://doi.org/10.1111/1467-9752.12349

Forbes, D. (2016). Critical integral contemplative education. In R. E. Purser, D. Forbes, & A. Burke (Eds.), *Handbook of mindfulness: Culture, context, and social engagement* (pp. 355–368). Springer International. https://doi.org/10.1007/978-3-319-44019-4

Forbes, D. (2019). *Mindfulness and its discontents: Education, self, and social transformation*. Fernwood.

Goldberg, S. B., Riordan, K., Sun, S., & Davidson, R. J. (2022). The empirical status of mindfulness-based interventions: A systematic review of 44 meta-analyses of randomized controlled trials. *Perspectives on Psychological Science, 17*(1), 108–130. https://doi.org/10.1177/1745691620968771

Greenwood, D. A. (2009). Place, survivance, and white remembrance: A decolonizing challenge to rural education in mobile modernity. *Journal of Research in Rural Education, 24*(10), 1–6.

Helmer, K. (2014). Disruptive practices: Enacting critical pedagogy through meditation, community building, and explorative spaces in a graduate course for pre-service teachers. *Journal of Classroom Interaction, 49*(2), 33–40.

Hemans, P. B. (2023). Embodying practices, empowering changes: A mindfulness for critical educators. UC San Diego. ProQuest ID: Hemans_ucsd_0033D_22117. Merritt ID: ark:/13030/m5wm92zf. Retrieved from https://escholarship.org/uc/item/6bj3f53x

Hoyt, M. (2016). Teaching with mindfulness: The pedagogy of being-with/for and without being-with/for. *Journal of Curriculum Theorizing, 31*(1), 126–142.

Hyde, A. M. (2013). The yoga of critical discourse. *Journal of Transformative Education, 11*(2), pp. 114–126. https://doi.org/10.1177/1541344613495591

Janesick, V. J. (2015). *Contemplative qualitative inquiry: Practicing the Zen of research*. Routledge.

Kabat-Zinn, J. (2003) Mindfulness-based interventions in context: past, present and future.
Clinical Psychology: Science and Practice, 10(2), 144–156. https://doi.org/10.1093/clipsy/bpg016

Kasson, E. M., & Wilson, A. N. (2017). Preliminary evidence on the efficacy of mindfulness combined with traditional classroom management strategies. *Behavior Analysis in Practice, 10*, 242–251. https://doi.org/10.1007/s40617-016-0160-x

Leon, A. Y., & Nadeau, D. (2018). "Embodying Indigenous resurgence: "All our relations" pedagogy. In S. Batacharya & Y. R. Wong (Eds.), *Sharing breath: Embodied learning and decolonization* (pp. 55–82). Athabasca University Press.

Long, A. C., Renshaw, T. L., & Camarota, D. (2018). Classroom management in an urban, alternative school: A comparison of mindfulness and behavioral approaches. *Contemporary School Psychology, 22*, 233–248. https://doi.org/10.1007/s40688-018-0177-y

Low, R. (2019). Mindfulness for teachers: Notes toward a discursive cartography. *History of Education Review, 48*(1), 91–108. https://doi.org/10.1108/HER-12-2018-0030

Nhất Hạnh, T. (1991). *Peace is every step: The path of mindfulness in everyday life.* Bantam.

Nhất Hạnh, T. (1998). *The heart of the Buddha's teaching: Transforming suffering into peace, joy, and liberation.* Broadway.

Nhất Hạnh, T. (2020, September 28). *The Moment is Perfect—Thich Nhat Hanh Lion's Roar.* Lion's Roar. https://www.lionsroar.com/the-moment-is-perfect/.

Orr, D. (2002). The uses of mindfulness in anti-oppressive pedagogies: Philosophy and praxis. *Canadian Journal of Education, 27*(4), 477–490. http://dx.doi.org/10.2307/1602246

Pewewardy, C., Lees, A., & Minthorn, R. Z. (Eds.) (2022). *Unsettling settler colonial education: The transformational Indigenous praxis model.* Teachers College Press.

Rendón, L. I. (2009). *Sentipensante (sensing/thinking) pedagogy: Educating for wholeness, social justice and liberation.* Stylus.

Reveley, J. (2016). Neoliberal meditations: How mindfulness training medicalizes education and responsibilizes young people. *Policy Futures in Education, 14*(4), 497–511. doi:10.1177/1478210316637972

Rocheleau, D. (2007). Neoliberal environments, technologies of governance and governance of technologies. In N. Heynen, J. McCarthy, S. Prudham, & P. Robbins (Eds.), *Neoliberal environments: False promises and unnatural consequences* (pp. 221–227). Routledge.

Roeser, R. W., Skinner, E., Beers, J., & Jennings, P. A. (2012). Mindfulness training and teachers' professional development: An emerging area of research and practice. *Child Development Perspectives, 6*(2), 167–173. https://doi.org/10.1111/j.1750-8606.2012.00238.x

Scott, J. C. (1990). *Domination and the arts of resistance: Hidden transcripts.* Yale University Press.

Spring, J. (2016). *Deculturalization and the struggle for equality: A brief history of the education of dominated cultures in the United States.* Routledge.

Tuck, E. (2013). Neoliberalism as nihilism?: A commentary on educational accountability, teacher education, and school reform. *Journal for Critical Education Policy Studies, 11*(2), 324–347.

Tuck, E., & Yang, K. W. (2012). Decolonization is not a metaphor. *Decolonization: Indigeneity, Education & Society, 1*(1), 1–40. https://doi.org/10.25058/20112742

Wilson, W. A., & Yellow Bird, M. (2005). *For Indigenous eyes only: A decolonization handbook.* School of American Research Press.

Wolfe, P. (2006). Settler colonialism and the elimination of the native. *Journal of Genocide Research, 8*(4), 387–409. https://doi.org/10.1080/14623520601056240

Wong, Y. R. (2018). "Please call me by my true names": A decolonizing pedagogy of mindfulness and interbeing in critical social work education. In S. Batacharya & Y. R. Wong (Eds.), *Sharing breath: Embodied learning and decolonization* (pp. 253–306). Athabasca University Press.

Yellow Bird, M. (2013). Neurodecolonization: Applying mindfulness research to decolonizing social work. In M. Gray, J. Coates, M. Yellow Bird, & T. Hetherington (Eds.), *Decolonizing social work* (pp. 293–310). Routledge.

Yellow Bird, M., Gehl, M., Hatton-Bowers, H., & Reno-Smith, D. (2020). Defunding mindfulness: While we sit on our cushions, systemic racism runs rampant. *Zero to Three.* https://www.zerotothree.org/resource/perspectives-defunding-mindfulness-while-we-sit-o n-our-cushions-systemic-racism-runs-rampant/

11

Challenging the Narrative

How Unexamined Behaviorist Beliefs Can Sabotage Trauma-Informed Practices

Jennifer Randhare Ashton, Jessica Sniatecki, and Maria Timberlake

Many children arrive at school having experienced trauma or adverse childhood events (ACEs), and research indicates a correlation with difficulties in school (Substance Abuse and Mental Health Services Administration [SAMHSA], 2023; Wall, 2021). Examples of ACEs include witnessing violence in the home; experiencing verbal, physical, and/or sexual abuse; incarceration of a parent; or having a family member with mental health and/or substance abuse challenges (CDC, 2023b). More than two-thirds of school-age children have experienced at least one traumatic event in their lifetime (SAMHSA, 2023), which can have a profound effect on students' performance and experience in school, including lower academic achievement, increased behavioral issues, and more frequent disciplinary involvement (SAMSHA, 2023; Wall, 2021). Although many negative outcomes have been linked with ACEs, they do not determine one's life trajectory. Social support, relationships with caring adults, and engaging school programs (CDC, 2023c; Logan-Greene et al., 2014) can help offset the potential impact of ACEs and promote resilience. These supports are most beneficial when paired with effective interventions and programming to help address trauma.

To mitigate the challenges of student behaviors in response to trauma, some schools are implementing a trauma-informed approach (TIA). TIAs encourage educators to reframe challenging behavior(s) from "consciously oppositional" (Sweetman, 2022, p. 5) to survival skills that are being misapplied in the school setting (Wall, 2021). Though trauma-informed approaches are promising, implementation when underlying normative assumptions have not been disrupted is likely to be unsuccessful and create frustration and disillusionment for students and educators alike. This chapter offers nuanced counterpoints to the dominant behaviorist discourses and reconceptualizes classroom management as a humanistic endeavor.

We, the authors, are currently college professors; two are former classroom teachers and the other is a former mental health counselor. We identify as female, nondisabled, white, educated, and work in teacher/counselor preparation programs at state university campuses with teacher candidates whose demographics are similar to our own. We teach that educators should not distance themselves from their students to manage their behavior and reject traditional behaviorist classroom management approaches built on a foundation of control and compliance.

MANAGEMENT AND CONTROL

Much of what is presented to educators about classroom management capitalizes on fears about losing control of unruly students and/or their classrooms. Strategies offered in college courses and required professional development workshops are historically built upon white, Western, Judeo-Christian behaviorist principles that view student behavior as a conditioned response or a rational choice (Harzem, 2004). Course texts offer strategies to manage challenging behavior through control and compliance without emphasizing the deeper work of listening and interpreting the communicative intent. Student behavior is undoubtedly an important topic, but the focus must be on recognizing the subjective cultural context and educators' internalized beliefs about motivation, obedience, and what comprises good behavior.

Employing a TIA (Emerson, 2022; Szarkowsi & Fogler, 2020) and humanistic (Orsati, 2016) approach can be a foundation for developing positive learning environments in which trust is built and support is provided. Aspiring and practicing educators must understand that norms around good behavior are socially constructed and upheld deliberately, though often unconsciously, by educators and students as well. Though these assumptions are strong and difficult to dismantle, it is possible to reject them.

TRADITIONAL CLASSROOM MANAGEMENT APPROACHES

Bad Behavior Should Be Punished

Behaviorism's influence on our schools and society is long-standing and so ingrained as to seem unremarkable. Even the most basic needs (i.e., rest, hydration and food, and belonging) are set up as rewards to be earned. Although it is not necessary for educators to identify all the political, cultural, economic, and historical factors that have shaped this paradigm, it is essential to identify and understand how they influence classroom management decisions. For example, early immigrants to the East Coast of the United States practiced Puritanism, a Calvinist movement that emphasized absolute obedience to God and "a strict moral discipline and purity as the correct form of Christian life" (Lydon, 1998, p. 423). Public schools were created as spaces of assimilation where cultural norms for children's behaviors (influenced by religious orthodoxy) dictated quiet, stoic, and prompt obedience to adult demands. Over time, existing systems of privilege and power further strengthened and shaped these norms by adding whiteness and able-bodiedness to the definition of well-behaved.

The belief in rewards and punishments is so culturally ingrained in educational spaces that contradictory research evidence has not changed practice. In fact, as schools and societies have become more diverse, the desire for control has only increased. Based on socialized experiences in P–12 education and pre-service preparation, many educators have internalized and rationalized a behaviorist approach to classroom management that features punishments such as time-outs, detention, expulsion, suspension, and disciplinary referrals to control students' behavior (Orsati, 2016). Modeled after our penal system, many schools have adopted ineffective and unquestioned zero-tolerance policies that act as a pedagogy of punishment (Ayers et al., 2017). Educators must recognize and understand this so that they can resist this grand narrative and problematic approach to conflict. Conflict is inevitable and to be expected in social settings such as schools, but responses to that conflict are socially mediated by cultural norms (Ayers et al., 2017). These seemingly logical punitive consequences can also lead to further traumatization in a school setting, compromising the potential benefits of existing TIAs and significantly limiting their effectiveness. To support students who have experienced trauma, Gorski (2020) implores educators to first map out all the ways in which students experience trauma at school.

The Trauma of Schools

Schools need to be acknowledged as a source of trauma in some children's lives. By not acknowledging schools as sources of systemic trauma, such as institutionalized racism, classism, ableism, and homophobia, schools continue to oppress and marginalize students with problematic curricula, mandated assessments, and policies (Gorski, 2020; Petrone & Stanton, 2021). Left unchecked, these systematic injustices risk re/traumatizing students with historically marginalized identities (Petrone & Stanton, 2021). For example, African American students are more likely to attend high-poverty schools that use a punitive approach, resulting in an overrepresentation in suspension and expulsion as well as a disproportionate number of subjective disciplinary referrals (Milner et al., 2010).

Students with marginalized identities have education trajectories filled with school faculty acting as agents in a system that pathologizes them and resorts to hyper-punishment to (ineffectively) curb undesired behaviors (Annamma, 2018). The predetermined consequences of punitive discipline policies often result in disengagement, dropout, and expulsion, which are directly correlated with future incarceration (Mallett, 2017). "Educators are either engaged in incarceration prevention or incarceration expansion. Period" (Laura, 2018, p. 25). Punitive responses are ineffective in addressing the underlying cause(s), often result in less compliance, and may even make the situation worse (Wall, 2021). There are also serious negative implications for the relationships between students and educators.

Even when educators shift to proactive strategies such as community building and collaboratively writing classroom expectations it is done with the goal of management and control, which makes it fundamentally very similar to overt behaviorist systems. Put very simply, "it is hard to have a good relationship with someone who is trying to control you" (Davies, 2019, p. 8). Regarding autism, for instance, academic research cites one gold standard evidence-based intervention—applied behavior analysis (ABA). ABA uses behaviorist stimulant/response training to modify behavior and is often presented as the best hope to have a *normal* life (Broderick, 2022). As with other marginalized identities, the meaning of autism and acceptable behavior are culturally and socially constructed based on problematic behaviorist assumptions of normalcy. This approach expects students to change fundamental aspects of their personalities to fit a socially constructed norm implying that they are inherently flawed and potentially causing further trauma.

Further, a perception is that conventional classroom management approaches are culturally neutral, but they are shaped by the cultural norms of the white middle class (Caldera et al., 2020; Orsati, 2016; Weinstein et al., 2004). When some students are seen as *bad* or as displaying inappropriate behavior and face consequences, the status of the students who are seen as *good* increases (Broderick & Leonardo, 2016). For *good* students, intangible benefits, such as less scrutiny and more leeway, positive adult attention, and default positive expectations, start to accrue. Therefore, students who successfully navigate the dominant system and make *good* choices not only avoid negative attention but find their privilege increasing.

A review of literature on classroom management professional development found a recent trend toward rethinking good versus bad behavior by focusing on the whole child and shifting away from narrow training in specific behavioral, cognitive, or affective responses (Freiberg et al., 2020). We agree with the sentiment articulated by Fox (1994), who questioned "the spiritual and ethical life of anyone whose work has never gotten [them] into trouble—if no issues of conscience have emerged or no clash of values has been experienced with the ongoing guardians of the status quo" (p. 13). Although this growing momentum toward humanistic approaches (Orsati, 2016) is encouraging, it is imperative that we push educators to examine their own philosophical and psychological beliefs about student behavior to ensure a deeper application of these holistic approaches (Freiberg et al., 2020) and less likelihood of doing further harm.

EFFECTIVELY ADDRESSING TRAUMA IN SCHOOLS

Though traumatic experiences are common among school-age youth, traditional behaviorist and punitive approaches typically ignore the impact of this trauma on behavior (Wall, 2021). Substantial evidence shows that adverse childhood experiences (ACEs) can lead to challenges later in life (CDC, 2023a, 2023b; Mosley-Johnson et al., 2019). ACEs have been correlated with physical and mental health issues in adulthood (CDC, 2023b) and increase risks for detrimental effects on psychological well-being, social well-being, and life satisfaction (Mosley-Johnson et al., 2019). Expanding awareness about how ACEs can influence academic outcomes has led to an influx of trauma-informed initiatives in K–12 schools; however, thoughtful implementation is required to maximize their effectiveness. Not only are punishment and exclusion practices ineffective at addressing the root cause of the child's behavior; they may also cause additional trauma (SAMHSA, 2014) and other unintended effects.

Trauma-Informed Approaches (TIAs) in Schools

Essential to implementing TIAs is the recognition that people respond to trauma in myriad ways. Hammond (2015) identifies five common reactions to trauma: fight, flight, freeze, hide, and appease. Students with less disruptive trauma responses are less likely to be identified as students in need of intervention as their responses may be viewed as good behavior. For example, a student with the "appease" reaction may be seen as quite helpful and cooperative, and their behaviors may not appear explicitly linked with trauma history. It is vital that educators are knowledgeable about all types of trauma reactions so that they do not overlook students who present in more socially acceptable ways.

TIAs typically contain "five distinct core components: (1) safe, supportive relationships, (2) structure and stability, (3) shared agency, (4) self-awareness and self-regulation, and (5) social-emotional learning and skill building" (Wall, 2021, p. 122). Supportive, healthy relationships with educators and other school staff can help children learn to build trusting, functional relationships. This approach also helps students gain a sense of control over their environment, feeling that their voice is heard. All school personnel can learn to identify triggers associated with their students' past experiences and make efforts to avoid them. Finally, TIAs emphasize skill development so that students can learn to challenge problematic thinking, manage challenging emotions, and engage in socially appropriate ways with others, both within the classroom and throughout their lives (Wall, 2021).

Individuals within a System

Although schools are using more TIAs to address behavior challenges, caution is warranted in relying on deficit-oriented lenses to evaluate students' individual needs. Khasnabis and Goldin (2020) suggest that TIAs often draw heavily from the medical field's definition of trauma and look for deficits within the child and then focus solely on individual behavior change using problematic behaviorist principles. Without acknowledging systemic factors, such as racism, homophobia, and ableism, we may pathologize and hold children (and their families) accountable for challenges that they did not cause. Systemic racism is endemic in education, employment, and medical systems in the United States; by not acknowledging and actively seeking ways to dismantle it, we are compounding the trauma that many children experience. The systems themselves become additional sources of trauma. Children of color, LGBTQ+ children, disabled children, and children experiencing poverty are often exposed to disciplinary practices that increase the likelihood of their future incarceration (Mallett, 2017). When students are described as the sum of their deficits, it leaves structural racism and ableism unchecked and significantly limits the effectiveness of TIAs (Khasnabis & Goldin, 2020). Until these systemic factors are explicitly addressed to reduce ongoing school-based trauma, the true potential of TIAs can never be realized.

Preparing Educators for TIAs

Attempting to implement TIAs when underlying behaviorist assumptions have not been disrupted is likely to fail, resulting in frustration and disillusionment. Educators must also acknowledge and process their own trauma; undergoing the training needed to implement TIAs may be triggering to some educators who have not done this work (Sweetman, 2016). They may also experience vicarious traumatization through hearing the stories of their students' trauma (Cavanaugh, 2016). Professional burnout and compassion fatigue are challenges that may arise for school personnel, particularly if they have insufficient institutional support (Cavanaugh, 2016; Sweetman, 2016). Facilitated workshops, mentoring programs, and supportive services from school personnel with clinical expertise (social workers, counselors, etc.) may be beneficial in helping school personnel avoid these outcomes.

TIAs in most schools focus on the individual child rather than the structural systems and fail to recognize the impact of systemic oppression within schools. Instead, they teach traumatized students how to cope with the existing flawed (behaviorist) system and may contribute to compounded trauma. This reactive approach is insufficient to create learning environments in which all students can thrive. Proactive TIAs could address both the trauma that students bring with them to schools and help to prevent further traumatization by the school system. This raises a valid question about the ethical implications of current TIAs for students who experience trauma via systemic oppression within schools. To truly help students feel safe and ready to learn, systemic change is needed that prioritizes removing triggers and addressing trauma that many students face daily, including those within the educational system itself. Implemented thoughtfully, TIAs can mitigate the effects of ACEs and limit the negative impact of further trauma that the educational system perpetuates. This deeper level work is difficult but essential.

> Work in the invisible world
> At least as hard
> As you do in the visible

This advice from Rumi in the 13th century summarizes our work to challenge the often-unexamined narratives of classroom management beliefs (Fox, 1994, p. 83). Critical, intentional reflection is required to disrupt the cultural messages about goodness, problematic behavior, and who deserves compassion and care in our schools and societies. The underlying norms and assumptions of behavior management must be examined and challenged before innovations such as TIAs can be implemented with success.

REFERENCES

Annamma, S. A. (2018). *The pedagogy of pathologization: Dis/abled girls of color in the school-prison nexus.* Routledge.

Ayers, W., Kumashiro, K., Meiners, E., Quinn, T., & Stovall, D. (2017). *Teaching toward democracy: Educators as agents of change.* Routledge.

Broderick, A. (2022). *The autism industrial complex. How branding, marketing and capital investment turned autism into big business.* Myers Education Press.

Broderick, A., & Leonardo, Z. (2016). What a good boy: the deployment and distribution of "goodness" as ideological property in schools. In D. Connor, B. Ferri, & S. A. Annamma (Eds.), *DisCrit disability studies and critical race theory in education* (pp. 55–70). Teachers College Press.

Caldera, A., Whitaker, M.C., & Conrad Popova, D. A. D. (2020). Classroom management in urban schools: Proposing a course framework. *Teaching Education, 31*(3), 343–361.

Cavanaugh, B. (2016). Trauma-informed classrooms and schools. *Beyond Behavior, 25*(2), 41–46.

Centers for Disease Control and Prevention (CDC). (2023, June 29a). *Fast facts: Preventing adverse childhood experiences.* https://www.cdc.gov/violenceprevention/aces/fastfact.html

Centers for Disease Control and Prevention (CDC). (2023, June 29b). *Help youth at risk for ACEs.* https://www.cdc.gov/violenceprevention/aces/help-youth-at-risk.html

Centers for Disease Control and Prevention (CDC). (2023, June 29c). *Risk and protective factors.* https://www.cdc.gov/violenceprevention/aces/riskprotectivefactors.html

Davies, N. (2019). The inexcusable fallacy of behaviourism in education. *Prospero, 25*(4), 8–9.

Emerson, A. (2022). The case for trauma-informed behaviour policies. *Pastoral Care in Education, 40*(3), 253–359. https://doi.org/10.1080/02643944.2022.2093956

Fox, M. (1994). *The reinvention of work: A new vision of livelihood for our time.* HarperCollins.

Freiberg, H. J., Oviatt, D., & Naveira, E. (2020). Classroom management meta-review continuation of research-based programs for preventing and solving discipline problems. *Journal of Education for Students Placed at Risk, 25*(4), 319–337. https://doi.org/10.1080/10824669.2020.1757454

Gorski, P. (2020). How trauma-informed are we, really? *Educational Leadership, 7*(2), 14–19. https://www.ascd.org/el/articles/how-trauma-informed-are-we-really

Hammond, Z. (2015). *Culturally responsive teaching and the brain: Promoting engagement and rigor among culturally and linguistically diverse students.* Corwin.

Harzem, P. (2004). Behaviorism for new psychology: What was wrong with behaviorism and what is wrong with it now? *Behavior and Philosophy, 32*, 5–12. https://www.jstor.org/stable/27759468

Khasnabis, D., & Goldin, S. (2020). Don't be fooled, trauma is a systemic problem: Trauma as a case of weaponized educational innovation. *Bank Street Occasional Paper Series, 43*(5), 44–57. https://doi.org/10.58295/ 2375–3668.1353

Laura, C. (2018). Against prisons and the pipelines to them. In E. Tuck & K. W. Yang (Eds.), *Toward what justice? Describing diverse dreams of justice in education* (pp. 19–28). Routledge.

Logan-Greene, P., Green, S., Nurius, P. S., & Longhi, D. (2014) Distinct contributions of adverse childhood experiences and resilience resources: A cohort analysis of adult physical and mental health. *Social Work in Health Care, 53*(8), 776–797. https://doi.org/10.1080/00981389.20142.944251

Lydon, J. (1998). Christian ethics, Protestant. In *Encyclopedia of Applied Ethics*, 2nd edition (pp. 423–434). Academic Press. https://doi.org/10.1016/B978-0-12-373932-2.00191-5

Mallett, C. A. (2017). The school-to-prison pipeline: Disproportionate impact on vulnerable children and adolescents. *Education and Urban Society, 49*(6), 563–592. https://doi.org/10.1177/0013124516644053

Milner, H. R., & Tenore, F. B. (2010). Classroom management in diverse classrooms. *Urban Education, 45*(5), 560–603. https://doi.org/10.1177/0042085910377290

Mosley-Johnson, E., Garacci, E., Wagner, N., Mendez, C., Williams, J. S., & Egede, L. E. (2019). Assessing the relationship between adverse childhood experiences and life satisfaction, psychological well-being, and social well-being: United States longitudinal cohort 1995–2014. *Quality of Life Research, 28*, 907–914. https://doi.org/10.1007/s11136-018-2054-6

Orsati, F. (2016). Humanistic practices to understand and support students' behaviors: A disability studies in education framework. In M. Cosier & C. Ashby (Eds.), *Enacting change from within: Disability studies meets teaching and teacher education.* Peter Lang.

Petrone, R., & Stanton, C. R. (2021). From producing to reducing trauma: A call for "trauma-informed" research(ers) to interrogate how schools harm students. *Educational Researcher, 50*(8), 537–545. https://doi.org/ 10.3102/0013189X211014850

Russell, E. W. (1974). The power of behavior control: a critique of behavior modification methods. *Journal of Clinical Psychology, 30*(2), 111–136. https://doi/10.1002/1097–4679(197404)30:2%3C111::AID-JCLP2270300202%3E3.0.CO;2-R

Skepple, R. G. (2014). Preparing culturally responsive pre-service teachers for culturally diverse classrooms. *Kentucky Journal of Excellence in College Teaching & Learning, 12*(6), 57–69. https://encompass.eku.edu/kjectl/vol12/iss2014/6

Substance Abuse and Mental Health Services Administration (SAMHSA). (2023, May 17). *Understanding childhood trauma.* https://www.samhsa.gov/child-trauma/understanding-child-trauma

Substance Abuse and Mental Health Services Administration (2014). *SAMHSA's concept of trauma and guidance for a trauma-informed approach.* Substance Abuse and Mental Health Services Administration.

Sweetman, N. (2022). What is a trauma informed classroom? What are the benefits and challenges involved? *Frontiers in Education, 7*, 1–8. https://doi.org/10.3389/feduc.2022.914448

Szarkowski, A., & Fogler, J. (2020). Supporting students with disabilities in trauma-sensitive schools. *Educational Leadership, 78*(2), 64–68. https://www.ascd.org/el/articles/supporting-students-with-disabilities-in-trauma-sensitive-schools

Wall, C. R. G. (2021). Relationship over reproach: Fostering resilience by embracing a trauma-informed approach to elementary education. *Journal of Aggression, Maltreatment & Trauma, 30*(1), 118–137. https://doi.org/10.1080/10926771.2020.1737292

Weinstein, C. S., Tomlinson-Clark, S., & Curran, M. (2004). Toward a conception of culturally responsive classroom management. *Journal of Teacher Education, 55*(1), 25–38. https://doi.org/10.1177/0022487103259812

12

Shaking Restorative Justice Clear from Retributive Justice Frameworks

Flynn Ross

Restorative justice practices have become commonplace in schools, often touted as a solution to address the racially disproportionate results of the zero-tolerance and exclusionary disciplinary practices that have dominated schools in the United States (Lodi et al., 2021). However, complaints are numerous that using restorative justice practice means that students have no consequences and "get away" with bad behaviors. This interpretation is in large part because restorative justice practices are viewed and implemented within a retributive justice mind-set that assumes that punishments and consequences are needed to change behaviors.

To better understand how restorative justice practices have been colonized, practitioners must understand the origins of the justice system that permeates both the United States legal and educational realms and how retributive justice beliefs dominate in the Western world.

I, Flynn Ross, the author of this chapter, am a white, Christian, female from New England. I include myself as a practitioner steeped in the Eurocentric practices of retributive justice as a teacher and teacher educator in colonized schools in the United States. Through practice, research, and experience I have learned how restorative justice practices have the potential to be transformative when they are implemented with fidelity and honor the cultural traditions from which they are derived.

In working with new teachers for more than 25 years as a teacher educator, I have found that we often must unpack and examine hidden assumptions and misconceptions before learners are open to new ideas. Therefore, in this chapter we will examine retributive justice, its origins and assumptions. Then I will share a general outline of how restorative justice practices are used in schools with some specific examples of successful programs. Resources will be shared throughout with the hope that interested practitioners will seek further readings, training, and experiences before claiming to implement restorative justice practices.

RETRIBUTIVE JUSTICE

Retributive justice is considered to have originated in 1755 BC in ancient Mesopotamia with Hammurabi's Code, a set of 282 laws set forth and carved in stone (Johns, 2008). The laws are considered the foundation of Judeo-Christian religious texts with the Jewish Torah and Christian Old Testament of the Bible. Retributive justice requires the offender to receive a punishment in proportion to the offense. For example, the idioms "eye for an eye" and "let the punishment fit the crime" describe retributions.

The criminal legal system in the United States is based on retributive justice. This narrow interpretation of justice is then further reinforced with the beliefs that punishments are deterrents that will shape behavior. Operant conditioning, developed by B. F. Skinner (1953), is part of the Western psychology cannon. It is a foundation for many educational psychology courses and is traditionally a part of K–12 discipline policies. For example, if a student is late to class, he might receive a detention; if he fights, he might receive a suspension. Taken to the extreme, zero-tolerance policies might require an expulsion for drugs or weapons brought to school. The assumptions behind these policies are that the consequences are so severe as to deter students from engaging in such behaviors.

These beliefs that high-stakes consequences will deter misbehavior assumes that the children and adolescents are in a rational, calculative state of mind to weigh the consequences against the behaviors. Most adults who work with children and adolescents laugh at the notion that their students always behave in rational ways, particularly if the children and adolescents have experienced trauma, mental distress, or are otherwise influenced by emotions. Yet we abide by school policies that punish students for behaviors that are not rational. And these punishments have been found to be so systematically biased by race and gender (Gershoff & Font, 2016) as to have U.S. Senate hearings in 2012 on the problem (Ending the School to Prison Pipeline, 2012).

HISTORY OF RESTORATIVE JUSTICE

Restorative justice is cited as having originated in Indigenous practices in New Zealand, Australia, and Canada. It was used to address the racial disparities in incarceration of youth in New Zealand in 1989 with the Family Group Counseling (Wood et al., 2021). In contrast to retributive justice and exclusionary practices—in which punishment often includes the removal of the offending perpetrator from the society—restorative justice is based on restoring harmony to the community through conflict resolution among the involved parties, including everyone in the community who is impacted. The cultural differences between the individualistic, hierarchical cultural assumptions of retributive justice and the collectivist, equality of restorative justice is stark. Restorative justice is based on a foundation of trust and strong relationships within a community from which accountability for one's actions can derive with the belief that humans desire to be connected and in community. Restorative justice is based much more on emotional relationships, respect, and honor of community rather than the calculated rationality of an individual avoiding punishment to shape behaviors.

However, all too often restorative justice practices are superimposed in schools using retributive justice mind-sets without having done the prior work of building relationships, trust, and community upon which restorative practices depend. For example, as students and the principal report, a local middle school was having too many issues at recess with the fifth graders, so they were all put in the gym and made to sit on the bleachers for recess time for a week. The principal called that restorative while she lectured them about their behavior. Another middle school sent students out of the classroom (exclusionary) to go to the "restorative room" to write a forced apology for the behavior that got them sent out of the classroom. Such examples are common across the United States. They are called "restorative," but they have much more to do with the "retributive" frameworks of punishments held by the teachers and administrators in authority.

Further, restorative justice practices have been co-opted and commercialized within the capitalist system of professional development within the education system in the United States; many consultants and nonprofit organizations provide workshops and training without crediting or financially compensating the Indigenous communities from which the practices originated.

Restorative justice practices rely on conflict resolution through community discussions built on trust and relationships with the goals of restoring harmony to the community and redressing the harm that was done. These conflict resolution practices are found in many cultural traditions across the globe. Connecting communities and families to traditional cultural practices and helping educators and families understand the difference from retributive justice assumptions are essential to implementing restorative practices in schools.

Many cultures have what is termed customary law, often unwritten laws that have governed social interactions through community elders and many systems of conflict resolution that share foundations with restorative justice practices. These include Xeer (hair), the customary laws of the Somali peoples in Africa and the diaspora. Xeer laws were revived and written down with the help of the Danish Deming Group's initiative, Civic Engagement in Reconciliation and State Formation in Southern Somalia (CERSF) (Leite, 2017). Similarly, the Indigenous customary laws of the Sami in Norway are given priority in many cases in the legal system under Articles 27 and 34 of the United Nations Declaration on the Rights of Indigenous Peoples (UNDRIP) to recognize Indigenous Peoples' laws (Lingaas, 2022). Connecting restorative justice practices in schools to cultural traditions in our students' communities holds great potential for healing and restoration.

RESTORATIVE JUSTICE PRACTICES IN SCHOOLS

Restorative justice practices prioritize building relationships and a foundation of trust as the groundwork for any community. In the tradition of collectivist cultures, interdependence, belonging, and group cohesion are highly valued. Restoring harmony and resolving conflicts are essential to restorative justice practices—"how to meet harm with care rather than the reproduction of harm through punishment" (Drake, 2024).

Restorative practices in schools usually consist of two distinctly identifiable phases. The first consists of building community with regular community meetings, in classrooms often called morning or daily meetings. Daily meetings provide an opportunity to build relationships, allow students to learn more about each other, and build the trust and shared respect essential for restorative justice. The second phase is then circles, or restorative meetings, in which conflicts or specific infractions are addressed with a trained facilitator, the perpetrator, victim(s), and others impacted by the incident.

For example, consider a classroom that regularly meets to build community, one in which the students and teacher have worked together to create a "classroom compact" (or an agreement on how to behave in the classroom). If one student calls another student a derogatory name, a restorative circle might be called by any member of the classroom. Everyone in the classroom would be expected to participate because everyone is impacted by the name calling as it is an infraction against their norms of respecting one another. Usually the teacher, or a trained staff member in the school, facilitates the restorative circle. They begin by sitting in a circle, revisiting the community agreements about respect and active listening. The circle often includes a talking piece, each person talking in turn, and a check-in on how everyone is doing. The circle then discusses the specific incident, problem solves, and reflects before closing (Restorative Resources, n.d.).

The discussion of the specific incident follows a set of questions answered by the perpetrator and victim and sometimes the observers/others impacted. The questions are (White, 2012):

- What happened?
- What were you thinking of at the time?
- What have you thought about since?
- Who has been affected by what you have done?
- In what way have they been affected?
- What do you think you need to do to make things right?

These questions stand in contrast to retributive justice questions that center on what law was broken, what evidence was there to prove a rule violation, and what the punishment should be. Retributive justice questions presume a hierarchical structure of compliance and punishment, with evidence being essential to prove that harm was done. In contrast, restorative justice acknowledges that harm may have been done, even if it wasn't intended, and the harm needs to be addressed to restore harmony to the community.

Examples

In one high-school incident, the teacher reported to the office that a Black male student waited outside her room for a white male student to leave class, hit him, and a fight ensued. The traditional exclusionary consequences: the Black male would receive a six-day suspension for starting a fight; the white boy, a two-day suspension for engaging in a fight. In a restorative practices circle, it was revealed that the white boy had urinated on the younger brother of the Black Muslim male in the gym lockers, and the Black male was defending his family honor by starting the fight. Through the restorative practices circle, the larger context of the fight and the cultural significance of the original offense were brought to light, everyone involved gained greater cultural understanding, resolution was found, and the boys remained in school rather than being suspended. Many similar examples show how restorative circles can lead to learning, increased understanding, and resolution that prevents future retaliatory actions.

More than 60 schools in the District of Columbia have committed to the restorative practices and participating in the training and foundational work of building community. They partner with the Department of Human Services and Office of the Attorney General to provide restorative alternatives to prosecution. RestorativeDC shares many of its materials (RestorativeDC, n.d.) and videos (School Talk DC, 2021) for a wider audience as well as providing training and materials.

In D.C., the retributive and exclusionary justice system of the criminal justice system is the default system; however, the restorative justice system is an option, especially in schools where the perpetrator and victim both agree to participate. This acknowledges the necessity of commitment and belief in the restorative justice practices by the participants for it to be successful. Helping students build skills for conflict resolution through facilitated restorative justice circles can empower students to communicate directly and address issues of bullying and disrespect earlier, ideally limiting the escalation of situations.

Challenges

Many groups and organizations are implementing and training others around restorative justice in schools, prisons, and globally, but there are no uniform standards of practice or accreditation bodies. Practitioners have widely varying levels of experience, training, and background. Fidelity in implementation of restorative justice practices is rare. This makes it difficult to conduct empirical research on the effectiveness of restorative practices because there is such a range of practices called "restorative" (Lodi, et al., 2021).

A COLLECTIVE JOURNEY

The RestorativeDC project recognizes that the collective process of implementing restorative justice practices is a journey, not a destination. The collective commitment to building inclusive schools that value and embrace all students, staff, and families requires engagement with all members of the community, time for listening and learning, and responsiveness to the local context and needs of the community. Achieving truly inclusive, safe, socially just schools is a worthy goal.

REFERENCES

Drake, R. (2024). Dreaming communities of care: Radical world-building with abolitionist organizers toward students' heartwholeness. In F. Ross & L. Malone (Eds.),

Decolonizing classroom management: A Critical examination of cultural assumptions and norms in traditional practices. Rowman & Littlefield, pp. 129–136.

Ending the School to Prison Pipeline, S. Hrg. 112–848. (2012). https://www.congress.gov/event/112th-congress/senate-event/LC1164/text?s=1&r=33

Gershoff, E. T., & Font, S. A. (2016). Corporal punishment in U.S. public schools: Prevalence, disparities in use, and status in state and federal policy. *Social Policy Report, 30*(1), 1–26. https://doi.org/10.1002/J.2379-3988.2016.TB00086.X

Johns, C. (2008). Babylonian law—The code of Hammurabi. *Avalon Project, Yale Law School*. https://avalon.law.yale.edu/ancient/hammpre.asp

Leite, N. (2017, October 12). *Reinvigoration of Somali traditional justice through inclusive conflict resolution approaches*. Accord. https://reliefweb.int/report/somalia/reinvigoration-somali-traditional-justice-through-inclusive-conflict-resolution

Lingaas, C. (2022). Indigenous customary law and Norwegian domestic law: Scenes of a (complementary or mutually exclusive) marriage? *Laws, 11*(2), 19. https://doi.org/10.3390/laws11020019

Lodi, E., Perrella, L., Lepri, G. L., Scarpa, M. L., & Patrizi, P. (2021). Use of restorative justice and restorative practices at school: A systematic literature review. *International Journal of Environmental Research and Public Health, 19*(1), 96. https://doi.org/10.3390/ijerph19010096

RestorativeDC. (n.d.). *Home*. https://restorativedc.org/

Restorative Resources. (n.d.). *Principles and practice of restorative circles*. https://www.restorativeresources.org/uploads/5/6/1/4/56143033/principles_and_practice_of_circle.pdf

School Talk DC. (2021). *Core processes of restorative justice circles.* [Video]. YouTube. https://www.youtube.com/watch?v=wDAc6Qkqhj0&t=159s

Skinner, B. F. (1953). *Science and human behavior*. Macmillan.

White, S. (2012, January 9). Time to talk: Using restorative questions. *International Institute for Restorative Practices.* https://www.iirp.edu/news/time-to-think-using-restorative-questions

Wood, W. R., Suzuki, M., Hayes, H., & Bolitho, J. (2021). Roadblocks and diverging paths for restorative justice in Australia and Aotearoa/New Zealand. In T. Gavrielides (Ed.), *Comparative restorative justice*. Springer, Cham. https://doi.org/10.1007/978-3-030-74874-6_10

13

Fostering Social and Emotional Bonds through Indigenous Storytelling

José Ortiz

In 2014, I was fortunate enough to attend a restorative justice circle at the high school where I was, at the time, completing my student teaching. As a first-generation Latino graduate student who was living and had attended K–12 schools in Los Angeles, California, I had experienced the traditional education model where student discipline was met with suspension, expulsion, or contact with law enforcement. As an emerging educator, restorative justice practices were a concept completely alien to me.

The restorative justice circle I witnessed at a high school in South Los Angeles was organized and facilitated by the school principal to address the struggles a Spanish teacher was facing concerning student conduct in the classroom. The teacher sobbed in front of students, openly sharing how disrespected they felt by the lack of student effort toward creating a respectful classroom environment and in getting classwork done. Students sat silently, actively listening. At one point, a student stood up and walked over to give the teacher a hug. Although restorative justice practices have shown to alleviate tensions that emerge in schools (Gregory et al., 2016), having witnessed that circle in person led to long-lasting questions concerning teacher vulnerability in the classroom.

Teachers often expect their students to show vulnerability when they are encouraged to share academic or social struggles they experience. A student disclosing struggles and a teacher actively listening and attending to those struggles can lead to a strong student-teacher relationship that can positively impact a student's academic trajectory (Hamre & Pianta, 2006;

David & Dupper, 2004). However, rarely do teachers return the favor and share struggles they may be facing in their teaching practice or more broadly, the personal struggles that come from social and political events that occur in society.

This chapter explores the social and emotional bonds that surface when teachers choose to be vulnerable in front of their students. I show how Latinx teachers leading a summer bridge program practice Indigenous storytelling to share their struggles dealing with social and political forces present in the United States. Although storytelling is already present in schools and has been practiced by teachers of color, it is important to highlight the emotional element present when individuals share personal experiences in front of a group.

INDIGENOUS STORYTELLING AND EMOTIONS

Storytelling is an informal, conversational approach that allows people to recount lived experiences in writing or aloud (Clandinin, 2006). Indigenous communities and cultures with strong oral traditions, in particular, employ storytelling to share their knowledge and experiences, values and traditions. Elders can often take a leading role in storytelling. Elders hold knowledge that comes from a long life of lived experiences. As such, elders employ storytelling to spread knowledge and awareness, to inform future generations of important, valuable life lessons (Iseke, 2013). Storytelling thus provides Indigenous People with the opportunity to keep their own story in existence, which is essential to subvert the dominant narrative that has historically and socially been constructed by white people in U.S. society (Delgado, 1995).

Although Indigenous communities typically practice storytelling outside a formal classroom setting, teachers have used storytelling to shift the power dynamics in the classroom and offer students the opportunity to share their own knowledge and experiences. Storytelling allows students, particularly students of color, to share a story oftentimes not valued or acknowledged in school. Centering a student's knowledge and lived experience in the classroom can empower students of color to inform and inspire significant social and systemic changes (Solórzano & Villalpando, 1998).

Fernández (2002), for example, presents a case where storytelling was used to inform teachers of the academic and social obstacles that Latina/o/x students face in U.S. schools. Over the course of two interviews, Fernández (2002) met and conversed with Pablo, a Midwestern university student, on Pablo's experience attending a public high school in Chicago, Illinois. Pablo revealed the lowered academic expectations and cultural deficit perspectives he and other Latina/o/x students encountered. Providing a student like Pablo with a platform to voice his lived experiences not only offers the potential to inform others who are unaware of the struggles that Latina/o/x students face, but it could also equip teachers and administrators with the tools needed to identify, address, and potentially prevent a hostile environment that negatively impacts Latina/o/x students' schooling experience from taking shape.

Although storytelling typically centers the lived experience of the person telling a story, emotions can be detected, heard and in some cases, felt by both storyteller and those reading or listening to a story. The emotions we develop and emit in our daily encounters are typically shaped by our lived experiences (Ahmed, 2015). Although storytelling involves someone recounting events that may have taken place in the past, being in the moment and retelling a story can lead one to relive past emotions felt (Reyes & Curry Rodríguez, 2012; Mead, 1934). For those listening who can also relate to a story being told, they too can relive past lived experiences, as well as the emotions once felt. As such, focusing on lived experiences can provide both teachers and students with an entry point to discuss emotions.

THE AQUETZA: YOUTH, LEADERSHIP, EDUCATION AND COMMUNITY EMPOWERMENT PROGRAM

I highlight the potential of Indigenous storytelling inspiring a discussion and examination of one's emotions by focusing on a free, weeklong, program known as *Aquetza.* Founded in 2012, Aquetza takes place every summer at the University of Colorado Boulder (CU Boulder) and seeks to "[implement] a culturally sustaining and academically enriching program for high school youth grounded in the historical narratives and contributions of Chicana/o people in the U.S." (Lopez & Ortiz, 2019, p. 5). Aquetza leaders historically have consisted of current and former CU Boulder undergraduate students, graduate students, and teachers from the Denver school district. For one week, Aquetza leaders organize a schedule where high-school students are immersed in a series of activities ranging from taking courses in history, literature, and health science, to having critical conversations examining social and political issues affecting their own cultural communities. Aquetza's curriculum aims to counter the dehumanizing practices that historically have existed in U.S. schools for students of color (Pizarro, 1998; Ruiz & Mills, 1997). Aquetza's goal is for students to reclaim their humanity and to reflect critically on their lived experiences.

Encuentro is a daily activity at Aquetza; the Spanish translates to "meeting" or an "encounter." Although Encuentros are meant to serve as an informal space for students to share a story, thought, or work completed during the class segment of the program, some routines were typically followed. An

Aquetza director would serve as the facilitator for every Encuentro and would begin by asking if anyone wanted to volunteer and present to the Aquetzeros (high-school students, CU Boulder students, and teachers attending Aquetza). If an Aquetzero chose to volunteer, they would walk to the front of a large lecture hall and present. Those not presenting were expected to be respectful, actively listen, and provide the presenter with constructive feedback. When a presenter finished, the facilitator would thank the presenter, ask for feedback from those listening, ask the presenter to take a seat, and open the floor to anyone else who wanted to present. The open space offered during the Encuentros provided the best opportunity to examine how students and teachers used storytelling to discuss and examine emotions present within stories shared.

Teachers Taking the Lead

To set expectations and model what an Encuentro presentation would look like, Aquetza teachers took the initiative and gave presentations during the first Encuentros. They modeled how relationships are rooted in trust and reciprocity (Valenzuela, 1999). If Aquetza teachers wanted students to eventually share their own stories, teachers first needed to establish trust by openly discussing their own lived experiences and encounters. Although there was no guarantee that students would reciprocate by sharing of stories after teachers did, the hope was that the back-and-forth conversation that usually arose during the Encuentros would spark student participation.

One of the first teachers to model an Encuentro presentation was Maria.
[1] On the second Encuentro, Maria proceeded to the front of the classroom, carrying along with her an acoustic guitar. As soon as the Aquetzeros grew silent, Maria shared how she would be performing a very significant song.

> I'm going to perform a song that is very powerful to me. The song is called *Cancion Mixteca* [composed by José López in 1912]. It's a song which was intended to describe indigenous people of Mexico and how these people were ripped apart from their land and it's a song that describes how much they miss the land they had. For me, it represents my parents. My parents are Mexican immigrants and it represents the sacrifice they made to come out here [the United States] and it's not just my parents. It's a sacrifice many Mexican parents make for us and sometimes that is not acknowledged.

Maria's decision to sing a song that reflects the struggles of Indigenous People of Mexico exemplifies the main purpose of storytelling: its goal is not only to highlight a struggle but also to reflect on the effects of that struggle (Brabeck, 2003). Maria's decision to connect a historical struggle to her parents adds an emotional layer to a collective experience. Holding back tears, Maria explained the pain she feels knowing that her parents miss their homeland. In addition, Maria also reflected on the current political climate and the negative rhetoric surrounding Mexicans in the United States (Costello, 2016; Treviño et al., 2017). Choosing to sing *Cancion Mixteca* in front of Aquetza students, many of whom share the same racial, ethnic, and cultural identities as Aquetza teachers, had the potential to spark personal student-teacher connections.

Maria proceeded to sing *Cancion Mixteca* and was met with a loud applause once finished. After the applause faded, Aquetza students did in fact reciprocate the trust Maria demonstrated by choosing to respond either with an affirming comment or sharing their own personal story.

Students Following Teacher's Lead

The Encuentro structure offered the opportunity for Aquetzeros to immediately respond to a presenter. Students took the time to express their thoughts and, in some cases, revealed emotions around the themes Maria touched on. One student immediately mentioned how she got "goosebumps" as soon as Maria finished singing. Another student whispered to a peer how the student started to cry during Maria's song. Many students commented, often breaking into laughter, how uncomfortably quiet the room was after Maria's presentation. One student, Gloria, connected to the personal meaning *Cancion Mixteca* had in Maria's life by mentioning her own parents' struggles of being away from their homeland.

> Everything you said came out perfectly and not only did you tell the story of your parents but you told the story of millions of other kids' parents and that's such a powerful thing [. . .] it shows that we're so connected at the root [. . .] it's just so powerful to speak other people's messages while knowing it's your own as well.

Gloria established a personal connection with Maria in noting the shared experience children of Mexican immigrants go through when seeing their parents struggle with not being able to go back and forth between countries. In the process, Gloria realizes that she is not alone and that Maria, as well as others, has an emotional connection that stems from a shared lived experience. Gloria demonstrates a transitioning from a micro to macro perspective regarding how emotions are influenced. Collins (1981, 1988) notes how emotions can typically be seen in the personal or micro interactions that form between a small group of people and not so much when discussing the influence social and political structures have in influencing emotions among a large group of people. Gloria's realization of the systems and structures that influence people's decision to migrate across borders potentially demonstrates how social and political structures cannot only influence peoples' experiences but their emotions as well. A social and emotional bond is thus established from teachers in Aquetza sharing their own story while also speaking to the story of students.

Indigenous storytelling offers the opportunity for students to realize the personal social connections that exist with their teachers that transcends the traditional academic schooling goals that have been the historical aim of schools in the United States (Finn, 1982). The impact Indigenous storytelling can have in establishing this social and emotional bond between teacher and student is captured in one student's comment. Responding to Maria's willingness to share an intimate personal story, one student said, "Wow, I wasn't expecting that. She's one of my instructors, and I can't believe she trusted us enough to tell us that."

DISCUSSION

I purposely describe the connection students and teachers reveal through sharing stories as "bonds" as opposed to "relationships." The reason for doing this revolves around the level of connection that surfaces between students and teachers. Student-teacher relationships are often defined as "the generalized interpersonal meaning students and teachers attach to their interactions with each other" (Claessens et al., 2017, p. 487). Although students should have a positive relationship with their teachers, research on student-teacher relationships often emphasize the importance relationships have in "establishing a classroom environment that is conducive to learning" (Pigford, 2001, p. 337). Although Aquetza teachers hoped that students gained knowledge conducive to their educational experience once leaving the program, the purpose of Aquetza stretched beyond academics, focusing more specifically on empowering students to make a positive individual or collective change centered around intentional collective identity.

The social and emotional interactions that occurred during the Encuentros move beyond a student-teacher relationship. To form a bond means that two or more people come to the realization that they relate to one another on a social level. Scheff (1990) describes bonds as a phenomenon that holds individuals and groups together in society. "Relationships" are presented as a connection that occurs between one teacher and one student, but "bonds" extend beyond the individual student-teacher framing, focusing specifically on how one can form a connection from experiences shaped by gender, race, and social class. Although most Aquetza teachers and students shared the same racial, cultural, and socioeconomic identities, it was the acknowledgement of and the personal reflection Aquetza participants took part in when discussing the lived experiences of people of color (POC) that in the end contributed to fostering social and emotional bonds.

With a primarily white teaching workforce in the United States (Ingersoll et al., 2021), teachers who do not identify as POC can go beyond establishing a teacher-student relationship with students of color by knowing of and empathizing with the social and political struggles POC experience in the United States. Although Indigenous storytelling is a practice historically and culturally grounded within Indigenous communities, white teachers choosing to be allies for POC and being present in social justice efforts to improve the lived experiences of POC can facilitate fostering a social and emotional bond in the classroom.

Indigenous storytelling provides a way to bridge micro and macro perspectives by allowing the one sharing a story to highlight how systems and structures present in larger society influence people's experiences on an individual level. In the process, students gain an understanding of an emotional connection that exists within a group of people. With an understanding of this collective experience, students hopefully can take the initiative to not feel alone in their struggles, inspiring them to connect with others to make that positive individual or collective change. With schools in the United States focusing heavily on the role emotions play in the learning process, it is important to not only consider how Indigenous practices can influence schools' approach for attending to students' emotions, but also in decolonizing current curriculum that emphasizes students' emotions in U.S. schools.

Often addressed under social-emotional learning (SEL) curriculum, educators are teaching students how to properly manage their emotions, solely focusing on how the acquisition of SEL skills can positively impact a student's academic performance (Bouffard et al., 2009; Durlak et al., 2011; CASEL, 2015). However, SEL programs are critiqued for 1) promoting a white, middle-class definition of emotions, 2) emphasizing an individual mentality, and 3) focusing on controlling rather than understanding one's emotions. In addition, a majority of SEL efforts in schools tend to focus on students; very little focus is directed at fostering teachers' SEL development (Katz et al., 2020). Indigenous storytelling can thus provide a way to not only decolonize SEL's practices but also to emphasize the role a teacher can assume in sparking conversations around emotions.

NOTES

1. Pseudonyms are used throughout the chapter.

REFERENCES

Ahmed, S. (2015). *The cultural politics of emotion*, 2nd edition. Routledge.

Bouffard, S., Parkinson, J., Jacob, R., & Jones, S. M. (2009). *Designing SECURe: A summary of literature and SEL programs reviewed in preparation for the development of SECURe*. Harvard Graduate School of Education, Harvard University.

Brabeck, K. (2003). Testimonio: A strategy for collective resistance, cultural survival and building solidarity. *Feminism & Psychology, 13*(2), 252–258. https://doi.org/10.1177/0959353503013002009

CASEL (2015). Effective Social and Emotional Learning Programs: Middle and High School Edition.

Claessens, L. C., van Tartwijk, J., van der Want, A. C., Pennings, H. J., Verloop, N., den Brok, P. J., & Wubbels, T. (2017). Positive teacher–student relationships go beyond the classroom, problematic ones stay inside. *Journal of Educational Research, 110*(5), 478–493. https://doi.org/10.1080/00220671.2015.1129595

Clandinin, D. J. (2006). Narrative inquiry: A methodology for studying lived experience. *Research Studies in Music Education, 27*(1), 44–54. https://doi.org/10.1177/1321103X060270010301

Collins, R. (1981). On the micro foundations of macrosociology. *American Journal of Sociology, 86*(5), 984–1014. https://doi.org/10.1086/227351

Collins, R. (1988). The micro contribution to macro sociology. *Sociological Theory, 6*(2), 242–253. https://www.jstor.org/stable/202118

Costello, M. B. (2016). *The Trump effect: The impact of the 2016 presidential election on our nation's schools*. Alabama Appleseed Center for Law and Justice.

David, K. S., & Dupper, D. R. (2004). Student-teacher relationships: An overlooked factor in school dropout. *Journal of Human Behavior in the Social Environment, 9*(1–2), 179–193. https://doi.org/10.1300/J137v09n01_12

Delgado, R. (1995). *The Rodrigo chronicles: Conversations about America and race*. NYU Press. https://doi.org/10.18574/nyu/9780814721025.001.0001

Durlak, J. A., Weissberg, R. P., Dymnicki, A. B., Taylor, R. D., & Schellinger, K. B. (2011). The impact of enhancing students' social and emotional learning: A meta-analysis of school-based universal interventions. *Child Development, 82*(1), 405–432. https://doi.org/10.1111/j.1467–8624.2010.01564.x

Fernández, L. (2002). Using critical race theory and LatCrit theory to document Latina/o education and resistance in urban public schools. *Qualitative Inquiry, 8*(1), 44–63. https://doi.org/10.1177/107780040200800102

Finn Jr., C. E. (1982). A call for quality education. *American Education, 18*(1), 31–36.

Gregory, A., Clawson, K., Davis, A., & Gerewitz, J. (2016). The promise of restorative practices to transform teacher-student relationships and achieve equity in school discipline. *Journal of Educational and Psychological Consultation, 26*(4), 325–353. https://doi.org/10.1080/10474412.2014.929950

Hamre, B. K., & Pianta, R. C. (2006). Student-teacher relationships. In G. G. Bear & K. M. Minke (Eds.), *Children's needs III: Development, prevention, and intervention* (pp. 59–71). National Association of School Psychologists.

Hoffman, D. M. (2009). Reflecting on social emotional learning: A critical perspective on trends in the United States. *Review of Educational Research, 79*(2), 533–556. https://doi.org/10.3102/0034654308325184

Humphrey, N. (Ed.). (2013). *Social and emotional learning: A critical appraisal.* Sage. https://doi.org/10.4135/9781446288603

Ingersoll, R., Merrill, E., Stuckey, D., Collins, G., & Harrison, B. (2021). The demographic transformation of the teaching force in the United States. *Education Sciences, 11*(5), 234. https://doi.org/10.3390/educsci11050234

Iseke, J. (2013). Indigenous storytelling as research. *International Review of Qualitative Research, 6*(4), 559–577. https://doi.org/10.1525/irqr.2013.6.4.559

Katz, D., Mahfouz, J., & Romas, S. (2020). Creating a foundation of well-being for teachers and students starts with SEL curriculum in teacher education programs. *Northwest Journal of Teacher Education, 15*(2), 5. https://doi.org/10.15760/nwjte.2020.15.2.5

Lopez, E. J., & Ortiz, J. (2019). Promoting transformative learning for Chicana/o and Latina/o high school youth. *Journal of Latinos and Education*, 1–15. https://doi.org/10.1080/15348431.2019.1612401

Mead, G. H. (1934). *Mind, self and society.* University of Chicago Press. https://doi.org/10.1177/000271623517900175

Pigford, T. (2001). Improving teacher-student relationships: What's up with that? *Clearing House, 74*(6), 337–339. https://doi.org/10.1080/00098650109599221

Pizarro, M. (1998). Contesting dehumanization: Chicana/o spiritualization, revolutionary possibility, and the curriculum. *Aztlan: A Journal of Chicano Studies, 23*(1), 55–76.

Reyes, K. B., & Curry Rodríguez, J. E. (2012). Testimonio: Origins, terms, and resources. *Equity & Excellence in Education, 45*(3), 525–538. https://doi.org/10.1080/10665684.2012.698571

Ruiz, D. M., & Mills, J. (1997). *The four agreements: A practical guide to personal freedom.* Amber-Allen.

Scheff, T. J. (1990). *Microsociology: Discourse, emotion, and social structure.* University of Chicago Press.

Solórzano, D. G., & Villalpando, O. (1998). Critical race theory, marginality, and the experience of students of color in higher education. *Sociology of Education: Emerging Perspectives, 21*, 211–222. https://doi.org/10.17763/haer.79.4.m6867014157m707l

Treviño, L. E. J., García, J., & Bybee, E. R. (2017). "The day that changed my life, again": The testimonio of a Latino DACAmented teacher. *Urban Review, 49*, 627–647. https://doi.org/10.1007/s11256-017-0412-2

Vadeboncoeur, J., & Collie, R. (2013). Locating social and emotional learning in schooled environments: A Vygotskian perspective on learning as unified. *Mind, Culture, and Activity, 20*(3), 201–225. https://doi.org/10.1080/10749039.2012.755205

Valenzuela, A. (1999). *Subtractive schooling: U.S. Mexican youth and the politics of caring.* State University of New York Press, Albany.

14

Dreaming Communities of Care

Radical World Building with Abolitionist Organizers Toward Students' Heartwholeness

Riley Drake

BEING SAFE OR FEELING SAFE?

"In schools, we talk about our students *being* safe, but we don't meaningfully pay attention to them *feeling* safe," lamented Staci Harrison,[1] a white woman and second-grade educator at a predominantly Black elementary school in a large, midwestern school district. Schooling across the United States functions to serve racial capitalism, a system in which racism and capitalism co-construct one another (Robinson, 1983), normalizing hierarchy, extraction, and the dehumanization of racialized bodies in schools. Students, particularly those who are Black, Indigenous, or people of color, are frequently rendered deficient, especially when they hold other marginalized identities such as queer or disabled. For those students who resist the reductive nature of schooling and the structural violence they are forced to endure as a result of racial capitalism (e.g., high rates of office discipline referrals, suspensions, and surveillance, among others), educators—particularly white educators—often attempt to extract their value, emphasizing instead what they believe students need to learn in order to *be safe*. Educators regularly implement social-emotional learning (SEL) to police and rectify perceived deficiencies, all the while neglecting how students *feel* as a result of and in systems of schooling.

In Spring 2022, Staci and Elena Cabrera, a Mexican American biracial woman and third-grade educator at an elementary school enrolling predominantly Latinx students in the same large, midwestern city, joined a Critical Participatory Action Research project I was facilitating to center students' social-emotional wholeness. Mindful of my identities and the protection that I, as a white woman, am afforded by whiteness, I recognized the ways that structural violence disproportionately impacts already vulnerable communities. For example, early in this project, a fatal shooting at a local high school in an economically disenfranchised, predominantly Black and Brown community escalated students' fears about gun violence. Prompted by Staci and Elena to share their emotions, Black and Brown students in both classrooms described feeling unsafe related to policing, guns, and incarceration; others talked about how schooling made them feel unsafe. In Staci's classroom, for example, several students voiced distress about district-identified school rules, which were "Responsible, Respectful, and Safe" and posted throughout the building. Staci interrogated students' resistance to school rules, and through dialogue, came to understand that students resented the rules created *for* them, not *by* or *with* them, as they often reproduced harm. One second-grade student provided clarity when she pointed to "Report problems to adults," a specific behavior noted underneath Safety, and dropped her head. "I hate that rule. It only gets kids in trouble, and then we get punished."

Later, when discussing the school rules, we returned to the student's comments and discussed the ways in which the school rules were inextricably connected with punishment. Together, we wondered how we might prefigure learning spaces that felt free and safe. bell hooks (2019) referred to this experience as "heartwhole," describing it as a deeply rooted connection she felt with nature and relationships inspired by values of belonging, such as reciprocal connection and openness to spirit, despite being in patriarchal spaces where she did not belong. Together, Staci, Elena, and I began to dream collective heartwholeness.

BUILDING WITH ABOLITIONIST ORGANIZERS

Following initial dialogues with students about their experiences feeling unsafe, we needed to get closer to those on the ground resisting policing, incarceration, gun violence, and the violence of schooling, which students had identified as intimately impacting them. We met with three local community organizers fighting for abolition, including Imani Alexander, a Black woman and cofounder of a local mutual aid fund centering Black women and liberation; and Jada Kirk and Nova Horton, Black femmes and organizers with the Black Liberation Movement (BLM). We disclosed what students had shared regarding feeling unsafe both in and out of school, our goals to prioritize heartwholeness, and requested their wisdom and expertise.

Imani, Jada, and Nova enthusiastically joined our team, and we engaged in radical world building (Agbebiyi et al., 2020; Butler, 1993, 1998), a collective process wherein we critically questioned, aimed to disrupt, and reimagined new ways (worlds) independent of schooling as racial capitalism. We conceived of classroom management as "a curriculum, a set of lessons that young people are learning from us" that teach them how to "power over others" (Shalaby, 2018). This understanding arose from students detailing their experiences with punishment, exclusion, and silencing powered over them, prompting us to imagine classroom communities centering care (Shalaby, 2017).

Through radical world building, the team identified three primary abolitionist practices that centered care related to students' experiences with violence:

- mutual aid, or the collective coordination of survival work enacted with social movements for justice (Spade, 2020);
- restorative justice, or an approach focusing on relationships, the need for repair when relationships are broken or violated, and the question of who within the community is responsible for meeting obligations and needs (Kaba, 2021); and
- healing justice, a political approach to community care and safety designed to address generational trauma resulting from structural violence and oppressive forces (Page & Woodland, 2023).

Organizers led and educators co-facilitated lessons, centering organizers' messages and practices.

PRACTICING MUTUAL AID

During Imani's visit to Staci and Elena's classrooms, she introduced mutual aid as solidarity, a direct disruption of racial capitalism. Imani explained mutual aid to students as giving what you have and taking what you need without notions of deservingness. Imani illustrated the practice of mutual aid with a seed burst activity, inviting students to combine wildflower seeds and wet paper mulch into clusters, which when dried, could be planted in students' communities as nourishment for and solidarity with the land, pollinators, and natural world who give of themselves to humanity. This activity illustrated mutual aid, then, as a means to keep one another safe through preserving and creating community.

In the second-grade classroom, Staci followed up on Imani's lesson by modeling the power of mutual aid in a community committed to care: when two students refused to come in from recess one day, Staci invoked mutual aid, asking the students what they needed. In community, the students shared that they were unable to play the role in a game that others had. Other students gave of themselves in response to the need: holding space and offering recommendations for the next recess. The two students listened, their shoulders relaxing, accepting what they needed from their peers. This was mutual aid in practice, and Staci and Elena drew from it often, activating students' reimagination of a community grounded in care.

PRACTICING RESTORATIVE AND HEALING JUSTICE

Nova and Jada introduced restorative justice as solidarity in conflict to directly challenge punishment, a hallmark of racial capitalism. They built upon students' earlier descriptions of feeling unsafe and described instances of interpersonal (Nova said she didn't like Jada's hair) and derivative forms of structural (Jada said she didn't like Black women's hair) harm. Jada and Nova asked students, nearly all of whom were Black or Latinx, to identify the differences between the harm, and students were quick to respond that the second way "was racist." Jada and Nova then role-played how they would respond to each type of harm and what it meant to take accountability for their actions. Their responses to one another, rooted in community accountability, transcended traditional apologies often modeled for young people in SEL lessons that are decontextualized and dismissive of structural harm, and illustrated how to meet harm with care rather than the reproduction of harm through punishment.

Later, Nova and Jada introduced students to healing justice practices. When students practiced a whole-body scan led by Nova, Elena participated, closing her eyes and breathing deeply with students. The lesson exceeded the time allotted, but Elena encouraged students to breathe and be in their bodies. Honoring one's body in this way, and spending the time to do so, challenges the racial capitalist logic to urgently control or "colonize" our emotions, as Prentis Hemphill teaches us, to be productive, and is a radical act for classroom communities in schools that prohibit authentic feeling and discourage embodiment (Young, 2021). Rather, being embodied allowed students to slow down to connect with themselves and *feel more* (brown, 2017). During this time and many times after, they were all connected in breath for the purposes of feeling and being.

DISRUPTING PUNISHMENT

Following lessons with Imani, Jada, and Nova, Staci and Elena wanted to challenge students to stretch their abolitionist muscles. They invited students to play two versions of Zombie Tag (Global Action Project, 2021). In the first version, or "The Capitalist Way," a volunteer Zombie chased others to tag them. While being chased, a student could yell out the name of another person, and the Zombie had to then chase the person whose name was called. If tagged, that person became the Zombie and chased others. In the second version, or "The Collective Way," the Zombie chased others, but this time, students could yell out the person's name about to be tagged, ensuring that person's safety, forcing the Zombie to chase someone else, who could also then be safe. After the game was over, Staci questioned: "If we want to practice the type of world we want to live in, what should we do about the Zombie, then? Do they need punishment? Or something else?" Several students shouted, "They need punishment!" Others appeared thoughtful, "They need something else."

In Elena's classroom, after the game, students were similarly processing what should happen to the Zombie. One student commented, "It's not really the Zombie's fault. They have to play the game, too." "Whose responsibility is it to right the wrong?" Elena asked, inviting students to question how accountability should be considered in community. "It's both. We all could say it's not right," offered a student. "Then what's the Zombie's responsibility?" Elena probed. "Remembering what others have told them," a student replied thoughtfully.

"Yes. We want to think about these questions. Am I thinking about my responsibility? The responsibility of others? That's restorative justice. Sometimes, things are situational. You might have to protect yourself sometimes. That's mutual aid. Sometimes you give and sometimes you ask for what you need. All of these together, we can go through the world and understand what our part is in that," Elena offered. Elena's synthesis of abolitionist practices demonstrated her firm belief in community care: everyone must accept accountability (albeit to varying degrees) to disrupt "the game" of racial capitalism and rather than punishment, community accountability may be the "something else" needed to "right the wrong."

SANCTIFYING COMMUNITIES OF CARE

In community with Imani, Jada, and Nova, Staci and Elena invited students to practice their abolitionist learning to reimagine their classroom communities as sacred sites of care. For example, Staci led students in creating a physical community of care, a tangible representation of their learning and reimagination of classroom rules. Students, who led the project, removed the decontextualized school rules from the wall in an act of willful defiance (Shange, 2019) and discussed and documented how they practiced safety together. They signed their names underneath their written agreements, indicating agreements designed *by* them to keep each other safe. This set of agreements was modified often, a living, breathing guide for the class, to be relevant for students' heartwholeness.

Along with Staci, Elena practiced a deepened commitment to a community of care. One day, she prompted the students to reflect deeply on community organizing: "You know doing the kind of work that the organizers do brings a lot of joy, like Imani said, but it is hard work. They have so much to do. What are some words of encouragement we can offer them?" Students shared affirmations with Imani, who was present in the classroom and humbly accepted their gratitude. With one prompt, Elena generated possibilities for students to practice care and demonstrate reciprocity for the labor of organizers. Elena's prompt invited students to expand their community of care to the broader community, particularly those working for abolition. Both Staci and Elena's commitments to community in and beyond school walls anchored their classrooms in care, moving beyond "Band-Aids" for social and emotional violence (Kaba, 2021), and toward radical imaginaries to shape and practice new visions of safety.

EXPERIMENTING IN CLASSROOMS

Staci and Elena had little experience with abolitionist organizing prior to connecting with Imani, Jada, and Nova, yet they were guided by process and a willingness to experiment, try and fail, and understand failure as generative. They recognized that our approach to centering students' heartwholeness was not a scripted program. Rather, dreaming heartwholeness *with* young people and community was a "necessary process for us to become, a process that will fundamentally reshape us and our relationships, and will have to, by its very magnitude, reshape the world" (Hemphill, 2022, p. 53). For educators with similar aspirations, they must acknowledge what is unknown and step forward anyway.

Next, educators must build this approach collectively and contextually. Importantly, students and their social and emotional worlds must be at the center. In addition to students, community organizers exist all over the nation, and many have reservoirs of localized, community knowledge and critical analyses of historical linkages between power and relationships they're willing to share. Educators must radically world-build with students and organizers to cultivate shared visions of safety and practice those visions to create the world we desire. Educators can use abolitionist questions (e.g., What is safety? Does punishment work?) and logic to reveal the forces deeply disturbing students' feelings of safety, and abolitionist care (e.g., mutual aid, restorative justice) to practice creating and sustaining safe communities.

As Elena noted, organizing can be both joyful and arduous labor: organizers must be compensated fairly for sharing their knowledge and skills. Beyond compensation, Elena, Staci, and I sought to practice reciprocity: we sought to understand organizers' goals and build interconnectedness by attending mutual aid events, connecting with coordinators to elevate their messaging and organizing, and purchasing their products. Instead of engaging in extraction, and giving nothing in return, brown (2017) invites us to question: "Are you actively practicing generosity and vulnerability to make the connections between you and others clear, open, available, durable? Generosity here means giving of what you have without strings or expectations attached. Vulnerability means showing your needs" (p. 91). Educators must be intentional about practicing reciprocity in collective approaches to heartwholeness.

Finally, educators must remember that they themselves do not get to determine whether their approach to heartwholeness is liberatory for students; the only people who can determine that are the students, who are the only ones able to liberate themselves (Darder, 2017), as Elena wisely noted. Educators must get political clarity about their roles and purpose, alongside their relational responsibility, and commit to experimenting while embracing the process. Perhaps, as educators committed to liberation, we all must be in process now, in all the messiness that it provokes, to understand that "every relationship with other people, or with the land we are on, is practice ground" (brown, 2022, para. 4) for our dreams of heartwholeness for the future.

NOTE

1. All names are pseudonyms.

REFERENCES

Agbebiyi, K., Hamid, S. T., Kuo, R., & Mohapatra, M. (2020). Abolition cannot wait: Visions for transformation and radical world-building. *Transform Harm.* https://transformharm.org/ab_resource/abolition-cannot-wait-visions-for-transformation-and-radical-world-building/

brown, a. (2017). *Emergent strategy: shaping change, changing worlds.* AK Press.

brown, a. (2022, March 29). Murmurations: Realizing our abolitionist dreams. *YES! Magazine.* https://www.yesmagazine.org/opinion/2022/03/29/accountability-abolition-adriennemaree-brown

Butler, O. (1993). Parable of the sower. Four Walls Eight Windows.

Butler, O. (1998). Parable of the talents. Seven Stories Press.

Darder, A. (2017). *Reinventing Paulo Freire: A pedagogy of love.* Routledge. https://doi.org/10.4324/9781315560779

Global Action Project. (2021). Rising together, moving forever: Curriculum & stories from Global Action Project. *Global Action Project.* https://www.global-action.org/curriculum

Hemphill, P. (2022). The wisdom of process. In T. Burke & B. Brown (Eds.), *You are your best thing: Vulnerability, shame resilience, and the Black experience* (pp. 43–53). Random House.

hooks, b. (2019). *Belonging: A culture of place.* Routledge.

Kaba, M. (2021). *We do this 'til we free us: Abolitionist organizing and transforming justice* (Vol. 1). Haymarket Books.

Kelley, R. D. (2002). *Freedom dreams: The Black radical imagination.* Beacon Press.

Page, C., & Woodland, E. (2023). *Healing justice lineages: Dreaming at the crossroads of liberation, collective care, and safety.* North Atlantic Books.

Robinson, C. J. (1983). *Black Marxism, revised and updated third edition: The making of the Black radical tradition.* UNC Press.

Shalaby, C. (2017). *Troublemakers: Lessons in freedom from young children at school.* The New Press.

Shalaby, C. [@CarlaShalaby]. (2018, August 25). *Too often, teachers think classroom management is something to do in order to get to the real teaching.* [Tweet]. Twitter. https://twitter.com/carlashalaby/status/1033450333568229376

Shange, S. (2019). *Progressive dystopia: Abolition, anti-Blackness, and schooling in San Francisco.* Duke University Press. https://doi.org/10.1515/9781478007401

Spade, D. (2020). *Mutual aid: Building solidarity during this crisis (and the next).* Verso Books.

Young, A. (Host). (2021, July 28). Prentis Hemphill on choosing belonging [Audio podcast episode]. *For the Wild.* https://forthewild.world/podcast-transcripts/prentis-hemphill-on-choosing-belonging-encore-281

15

Creating Harmonious Classroom Communities by Embracing Community Cultural Wealth and Connection-Building

Violet Jiménez Sims and Dana Turnquest

We approach this chapter through our worldviews of multiple marginalized identities.

I, Violet, am a Dominican-born U.S. immigrant, bilingual and bicultural woman. I am racially Black and ethnically Latino/Hispanic in the U.S. context. As a first-generation college-educated person, I am also a first-generation professional who has spent more than two decades navigating and challenging the unwritten rules and coded language often found in primarily white spaces. I draw from my experiences and research to center cultural sustainability and cultivate liberatory practices in public education settings.

I, Dana, am a Harlem-born, first-generation college-educated Black man. As one of four children and the only son of a single mother, I looked at education very purposefully. My worldview is shaped by a Black male experience of duality where education and cultural pride have echoed throughout my life but do not always align. I developed a critical lens as I discovered similar data trends in educational systems and criminal justice systems, especially as it impacts people who look like me. This critical lens shows up in my educational practices where I aim to make public education more transformative than conformative.

Using the community cultural wealth (CCW) framework (Yosso, 2005) as an anchor, and drawing from its predecessors, including African and Indigenous pedagogies such as Ubuntu and In Lak'ech which center wholeness, community, and harmony over individualism, we assert that viewing students through an asset lens and understanding the cultural wealth students bring into the classroom can be leveraged to build authentic connections and inform classroom procedures that align with decolonized classroom community practices. Decolonizing classroom management includes moving away from behaviorist and deficit perspectives, including redefining the terms systematically used to describe student behaviors, and shifting adult mind-sets. Impactful tools exist that are underused, or sometimes misused, yet crucial for the success of every classroom community.

BACKGROUND—SHIFTING FROM BEHAVIORIST, DEFICIT PERSPECTIVES TO ASSET-BASED CONSTRUCTIVIST CLASSROOM COMMUNITIES

The term "behavior management" has long described systems for dealing with modifying human behavior from corporate settings to schools that is deemed challenging (Adam & Scott, 1971; Bourdon, 1977; Wielkiewicz, 1986), a perspective grounded in behaviorism. Behavior management aims for task completion, regulation, and control. Classroom management is an evolution of behavior management. Both these terms typically center a system of rewards and punishments. A close look at status quo classroom management practices affecting children of color reveals parallels to criminal justice systems, including the associated recidivism, time lines, and responses to behavior. Antiquated and punitive-heavy systems create a school-to-prison nexus (Kautz, 2023) that serves as a foundation for the school-to-prison pipeline.

Community cultural wealth (CCW) uses critical race theory to contextualize the experiences of communities of color who enact community cultural wealth as they challenge deficit structures along the PK–20 education pipeline (Acevedo & Solórzano, 2021). Yosso (2005) defines CCW as an array of knowledge, skills, abilities, and contacts that communities of color possess and use to survive and resist all forms of oppression. This perspective legitimizes experiential knowledge and resilience and challenges deficit perspectives. Yosso and Solórzano (2005) note that such knowledge is a strength and draws "explicitly on the lived experiences of people of color by including such methods as storytelling, family histories, biographies, scenarios, parables, *cuentos*, *testimonios*, chronicles, and narratives" (p. 123). The core types of capital within the CCW framework are aspirational capital, linguistic capital, familial capital, social capital, navigational capital, and resistant capital (Yosso, 2005).

Culture can be defined as behaviors and values that are learned, shared, and exhibited by a group of people (Yosso & Solórzano, 2005). All students have valuable experiential knowledge connected to their home and community cultures that educators can build on to facilitate a shared classroom culture that is additive and harmonious. A CCW lens, combined with the community-oriented worldviews that characterize African and Indigenous pedagogies, can ground constructivist approaches and strategies to building harmonious classroom communities.

DISTRICT, SCHOOL-WIDE, AND CLASSROOM PRACTICES

Behavior management ensures conformity instead of transformation. Conformity shows up when punishments are applied for anything that challenges compliance. Schools may purport to have social justice imperatives, but without intentional inclusion and honoring of CCW, they can end up further marginalizing students and stifling equity efforts (Locke et al., 2017) as too many efforts usurp the language of equity while still engaging in colonized practices. Garnett et al. (2022) uncovered educator frustrations when restorative practices in schools and districts are a disjointed combination of interventions that lack integrity and become buzzwords. "Building relationships" is one well-meaning phrase that is overused and applied subjectively and with varying success as efforts become sound bites and superficial implementation falls short. When there is an overreliance on intuitive relationships without understanding of CCW and intentional connection-building practices, once boundaries are crossed, relationships fall apart, and classroom communities begin to unravel. Building better, harmonious learning communities is possible in any climate and with teachers of all backgrounds via practices that establish meaningful connections rather than simply encouraging people to build relationships grounded in their own interpretation.

At systemic levels, shifting adult behaviors and perspectives is possible through professional learning and coaching. Practices for building connections are easier—more concrete—to teach and model than simply encouraging practitioners to build relationships. Using CCW to build connections is accessible to all levels of understanding, to digest, to quantify, to bridge cultural gaps, and to not violate; connections are less likely to be severed compared to relationships. There are practical ways to use community assets in the classroom (Yosso & Solórzano, 2005). Centering CCW and establishing connections takes a realistic (Bell, 1992) but optimistic approach as we face the reality of working within existing systems while dismantling colonized views and building a more inclusive system.

RECOMMENDATIONS FOR PRACTICE/APPLICATION OF CCW FOR BUILDING CONNECTION

A concrete step for creating a classroom community where learning is optimal is to decriminalize and objectify behavior categories and discipline-related language. Words commonly used on school or district-wide discipline referrals to define classroom and school transgressions such as trespassing, loitering, assault, battery, disrespect, disruptive, and insubordination are either criminal offenses or descriptions of feelings about behavior. Although the work needed to shift this parallel to the criminal justice system is most impactful at the systemic level, language use can be intentional at the classroom level regardless of where district efforts are on the continuum of antiracist and decolonized practices. Racial microaffirmations—subtle verbal and/or nonverbal strategies people of color consciously engage (with other people of color) to affirm each other's value, integrity, and shared humanity—are compatible with CCW as extensions of linguistic and resistant capital (Acevedo & Solórzano, 2021) and can be curated in classroom conversations. Some general categories can replace criminal language and describe student behaviors concretely: out of assigned area or out of bounds (instead of trespassing or loitering), harmful language or gestures (instead of disrespect), physical aggression or altercation (rather than assault/battery), and misuse or damage to resources; in essence, only observable behavior should be recorded. When there is harm or disruption, the above categories serve as examples describing the behavior, not others' feelings about it or authority and hierarchy. A guiding question for choosing intentionally restorative communal language should be, "What harm was done?," not "What orders were not followed?"

Further, the mind-set of classroom management must shift from an operant strategy, requiring punishment, to a restorative and teaching strategy that empowers processing. Restorative strategies lead to a longer lasting impact and development of intrinsic motivation. A challenge with operant strategies is that they decrease in effectiveness when the motivator is absent. In contrast, an effective, proactive, and equitable tool that can be used in classrooms of all age groups is circles (Boyes-Watson et al., 2021). Although circles were mainly introduced in educational spaces as a strategy to connect regarding social and emotional issues, traditionally circles have been used for everything from morning meetings to judicial proceedings dating back to Indigenous times. "Circles have value in school classrooms, both for post-incident peacemaking and as a proactive pedagogy for citizenship, academic learning, and developing mutual understanding" (Parker & Bickmore, 2020, p. 1).

This section will expand on using circles for the purpose of Tier 1 proactive peace education. Circles have the potential to create harmonious classroom communities and contribute to dismantling colonized, behaviorist, punitive approaches to discipline and classroom management. "At its core, restorative community building Tier 1 RP circles aspire to value all voices equally, foster participant self-awareness and empathy for others, and encourage collective ownership of the circle space by all participants" (Garnett et al., 2022, p. 113).

Circles are extremely useful for fostering equality, equity, safety and trust, responsibility, facilitation skills, building connections, and ownership (Costello et al., 2019). Another imperative reason to amplify the use of circles in classrooms is communication. Effective communication should be explicitly taught, especially because it is an expectation that adults place on students and is necessary for conflict resolution. Adults in students' spheres of influence expect them to learn how to navigate interpersonal issues through adult modeling. But what if the role models are not skilled communicators when it comes to conflict resolution, problem solving, or emotional regulation? The framework for circles explicitly teaches how people communicate in groups and how to optimize interpersonal communication, benefiting both adults and students.

A competency that educators should master is the art of asking affective questions (Costello et al., 2019), both proactively and as a response to classroom community issues or harm done. Because the restorative framework follows the same sequence that operant strategies do (antecedent, behavior, consequence), instead of focusing on the behavior using a reward system, as PBIS would, affective questions help students tell their story. This focus on the antecedent scaffolds articulating aspirations, cultural and linguistic pluralism, accountability, conflict resolution, and building connection—along with other forms of CCW capital. Table 15.1 connects theory to practice by illustrating strategies, practices, and sample questions that align with the CCW framework and can be used to build harmonious classroom communities and facilitate Tier 1 circles.

Whereas academia tends to focus on intellectual abilities, emotional intelligence and emotional literacy are essential to harmonious communities; adaptability, voicing frustration, tolerance, empathy, and other expected interpersonal skills can be explicitly taught. These skills are intuitive to restorative practices and essential to learning communities (Schumacher, 2014); their absence becomes a barrier in classrooms. Basic tenets of classroom circles should precede activities and interventions to teach both group communication and the emotional intelligence essential to interpersonal relationships and community learning. Four such tenets include respect the speaker, space, or conversation; listen with empathy and for understanding; speak your truth and with purpose; and contribute to and share the space.

Table 15.1. Strategies, Practices, and Sample Questions That Align with the CCW Framework.

Community Cultural Wealth (CCW) Capital	From Theory to Practice: Connected Strategies/Practices/Sample Circle Questions
Aspirational Capital	*Appreciate/build on*: hopes and dreams in the face of barriers
	Facilitate/teach: setting goals, connections as networking, nurturing a culture of possibility
	Sample circle question: What would be your dream career? If money wasn't an obstacle, which college would you attend?
Linguistic Capital	*Appreciate/build on*: the intellectual and social skills inherent to speaking more than one language and/or dialect
	Facilitate/teach: intentionally leverage linguistic capital for different purposes
	Sample circle question: When is code switching appropriate or needed?
Familial Capital	*Appreciate/build on*: the cultural knowledge developed through immediate, extended, and/or chosen family
	Facilitate/teach: co-create an inclusive classroom climate and culture
	Sample circle question: Who is someone you look up to in your family and why? Who is someone not related to you but who you consider family?
Social Capital	*Appreciate/build on*: knowledge of community resources and supports
	Facilitate/teach: education resources and supports that align with students and families' goals and aspirations, "lifting as we climb"
	Sample circle question: Outside of your home (or this classroom) is there a place you go when you need support, refuge, or an outlet?
Navigational Capital	*Appreciate/build on*: skills of maneuvering institutions, resilience of marginalized groups
	Facilitate/teach: concepts of mutual aid, benefit societies, cooperation
	Sample circle question: Who is in your positive sphere of influence? Does that list need to grow/shrink?
Resistant Capital	*Appreciate/build on*: knowledge and skills developed through challenging inequality
	Facilitate/teach: self-advocacy, self-value, conflict resolution
	Sample circle question: What's important to you, why is it important to you, and what happens if you don't have that?

Some may challenge the universal use of classroom circles and restorative procedures for multilingual learners (MLLs) and neurodivergent students. Yet, using language in context is integral to language acquisition. Krashen and Terrell (1983) compiled research indicating that language can be acquired naturally when the input is high interest and the environment is conducive to learning. Language is a social semiotic system—a resource for meaning across the changing contexts of human interaction (Halliday & Webster, 2003). Consistent use of circles not only encourages quieter MLLs to participate, but in a special needs classroom of primarily autistic students, as the teacher gained the capacity to facilitate circles, students with autism were capable of participating in focused listening and speaking circle activities with scaffolding and support (Parker & Bickmore, 2020).

When circles are integrated into classroom communities and shared tenets become part of common language, a culture of structured, safe dialogue is established. Good communication and processing, or using affective statements and questions, are not dependent upon advanced language skills. Consider that empathy is a foundational skill, yet a main ingredient for effective communication, problem-solving, and processing. As empathy grows within classroom communities, the impact on multilingual learners and those who struggle with social interactions is positive. Once a safe space is created, any attempts to contribute to the space will be reinforced with enthusiasm. Imagine the student who never shares but just quietly observes every group discussion. Now imagine the first time that student decides to contribute to the space, and her comments are rewarded with positive feedback and microaffirmations.

As the term "relationship building" echoes through the halls of public education, the seemingly simple concept may be elusive to educators for numerous reasons. In addition, quality relationships require building from both parties. So, if a student does not wish to build a relationship with an educator, the educator's efforts may fall flat. Unfortunately, the word relationship can generically describe any two related things; the concept is easier said than done.

A shift in thinking from the esoteric concept of building relationships to a focus on establishing connections can support educators' ability to curate harmonious classrooms. Simply put, a connection is the depth of information that you have learned about an individual you have met. Connections do not require memorization, common interest, knowledge, or shared backgrounds. Connection is simply created by your authentic desire to want to connect, and in doing so, lead you to inquire about something of value to that person. For example, a parent who wants to hear all about their first-grader's day at school shows authentic enthusiasm toward the information shared, which creates a bond that provides material for the foundation of a long-term relationship. Authentic responses and inquiries strengthen connections. Where time can be a cause of contention in certain relationships, a strong connection can reunite two people after many years. Negative connections can also have lasting impact, and both are based on the depth of the interaction. So, dig without prying for the purposes of discovery but not excavation.

Now that society has moved into the social age, it is important for school systems and classroom educators to recognize and abandon the approaches that worked during the industrial age or even the information age but no longer work for today's students. In the industrial age, job loyalty and school compliance were valued. In the social age, districts, schools, and classrooms can no longer rely on outdated compliance tactics and monocultural values. Antiquated systems such as PBIS yield short-term effects for basic behaviors, but educators who are intentional about integrating CCW, building connection, using restorative practices, and modeling communication skills can cultivate intrinsic motivation and harmonious learning communities.

Social justice work is complex and ongoing (Acevedo & Solórzano, 2021). A CRT analysis acknowledges that despite the "peaks of progress" present throughout U.S. history, structural racism will continue to adapt to keep communities of color in their place (Bell, 1992). Building harmonious classroom communities centered on African and Indigenous pedagogies and decolonizing classroom management in public schools requires a comprehensive, systemic approach. Although dismantling and simultaneously rebuilding a system from within takes intentional and strategic efforts at the district, school, and classroom levels, all educators can interrupt systemic discrimination and discipline bias. Hopefully, some practical strategies shared in this chapter can support continuous efforts to dismantle oppressive structures and decolonize institutional practices and perspectives.

REFERENCES

Acevedo, N. & Solórzano, D. G. (2021). An overview of community cultural wealth: Toward a protective factor against racism. *Urban Education, 58*(7), 1–19. https://doi.org/10.1177/00420859211016531

Adam E., & Scott, W. E. (1971). The application of behavioral conditioning procedures to the problems of quality control. *Academy of Management Journal, 14*(2), 175–193. https://doi.org/10.2307/255305

Bell, D. (1992). Racial realism. *Connecticut Law Review, 24*(2), 363–379.

Bourdon, R. D. (1977). A token economy application to management performance improvement. *Journal of Organizational Behavior Management, 1*(1), 23–37. https://doi.org/10.1300/J075v01n01_02

Boyes-Watson, C., Pranis, K., Henson, M., Lima, C., Morris, K., Ozaki, K., Rothstein, S. M., Salomon, A. R., Stewart, J., & Warren, E. (2021). *Circle forward supplement*. Living Justice Press.

Costello, B., Wachtel, J., & Wachtel, T. (2019). *Restorative circles in schools: A practical guide for educators*. International Institute for Restorative Practices.

Garnett, B. R., Kervick, C. T., Moore, M., Ballysingh, T. A., & Smith, L. C. (2022). School staff and youth perspectives of Tier 1 restorative practices classroom circles. *School Psychology Review, 51*(1), 112–126. https://doi.org/10.1080/2372966X.2020.1795557

Halliday, M. A. K., & Webster, J. (2003). *On language and linguistics*, 1st edition. Bloomsbury.

Kautz, M. B. (2023). From segregation to suspension: The solidification of the contemporary school-prison nexus in Boston, 1963–1985. *Journal of Urban History, 49*(5). https://doi-org.ezproxy.lib.uconn.edu/10.1177/00961442221142059

Krashen, S. D., & Terrell, T. D. (1983). *The natural approach: Language acquisition in the classroom*. Alemany Press.

Locke, L. A., Maxwell, G., & Tello, M. (2017). "You don't come to this school . . . to show off your hoodies": Latinas, community cultural wealth, and an early college high school. *Qualitative Report, 22*(9), 2404–2427. https://doi.org/10.46743/2160–3715/2017.2496

Parker, C., & Bickmore, K. (2020). Classroom peace circles: Teachers' professional learning and implementation of restorative dialogue. *Teaching and Teacher Education, 95*. https://doi.org/10.1016/j.tate.2020.103129

Schumacher, A. (2014). Talking circles for adolescent girls in an urban high school: A restorative practices program for building friendships and developing emotional literacy skills. *Sage Open, 4*(4). https://doi.org/10.1177/2158244014554204

Wielkiewicz, R. M. (1986). *Behavior management in the schools: principles and procedures*. Pergamon Press.

Yosso, T. J. (2005). Whose culture has capital? A critical race theory discussion of community cultural wealth. *Race, Ethnicity and Education, 8*(1), 69–91. https://doi.org/10.1080/1361332052000341006

Yosso, T. J., & Solórzano, D. G. (2005). Conceptualizing a critical race theory in sociology. In M. Romero & E. Margolis (Eds.), *The Blackwell Companion to Social Inequalities* (pp. 117–146). Blackwell. https://doi.org/10.1002/9780470996973.ch7

16

A Collaborative Approach of Ubuntu

Dismantling Colonial Classroom Management Practices in South African Schools through the Spirit of Ubuntu

Amy Sarah Padayachee and Samantha Kriger

Globally, classroom management trends have revealed a repositioning of deeply rooted colonial practices to that of decolonized approaches and strategies. Literature suggests a significant shift toward classroom management practices substantially adapted to multiculturalism, inclusivity, and education reform, which have collectively been placed at the forefront of educational endeavors (Paseka & Schwab, 2019; Torres & Tarozzi, 2020), although these visions are far from being fully realized (Sorkos & Hajisoteriou, 2021). Glaring disparities remain in the existent practices of educational practitioners in developing countries such as South Africa.

In this chapter, we advance the notion that South Africa, like other developing countries, still employs punitive classroom management practices that reflect jarring notions of colonization. To this end, the book chapter illuminates Ubuntu, an African philosophy used to promote decolonization in classroom management practices.

It is germane to briefly highlight the reality of educational practices in South African classrooms. Since 1994, the South African education system has undergone a major process of education reform aimed at decolonizing a system that was entrenched in racial pedagogies. The shift to a democratized system of education was buttressed by the establishment and implementation of democratic educational acts and laws that govern all aspects of educational delivery, including that of classroom management practices. It is, however, noteworthy that the South African Schools Act (84 of 1996) advanced the notion of multicultural education approaches devoid of ethnocentric views that once governed the South African education landscape. Despite such reform, countries such as South Africa remain inherently unpredictable in the shift toward decolonized education practices.

As the authors of this chapter, we are uniquely situated to write about school practices in South Africa, having taught for 30 years during this reform period as did classroom teachers and teacher educators in hundreds of schools. We are female academics of color who currently serve as lecturers to preservice teachers completing a bachelor of education program at a South African University of Technology in Cape Town. Both authors, having completed their doctoral degrees in education, share research interests in education management—in particular, the transformation of the South African education system.

Ideally, decolonized classroom management practices should be aimed at restitution, reconciliation, and accountability. Debunking the myth that South African classroom management strategies display elements of decolonization, this book chapter emerged from a study conducted by Padayachee and Gcelu (2022) and is deeply rooted in the collaboration theory (Chrislip & Larson, 1994) that articulates the potential of Ubuntu to redress past imbalances, heal breaches, and restore the damage caused by the imposition of colonial management practices.

PUNITIVE CLASSROOM MANAGEMENT PRACTICES

During apartheid, school discipline in South Africa's racially segregated schools was characterized by corporal punishment and colonial use of physical violence to control students. With the introduction of the South African Schools Act (84 of 1996) and its agenda of education transformation, corporal punishment, colonial educational segregation, and Eurocentric curricula were replaced in every domain with more democratic practices. Harber and Mncube (2011) illuminate that schooling was a significant site in the struggle against apartheid, and there is no doubt that postapartheid governments since 1994 have attached considerable importance to educational reform. The South African National Curriculum (2007) intended to harness the full potential of every student as a confident, independent, literate, numerate lifelong citizen with the ability to participate actively in a global society with criticism and compassion (Joubert et al., 2015). The curriculum was intended to not only transform South Africa's pedagogy, but also our political culture, from domination, obedience, and division to equality, self-discipline, and cooperation (Chisholm, as cited by Mattes, Denemark, & Niemi, 2012). Yet despite such far-reaching aims and objectives, the curriculum has failed to address the imbalances that continue to weigh heavily on classroom management practices.

Research on school management practices (Padaychee & Gcelu, 2022) reveals that despite the implementation of policy and legislation aimed at education reform, many elements of colonization remain embedded in school management practices. The extent to which historical inequalities have seeped through the South African education landscape is seen in many violent acts of student resistance. Glasser (1992) succinctly states that student rebellion is against a system of education that does not sufficiently take their needs into account—to students, the educators represent this system. If the system is to be changed, teachers must change what they do. It is important to understand that many deficits in educational policies stem from the inability of policy makers to take into consideration the culture of violence created by a system fraught with disparities in education that cannot be dislodged from the apartheid regime.

UBUNTU

Ubuntu is an Indigenous philosophy that may offer a way out of the cycles of violence by bringing the values of collective humanism to schools. Although Ubuntu is an Nguni Bantu word, it is also found in several African languages, including isiZulu and isiXhosa. Ubuntu is also a South African ideology that, when translated, simply means "humanity toward others."

There are many descriptions of what Ubuntu is and what it means to African people; however, this description by anti-apartheid activist Archbishop Desmond Tutu (1999) describes the essence of Ubuntu, which is embedded in the essence of humanity such that any person, regardless of nationality, can ascribe to it (pp. 34–35):

> Ubuntu is very difficult to render into a Western language. It speaks to the very essence of being human. When you want to give high praise to someone we say, "Yu, u Nobuntu"; he or she has Ubuntu. This means that they are generous, hospitable, friendly, caring, and compassionate. They share what they have. It also means that my humanity is caught up, is inextricably bound up, in theirs. We belong in a bundle of life. We say, "a person is a person through other people" (in Xhosa Ubuntu umgamntu ngabanye abantu and in Zulu Umuntu ngumuntu ngabaye). I am human because I belong, I participate, and I share. A person with Ubuntu is open and available to others, affirming of others, does not feel threatened that others are able and good; for he or she has a proper self-assurance that

comes with knowing that he or she belongs in a greater whole and is diminished when others are humiliated or diminished, when others are tortured or oppressed, or treated as if they were less than who they are.

That excerpt speaks of the principles of Ubuntu: humanity, belonging, and sharing. We forward the notion of the African philosophy of Ubuntu as a lens through which classroom management practices should be viewed. Research is now available that provides concrete suggestions of what "ubuntu" pedagogy focusing on the development of culturally responsive and caring classrooms might look like (Biraimah, 2016; Ngubane & Makua, 2021).

UBUNTU IN THE CLASSROOM

In a classroom based on Ubuntu principles, learning takes place through interactions with others; learners are nurtured and developed for them to construct knowledge and acquire skills, values, and attitudes in the classroom through cooperation and taking responsibility for one another's success (Maphalala, 2017). When teachers understand and embrace Ubuntu, it is likely that Ubuntu values can empower them to combat exclusion and employ pedagogies that aim to reach all learners in the classroom. The infusion of Indigenous methodologies and pedagogies into the curriculum should not exclude or diminish the value of traditional Western methodologies and pedagogies that have been used in schools for decades (Nxumalo & Mncube, 2018). Rather, inclusive pedagogies thrive on the connectedness between learners, teachers, and a community of learning, which all provide a positive environment. They, in turn, positively influence learners' self-worth, self-belief, and achievement (Ngubane & Makua, 2021). Ubuntu pedagogy rejects exclusion, marginalization, and inequality in the teaching and learning spaces (Phasha, 2016). Further, the interchanges of Ubuntu and other Indigenous convergences are in stark contrast with an education system that encourages learners to outperform one another (Vandeyar & Mohale, 2022).

Letseka (2013) opines that Ubuntu in education is considered African cultural capital that provides for the dissemination of Indigenous knowledge that is pivotal for integration into our African conception of inclusion. That, in turn, fosters and promotes inclusivity, equality, and social justice in our education system. Because the agenda of most developing countries such as South Africa is that of transformation, Ubuntu as a philosophy can be used to redress past imbalances in the way in which we manage our classroom practices.

Today, South African classrooms proudly embrace diversity and inclusion. Ubuntu supports the use of local languages instead of European or foreign languages, such as the once compulsory language, Afrikaans, as mediums for instruction or systems of communicating information in class (Omodan & Diko, 2021). Ubuntu also reflects on critical thinking in which students learn not just to pass their exams but, more important, learn for the change, growth, creativity, and freedom through actions for others (Venter, 2004; Hungwe, 2021). Ubuntu classroom practices make it possible to draw on and integrate traditional knowledge, science, and technology to design a curriculum that suits community needs (Seehawer, 2018). Further, decoloniality challenges how knowledge is produced to unveil the many ways in which Eurocentrism has distorted the original meaning of curriculum as a way of knowing, learning, and passing down knowledge from generation to generation (Omodan & Diko, 2021). Ubuntu classroom practice also advocates for community participation involving learners, parents, and teachers, whereby all members work together to learn new things through group discussions and joint learning (Hapanyengwi-Chemhuru & Shizha, 2012).

According to Mbjigi (1997), the five key elements of Ubuntu are survival, solidarity, compassion, respect, and dignity. Rather than a Eurocentric approach to teaching and learning, by incorporating Ubuntu, every nation and nationality will be tied together in the sense of togetherness by weaving their history, culture, art, economic, and spiritual wealth (Ali & Shisigu, 2020).

Philosophy plays a crucial role in determining the aims and objectives of learning content and ultimately, curricula of a schooling system. How students receive this depends on how they relate to this content and how relatable the learning experience is. An important point of consideration is that though African philosophy is in existence, it is only the Eurocentric philosophy that Africans learn in school (Ali & Shishigu, 2020). Although Ubuntu is inextricably linked to a value system that, in turn, translates to "I am, because you are," globally humanity extends to the very same value system and supersedes boundaries and nationality.

Ubuntu can be adopted to change the narrative of colonial practices worldwide by focusing on the collective stance of solidarity. The philosophy of Ubuntu is deeply rooted in collaboration theory (Chrislip & Larson, 1994) as it draws on a connectedness of various domains, backgrounds, Indigenous knowledge systems, and cultural capital to reshape our classroom management practices and ultimately our educational landscape. Despite policy implementation, classroom management and adopted practices must be viewed holistically and practically. An African child is born into a world consisting of people who are connected, not necessarily by blood, and this makes the child a relative of many people in the community (Akabor & Phasha, 2022). Schools should, therefore, approach classroom management with the Ubuntu philosophy at the forefront of the endeavor: a collaborative approach in which interpersonal values, intrapersonal values, and environmental values are taken into account.

Chrislip and Larson (1994) assert that collaborative leadership operates under the premise that if you bring the appropriate people together in constructive ways with good information, they will create authentic vision and strategies to address the shared concerns of the organization or community. Ubuntu espouses the idea of the collective achievement of the goals of the organization; it does not relegate an individual's own goal as secondary but confirms the idea that achieving individual goals and group goals are equally critical and go hand in hand (Frempong & Kadam, 2022).

SCHOOL GOVERNANCE IN SOUTH AFRICA

It must be noted that in South African public schools, governance is predominantly bestowed upon school governing bodies. They comprise the communities that serve as the decision-making bodies of schools. Classroom practices are, therefore, influenced by the communities that individual schools serve. The teacher, then, must build a sense of community in the classroom based on collective responsibility.

The development and implementation of democratic policies, legislation, and curricula aimed at redressing decolonized educational spheres is highly influenced by values of Ubuntu such as respect, value, dignity, honor, humanity, and tolerance. Moreover, the management of educational practices, through the lens of Ubuntu, should be one based on collaboration of all related stakeholders; parents, guardians, community leaders and activists, religious leaders, local government officials, and all those with a vested interest.

For societies in developing countries, education was conceptualized, designed, and implemented as an instrument of a colonial rule founded on unequal rights and marginalization of the colonized, for whom education was not considered a right under the colonial system (Oviawe, 2016). These imbalances in education remain evident. The inclusion of Ubuntu in classroom management practices is a means by which the marginalized take back their rightfully owned educational spaces, spaces where education remains relevant to the students it serves and to those who challenge colonial practices that have no relevance or use in the present education system.

Similarly, oppressive forms of classroom management such as corporal punishment have no place in society, yet despite its abolishment and the transition toward democratic practices that reflect values of human dignity, many institutions still employ punitive punishment as a form of classroom management. On the contrary, Ubuntu principles value interconnectedness among people and create awareness of positive behaviors (Msila, 2015; Mbhele,

2015). Ubuntu, if adopted in its true sense, would address such issues while drawing on a sense of moral obligation and, in turn, exemplify true humanity. Lefa (2015) postulates that Ubuntu is regarded as the soul force that drives almost every facet of societal life in African societies and that creates the relationship between the African community.

The findings from a study conducted by Padayachee and Gcelu (2022) reveal that despite evident colonial practices that still govern classroom management in many educational institutions, the driving force that can be used to shift the traditional form of classroom management practices is Indigenous knowledge deeply rooted in the sociocultural milieu of African people (Ali & Shishiqu, 2020). Findings from the study indicate that in African communities, parents and elders view all children in the community as their own and their well-being as the responsibility of the entire community. This stems from the African proverb, "It takes a village to raise a child." South African schools are served largely by their communities and are often the driving force ensuring that classroom practices reflect social and cultural norms. It should be noted that Ubuntu fosters cohesiveness, collaboration, getting along with others, and coexistence for the good of the collective, so when classrooms become learning communities, learners are accountable to one another to achieve the shared goals of the classroom, the school, and the education system as a whole (Maphalala, 2017). In African culture the community always comes first (Venter 2004) in contrast to the individualism of Eurocentric societies. By evoking the principles of Ubuntu, Indigenous knowledge systems serve as a premise for dismantling colonial classroom practices. Epistemologies that inform knowledge construction in the classroom can be broadened to include philosophies of African origin (Vandeyar & Mohale, 2022) for the benefit of the community.

Research further suggests that compassion, reciprocity, dignity, harmony, and humanity serve as the overarching framework for decolonizing punitive classroom management practices in the interests of building and maintaining a community with justice and mutual caring (Lefa, 2015). According to Jansen (2018), cultivating humanity in the 21st century involves emotional presence, which focuses on sensing learners' needs and concerns and responding to them.

CONCLUSION

As authors based in South Africa, we identify with the philosophy of Ubuntu and how Indigenous knowledge and value systems allow students to position themselves culturally and socially. Traditional classroom practices such as corporal punishment that widen the gap of marginalization and discrimination have no place in society. As human beings, our identities are often shaped by those around us, which resonates with the essence of Ubuntu. As a matter of fact, a well-rounded, respectable, and respected human being in the African context is the one who is honest, caring, good mannered, regards others, self-disciplined, courageous, tolerant, and empathetic (Nziramasanga, 1999). These are the values that our classroom practices should reflect in society. Further, Samkange and Samkange (2013) note that the African philosophy of education enables us to challenge the status quo in terms of assumptions, beliefs, and viewpoints about the function and relevance of schooling to an educated African. In providing holistic, democratic schooling, education that allows students to challenge the status quo of every colonial practice, Ubuntu must be incorporated in our classroom management practices.

As we conclude this chapter, we therefore advance the notion that classroom management practices should be based on principles of Ubuntu by understanding that our essence as humans is intricately intertwined with recognition of the humanity of others, and as such lifelong sustainable education reform is underpinned by the Ubuntu philosophy.

REFERENCES

Akabor, S., & Phasha, N. (2022). Where is Ubuntu in competitive South African schools? An inclusive education perspective. *International Journal of Inclusive Education*, 1–17. https://doi.org/10.1080/13603116.2022.2127491

Ali, T., & Shishigu, A. (2020). Implications of Ubuntu/synergy for the education system of Ethiopia. *Education Research International, 2020*, 1–11. https://doi.org/10.1155/2020/8838077

Biraimah, K. L. (2016). Moving beyond a destructive past to a decolonised and inclusive future: The role of Ubuntu-style education in providing culturally relevant pedagogy for Namibia. *International Review of Education, 62*, 45–62. https://doi.org/10.1007/s11159-016-9541-1

Chrislip, D., & Larson, C., 1994. *Collaborative leadership*. Jossey-Bass.

Frempong, G., & Kadam, R. (2022). Educational paradigm with Ubuntu mindset: Implications for sustainable development goals in education. *Active Learning-Research and Practice for STEAM and Social Sciences Education*, 237. https://doi.org/10.5772/intechopen.104929

Glasser, W. (1992). *Quality school: Managing students without coercion*, 2nd edition. Harper Perennial.

Hapanyengwi-Chemhuru, O., & Shizha, E. (2012). Unhu/Ubuntu and education for reconciliation in Zimbabwe. *Journal of Contemporary Issues in Education, 7*(2), 17–27. https://doi.org/10.20355/C5XW2D

Harber, C., & Mncube, V. (2011). Is schooling good for the development of society? The case of South Africa. *South African Journal of Education, 31*(2), 233–243

Hungwe, J. P. (2021). The (In)compatible nexus between Ubuntu and critical thinking in African philosophy of education: Towards Ubuntu critical thinking in African higher education. In B. I. Omodan & N. Diko, Conceptualisation of Ubuntugogy as a decolonial pedagogy in Africa. In *Mediating learning in higher education in Africa* (pp. 23–40). Brill. https://doi.org/10.1163/9789004464018_003

Jansen, J. (2018, September 26). Presence as a powerful form of classroom communication. Optentia research day: Cultivating humanity. [Webinar and Slideshow Presentation].

Lefa, B. J. (2015). The African philosophy of Ubuntu in South African education. *Studies in Philosophy and Education, 1*(1), 15.

Letseka, M. (2013). Educating for ubuntu/botho: Lessons from Basotho Indigenous education. *Open Journal of Philosophy, 3*(02), 337–344. https://doi.org/10.4236/ojpp.2013.32051

Maphalala, M. C. (2017). Embracing Ubuntu in managing effective classrooms. *Gender and Behaviour, 15*(4), 10237–10249. https://hdl.handle.net/10520/EJC-c1eb0d3be

Mattes, R. B., Denemark, D., & Niemi, R. G. (2012). Learning democracy? Civic education in South Africa's first post-apartheid generation. Presented at the seventh general conference of the European Consortium for Political Research.

Mbhele, N. (2015). Ubuntu and school leadership: Perspectives of teachers from two schools at Umbumbulu Circuit. Master's thesis, University of KwaZulu, Natal, South Africa.

Mbiji, L. (1997). *Ubuntu: The African dream in management.* Knowledge Resources.

Ngubane, N., & Makua, M. (2021). Ubuntu pedagogy—transforming educational practices in South African through an African philosophy from theory to practice. *Inkanyiso: Journal of Humanities and Social Sciences, 13*(1). https://hdl.handle.net/10520/ejc-uz_inka-v13-n1-a2

Nxumalo, S. A., & Mncube, D. W. (2018). Using Indigenous games and knowledge to decolonise the school curriculum: Ubuntu perspectives. *Perspectives in Education, 36*(2), 103–118. https://doi.org/10.18820/2519593X/pie.v36i2.9

Nziramasanga, C. T. (1999). [Presidential Report] Zimbabwe: Report of the presidential commission of inquiry into education and training. https://unesdoc.unesco.org/ark:/48223/pf0000173101

Omodan, B. I., & Diko, N. (2021). Conceptualisation of ubuntugogy as a decolonial pedagogy in Africa. *Journal of Culture and Values in Education, 4*(2), 95–104. https://doi.org/10.46303/jcve.2021.8

Oviawe, J. O. (2016). How to rediscover the Ubuntu paradigm in education. *International Review of Education, 62*(1), 1–10. https://doi.org/10.1007/s11159-016-9545-x

Padayachee, A. S., & Gcelu, N. (2022). Collaboration: The key to managing discipline in South African schools. *South African Journal of Education, 42*(4), 1–9. https://doi.org/10.15700/saje.v42n4a2139

Paseka, A., & Schwab, S. (2019). Parents' attitudes towards inclusive education and their perceptions of inclusive teaching practices and resources. *European Journal of Special Needs Education, 35*(2), 254–272. https://doi.org/10.1080/08856257.2019.1665232

Samkange, W., & Samkange, C. (2013). Philosophies and perspectives in education: Examining their roles and relevance in education. *Greener Journal of Educational Research, 3*(10), 454–461. https://www.gjournals.org/GJER/archive/dec-2013-vol-310/samkange-andsamkange.html

Seehawer, M. (2018). South African science teachers' strategies for integrating indigenous and Western knowledges in their classes: Practical lessons in decolonisation. *Educational Research for Social Change, 7*(0), 91–110. http://dx.doi.org/10.17159/2221–4070/2018/v7i0a7

Sorkos, G., & Hajisoteriou, C. (2021). Sustainable intercultural and inclusive education: Teachers' efforts on promoting a combining paradigm. *Pedagogy, Culture & Society, 29*(4), 517–536. https://doi.org/10.1080/14681366.2020.1765193

Torres, C. A., & Tarozzi, M. (2020). Multiculturalism in the world system: towards a social justice model of inter/multicultural education. *Globalisation, Societies and Education, 18*(1), 7–18. https://doi.org/10.1080/14767724.2019.1690729

Tutu, D. (1999). *No future without forgiveness*. Image, Doubleday.

Vandeyar, S., & Mohale, M. A. (2022). Philosophy of ubuntu and collaborative project-based learning in post-apartheid South Africa: A case study of underperforming learners at Hope Saturday school. *South African Journal of Education, 42*(4). https://doi.org/10.15700/saje.v42n4a2080

Venter, E. (2004). The notion of Ubuntu and communalism in African educational discourse. *Studies in Philosophy and Education, 23*, 149–160. https://doi.org/10.1023/B:SPED.0000024428.29295.03

Epilogue

Decolonial Theory to Practice
Toward Shared Anticolonial Futures

Rebecca Sockbeson, Fiona Hopper,
Bridgid Neptune, Starr Kelly

DR. REBECCA SOCKBESON

Penobscot Indian Nation and Alexis Nakota Sioux Nation, professor Indigenous Peoples education, University of Alberta

FIONA HOPPER

White settler, social studies teacher leader, and Wabanaki studies coordinator, Portland Public Schools

BRIDGID NEPTUNE

Passamaquoddy Tribe, Wabanaki studies curriculum consultant

STARR KELLY

Citizen of the Kitignan Zibi Anishinabeg First Nation, former curator of education at the Abbe Museum

These concluding words nod to the future while remaining rooted in the past and organized here through personal narratives by coauthors in an attempt to nurture the relationships between theory and practice as we look to ground and honor the excellent intellectual work of decolonization in this collection with an example of what this might look like. Through the local action of Indigenous education initiatives in Maine, Wabanaki Peoples and white educators worked together making tremendous efforts and reaching classroom instruction in the state of Maine. We begin with my reflections (Rebecca) taking up the possibilities of how genocide and land acknowledgments can become a dynamic catalyst for decolonizing classroom management. Then we turn to the story of more than 10 years of curricular development in the making, a Wabanaki-led, yet collaborative project organized to support educating classroom teachers for compliance with Wabanaki Studies Law K–12 state legislation expecting teachers in Maine to teach about the Wabanaki people, our history, culture, governance, and place.

Rebecca

As I look to the future of decolonized classrooms, I feel a deep urgency for the type of intellectual engagement this edited book offers and see a timeliness for us to put to action the critically important theories of anticolonialism and their imbedded intersectionality of anti-oppression, the height of which is love, humanity, and compassion. We face national discourses outlawing critical race theory in schools, diminishing abortion rights, eroding of 2SLGBTQ rights, and increasing mass school shootings with associated fatalities are at an all-time high while the government continues to protect gun ownership rights. Here is when I pause to remember the first era of policy in this country against my ancestors, that of genocide, and I am painfully reminded of how colonial violence has a lived legacy today manifested in this national discourse.

This history of genocide is inextricably linked to national discourses that attempt to take humanity away from marginalized people: understanding that history helps to make sense of how we got here. As seen in the original colonial document (figure 1), bounties for the scalps of Wabanaki began being paid in the early 1700s when Queen Anne of England ruled that colonists would be compensated for the scalps of Native Americans. This genocidal law compensated colonial bounty hunters richly for killing Indigenous men, women, and children (Davey & Thunder Woman, 2006; Sockbeson, 2017a). A bounty offering up to £50 (about $17,529 today) for live capture of Penobscot people and £40 for Penobscot scalps was issued in 1755, about 100 years after Wabanaki were legally prohibited from using guns (Paul, 2000).

By His HONOUR

SPENCER PHIPS, Esq;
Lieutenant-Governour and Commander in Chief, in and over His Majesty's Province of the *Massachusetts-Bay* in *New-England*.

A PROCLAMATION.

WHEREAS the Tribe of *Penobscot* Indians have repeatedly in a perfidious Manner acted contrary to their solemn Submission unto His Majesty long since made and frequently renewed;

I have therefore, at the Desire of the House of Representatives, with the Advice of His Majesty's Council, thought fit to issue this Proclamation, and to declare the Penobscot Tribe of Indians to be Enemies, Rebels and Traitors to His Majesty King *GEORGE* the Second: And I do hereby require His Majesty's Subjects of this Province to embrace all Opportunities of pursuing, captivating, killing and destroying all and every of the aforesaid Indians.

AND WHEREAS the General Court of this Province have voted that a Bounty or Incouragement be granted and allowed to be paid out of the Publick Treasury, to the marching Forces that shall have been employed for the Defence of the *Eastern* and *Western* Frontiers, from the *First* to the *Twenty-fifth* of this Instant *November*;

I have thought fit to publish the same; and I do hereby Promise, That there shall be paid out of the Province-Treasury to all and any of the said Forces, over and above their Bounty upon Inlistment, their Wages and Subsistence, the Premiums or Bounty following, viz.

For every Male *Penobscot* Indian above the Age of Twelve Years, that shall be taken within the Time aforesaid and brought to *Boston*, *Fifty Pounds*.

For every Scalp of a Male *Penobscot* Indian above the Age aforesaid, brought in as Evidence of their being killed as aforesaid, *Forty Pounds*.

For every Female *Penobscot* Indian taken and brought in as aforesaid, and for every Male Indian Prisoner under the Age of Twelve Years, taken and brought in as aforesaid, *Twenty-five Pounds*.

For every Scalp of such Female Indian or Male Indian under the Age of Twelve Years, that shall be killed and brought in as Evidence of their being killed as aforesaid, *Twenty Pounds*.

Given at the Council-Chamber in *Boston*, this Third Day of *November* 1755, and in the Twenty-ninth Year of the Reign of our Sovereign Lord *GEORGE* the Second, by the Grace of GOD of *Great-Britain, France* and *Ireland*, KING, Defender of the Faith, &c.

By His Honour's Command,
J. Willard, Secr.

S. Phips.

GOD Save the KING.

BOSTON: Printed by *John Draper*, Printer to His Honour the Lieutenant-Governour and Council. 1755.

The critically important theories of decolonization can be realized and supported in education systems so that decolonizing classroom management can be maximized. This colonial document calling for and paying out compensation for the genocide of my ancestors is intended to link the present with the history, and I call for that history to be visible and constant (Sockbeson,

2019). I position the following questions to be taken up as a rationale for this concluding discussion of the book:

What is a decolonized classroom management when

- students are not taught who the Indigenous Peoples and original inhabitants were of the land on which their schools rest?
- students are not taught that the Indigenous Peoples of the land survived genocide?
- students and teachers do not have a relationship or an awareness with the people Indigenous to the land on which their schools operate?
- teachers are also not educated to deliver Indigenous content in their teacher preparation programs?

In light of this, I offer a pedagogical approach that can make further use of the multitude of land acknowledgments currently being used. Here, the classroom has the potential to serve as a vessel of decolonial content delivery, and this depends on a multitude of factors (Ambo & Beardall, 2023). Land acknowledgments have been normalized, recited in classrooms throughout universities in both Canada and the United States, and other educational spaces more or less as a routine practice. They often reflect the theories of decolonization and/or how universities make sense of their relationship with the Indigenous Peoples and territories they occupy. These acknowledgements are placed in course outlines, opening remarks by educators, administrative leaders, and other community members. They are taken up in a range of ways from empty talk without any action to reference points of commitment and institutional accountability, depending on their construction. We begin with the University of Southern Maine's land acknowledgment (USM, 2024) situated on Wabanaki territory, the very academic home space of this book, to shed light on the possible classroom practice of decolonization. I highlight the exemplary decolonial gems in bold:

> We acknowledge the land and water that the University of Southern Maine campuses occupy, as well as the ancestral and contemporary peoples indigenous to these places in the Dawnland. **Campus lands were the ancestral fishing, hunting, and agricultural grounds inhabited by the Abenaki and Wabanaki People for thousands of years.**
>
> We recognize that we are on indigenous land. In addition to the Abenaki, the broader place we now call Maine is home to the sovereign people of the Wabanaki Confederacy: the Penobscot, Passamaquoddy, Maliseet, and Mi'kmaq Peoples. **We exist on their unceded homelands.**

> We also acknowledge the **uncomfortable truths of settler colonialism, among them that the peoples indigenous to this place were often forcibly removed from this place.**
> **Harm from the physical and cultural genocide of Native people here** and throughout the land we now call Maine continues and is felt by members of the Wabanaki Confederacy who live here today, including our own Wabanaki students, staff, and faculty.
> To participate in the healing process, please visit the organization Wabanaki REACH at mainewabanakireach.org.
> **We all have work to do.**

The land acknowledgment can serve as an important institutional space of engagement, where a classroom can be managed through and within a decolonial lens. Consider how these land acknowledgments can effectively present the difficult knowledge, the hard truth of the respective Indigenous territories that classrooms occupy. As a nod to the future, we encourage educators to use their respective institutional land acknowledgement in their classroom to guide the critical discussions necessary to realize decolonization. I offer these questions for critical reflections as an example of how take up this discussion:

- Do you know your institutional land acknowledgment; what is your relationship to it?
- Who wrote it; were Indigenous scholars and/or educators to the territory of your school involved in the construction of the statement?
- How can your land acknowledgment be used to discuss the colonial dispossession of land and the attempted genocide of the Indigenous People?

A Vision for the Future: Decolonial Work Is Constant

Fiona, Brigid, and Starr

In 2019, almost 20 years after the development of the Wabanaki Studies law, a part-time position was created in Portland Public Schools, the first-ever Wabanaki Studies coordinator in the state of Maine. Part of my (Fiona) responsibility in this position was to collaborate with numerous Wabanaki educators. Through that collaboration, we developed a process for cross-cultural curriculum creation that centers relationship building and collaboration and includes multiple layers of accountability. The importance of relationships is something I've learned from and witnessed in Wabanaki communities over and over again. Centering relationships with historically marginalized communities is not how education has traditionally done business. It's not how the culture I grew up in operates. Centering relationships requires schools, particularly those leading them, to listen, grow, and demonstrate a willingness to change.

In 2018, Bridgid and I (Fiona) worked together to convene a group of 10 Wabanaki advisers who have met regularly ever since to discuss and review curriculum. The advisory has been essential to the curriculum development process because it ensures that it is guided by multiple voices and perspectives, not, as is so often the case in dominant white culture, just one. The K–12 curriculum in its entirety includes contributions from more than 65 citizens of Wabanaki nations, 35 teachers, and multiple community partners. All told, more than 100 people helped in large and small ways to make this curriculum possible. This is an unprecedented level of collaboration for any curriculum, let alone one initiated by a local school district.

Each grade level unit begins with a question that emerged from discussions with the advisory group. Once the advisers reviewed the questions, I assembled a group of educators to begin developing grade-level units related to each question. We met every other month for two years. The first step in our process was to hear a presentation from a Wabanaki knowledge holder with expertise related to the central question of a grade-level unit. Afterward, each educator submitted ideas for how to present the knowledge that was shared to the specific grade level tagged for that unit. Starr Kelly, former curator of education at the Abbe Museum and citizen of the Kitignan Zibi Anishinabeg First Nation, and I reviewed all the teachers' submissions and wove them into a single unit overview.

Those overviews were then reviewed by the initial group of teachers, then the advisers, before being turned over to unit writers (Portland Public School teachers and me) who transformed them into full-fledged units ready for classroom use. The finished units were then returned to the original Wabanaki knowledge holder for final review. After final revisions, the units were shared with all grade-level teachers for implementation, but not before those teachers engaged in professional development to prepare them to teach the units. The final step in the process involves individual meetings with grade-level teams to collect feedback on the units. Those meetings precede classroom walkthroughs with the advisory group. At this point, conversations generate further revision and review in recognition of curriculum as a living, changing, evolving document.

Each unit has called for unique supporting materials, particularly at the elementary level. I've commissioned the creation of original artwork and maps from Wabanaki and non-Wabanaki artists to meet the need for high-quality teaching materials. Books, too, have been needed at every grade level to provide students with accurate information from contemporary Wabanaki and Indigenous authors. All of this, including payment for advisers, presenters, and reviewers and funding for the Wabanaki Studies coordinator position has meant a significant investment from Portland Public Schools. Although dollars are important, the creation of a curriculum of this depth and magnitude is a collaborative endeavor that is only as strong as the relationships that underpin it. Without relationships, there is no curriculum, and without a curriculum that teaches students the history of the land and the people who have been here since time immemorial, decolonization, in all its forms, is a mirage.

As the Portland Public Schools enters its second year of phased implementation of Wabanaki Studies, I (Fiona) have been encouraged by the positive teacher response. It is one thing to create a beautiful curriculum, but it is another to get it to become reality for students. Time and time again I hear from teachers how much students love the curriculum and how much they are learning alongside their students. Nearly 25 years later, Wabanaki Studies is becoming part of common practice, part of standard operating procedure, part of what students, Indigenous and non-Indigenous alike, can expect to learn in school. This curriculum is creating the conditions for decolonization because the cross-cultural relationship building and truth ushered into these classrooms offers restorative practice an opportunity to flourish. Truth telling and relationship building create the conditions for healing and repair.

Taking theory into practice through curriculum design has many challenges including questions of accessibility for other districts across the state while maintaining the integrity of the Indigenous cultural intellectual property (ICIP) it is based on and the relationships that supported its creation. We hope to find a long-term academic home for this collaborative masterpiece that allows educators from across Maine and across the country to learn from the journey we've been on. In the meantime, we continue to grow relationships, join hands, and keep on the lookout for ongoing ways to participate in the restoration of community. Together.

Rebecca

As we work together toward shared anticolonial futures, I offer a few of the 15 teacher oath statements I developed last year for the Alberta Teachers Association Magazine, found at https://teachers.ab.ca/news/addressing-anti-indigenous-racism-schools, that are particularly relevant to decolonizing classroom management to support teachers in their attempts to address anti-Indigenous racism in schools:

1. I have the will and commitment to learn from and stay with my personal discomfort. I understand that feeling guilty serves neither me nor Indigenous people.
2. I actively recognize the wrongdoing associated with the Indian residential school system, sixties scoop (in a U.S. context, this may read Indian

Child Welfare Act violations leading to illegal Indian child apprehensions), and other aspects of the oppressive history of Canada's treatment of Indigenous Peoples.
3. I am responsible for what I do today and choose to interrupt oppressive colonial history through my commitment to teach the truth about it.
4. I care about others without co-opting or prying into their cultural ways or practices. I recognize that Indigenous culture has been continuously objectified, stolen, and outlawed, therefore it is inappropriate to feel entitled to seek sensitive cultural information directly from individuals. I instead practice self-inquiry into my motives while focusing on my commitment to learning from Indigenous scholarship in the fields of Indigenous education and Indigenous studies.
5. I respect the space of Indigenous ceremony, including smudge, without attempting to re-create it.
6. I courageously take opportunities to learn, question, and develop professionally in Indigenous education and Indigenous studies and to respect what is being called for by Indigenous leaders and educators in this area.
7. I release Indigenous students from expectations that they be experts or knowledgeable about anything Indigenous.
8. I critically rethink the world around me, including taking for granted how things are done.
9. I expect no praise for teaching truth and take it as a responsibility and part of a legacy of my own contribution to a more just future.

Decolonizing classroom management will require holding up mirrors and understanding in critical ways our relationship with the land and peoples Indigenous to it. As Chalga Tulku (2003) warns, "Trying to change the world without changing our minds is like trying to clean the dirty face in the mirror by scrubbing the glass" (p. 4). The examples we have shared, reexamining and unpacking land acknowledgments, truly collaborative curriculum development, and the samples of statements from teacher oaths, are a few of the many creative and authentic ways to move toward decolonizing teacher education in a spirit of facing the difficult truths head on with love and humanity.

To learn more about the Wabanaki Studies curriculum development process, please see the following articles and videos:

American Civil Liberties Union. (2022). *The Wabanaki studies law: 21 years after implementation*. https://www.aclumaine.org/sites/default/files/field_documents/2022_wabanaki_report-digital.pdf

Hopper, F. (2020, July 2). Confronting place-ignorance in education. Wabanaki Reach. https://www.wabanakireach.org/confronting_place_ignorance_in_education

Hopper, F. (2021). Finding a riverview: Anti-racist education, decolonization, and the development of a district-wide Wabanaki studies curriculum. *Journal of School & Society,* 7(1) 47–56.

Portland Museum of Art. (2020, December). Evening for educators: Stories of Maine. Vimeo. https://vimeo.com/505266012

Portland Museum of Art (2023, January 11). A new era in Wabanaki studies education in Maine: How do we tell the stories of Wabanaki cultures in the classroom? https://www.portlandmuseum.org/magazine/wabanaki-studies

Sockbeson, R. (2019). Main Indigenous education left behind: A call for anti-racist conviction as political will toward decolonization. *Journal of American Indian Education,* 58(3), 105+.

The curriculum and the ICIP included in it is protected by an MOU between the Portland Public Schools and the Wabanaki advisers and is not available for open-source sharing.

REFERENCES

Ambo, T., & Rocha Beardall, T. (2023). Performance or progress? The physical and rhetorical removal of Indigenous Peoples in settler land acknowledgments at land-grab universities. *American Educational Research Journal,* 60(1), 103–140.

Davey, R., & Thunder Woman, Y. (Directors). (2006). *The canary effect* [Motion Picture]. USA: Bastard Fairy Films.

Paul, D. (2000). *We were not the savages: A Mi'kmaq perspective on the collision between European and Native American civilizations,* 2nd edition. Halifax: Fernwood.

Sockbeson, R. (2019). Maine Indigenous education left behind: A call for anti-racist conviction as political will toward decolonization. *Journal of American Indian Education,* 58(3), 105+.

Tulku, C. (2003). *Change of heart: The Bodhisattva peace training of Chagdud Tulku.* S. Drolma (Ed.). Junction City, CA: Padma Publishing.

University of Southern Maine (2024). Land acknowledgment. https://usm.maine.edu/president/land-acknowledgment/

Contributors

Jennifer Randhare Ashton, Marie Battiste, Maggie R. Beneke, April Coloma Boyce, Katie Brooks, Jade Calais, Ronald Cunningham, Brian Dinkins, Riley Drake, Brooke Harris Garad, Matthew Green, Patricia Benitez Hemans, Erica Holyoke, Fiona Hopper, Starr Kelly, Samantha Kriger, Danielle Madrazo, Larissa Malone, Erika McDowell, Bridgid Neptune, Brandie Oliver, José Ortiz, Amy Sarah Padayachee, Flynn Ross, Adam Schmitt, Violet Jiménez Sims, Jessica Sniatecki, Rebecca Sockbeson, Dina Strasser, Maria Timberlake, Dana Turnquest.

About the Editors

Flynn Ross is professor and chair in the teacher education department at University of Southern Maine. She is founding director of the Maine Teacher Residency for statewide paid teacher residency positions funded by the U.S. Department of Education and state appropriations. She is also founder of the Equity and Excellence in Maine Schools Web-based clearinghouse of resources for Maine educators. She earned a master's and doctorate degree from Teachers College Columbia University.

Larissa Malone is associate professor of social and cultural foundations of education at University of North Carolina Wilmington. Dr. Malone earned a PhD in cultural foundations of education at Kent State University, an MA in education from Walsh University, and a BA in international studies from Case Western Reserve University. Dr. Malone founded Maine Black Educators Collective, a grant-funded organization that holds the mission of supporting Black educators through educational opportunities, social-emotional connection, and advocacy, and received the inaugural Maine Education Association's 2022 Human and Civil Rights Award for this initiative.

www.ingramcontent.com/pod-product-compliance
Lightning Source LLC
Chambersburg PA
CBHW020738230426

43665CB00009B/484